An Anti-Communist on the Eastern Front

The Memoirs of a Russian Officer in the Spanish Blue Division (1941–1942)

Vladimir Ivanovich Kovalevskii

Edited by Oleg Beyda and Xosé M. Núñez Seixas

Translated by Richard W. Harrison

Pen & Sword
MILITARY

An imprint of
Pen & Sword Books Ltd
Yorkshire – Philadelphia

Pen & Sword
MILITARY

First published in Great Britain in 2023 by
PEN & SWORD MILITARY
An imprint of
Pen & Sword Books Ltd
Yorkshire – Philadelphia

Copyright © Vladimir Kovalevski 2023

ISBN 978 1 39906 208 4

The right of Vladimir Kovalevski to be identified as Author of this work has been asserted by him in accordance with the Copyright, Designs and Patents Act 1988.

A CIP catalogue record for this book is available from the British Library

All rights reserved. No part of this book may be reproduced or transmitted in any form or by any means, electronic or mechanical including photocopying, recording or by any information storage and retrieval system, without permission from the Publisher in writing.

Typeset in Chennai, India
by Lapiz Digital Services.

Printed and bound by CPI Group (UK) Ltd, Croydon, CR0 4YY

Pen & Sword Books Ltd incorporates the imprints of Pen & Sword
Archaeology, Atlas, Aviation, Battleground, Discovery, Family History, History, Maritime, Military, Naval, Politics, Social History, Transport, True Crime, Claymore Press, Frontline Books, Praetorian Press, Seaforth Publishing and White Owl

For a complete list of Pen & Sword titles please contact

PEN & SWORD BOOKS LTD
47 Church Street, Barnsley, South Yorkshire, S70 2AS, England
E-mail: enquiries@pen-and-sword.co.uk
Website: www.pen-and-sword.co.uk

Or

PEN AND SWORD BOOKS
1950 Lawrence Rd, Havertown, PA 19083, USA
E-mail: Uspen-and-sword@casematepublishers.com
Website: www.penandswordbooks.com

Contents

List of Plates vii
Preface ix

INTRODUCTION: 'WHITE, BLUE AND RED': RUSSIAN
EMIGRANTS, THE SPANISH BLUE DIVISION AND THE USSR 1

    'The Ongoing Defeat': Officers as Taxi Drivers 3
    'It's Strangely the Same': General Franco's Russian Soldiers 8
    'Sandcastles': Russian Émigrés and Operation Barbarossa 25
    'German Prohibitions, Spanish Needs': Émigrés in the Blue Division 29
    'The Young Lady is *Mucho* Beautiful!': Spaniards on the Russians,
    Russians on the Spaniards 36
    'Bygone Natures': Russians on Russians and About Themselves 41
    'The Riddle of a Life': Vladimir Ivanovich Kovalevskii 50
    'A Tale of a Manuscript', or There and Back Again 56
    'The Mirror of Trauma': The Russian View of Spanish Warfare 60

THE 'BLUE DIVISION' AND THE CAMPAIGN IN RUSSIA
BY VLADIMIR IVANOVICH KOVALEVSKII 75

Preface 79

Part One: The Path 81
    June 1941. San Sebastián 83
    Burgos 88
    On the Road to Germany 92
    Camp Grafenwöhr (Bavaria) 95
    On the Road to Russia 102

Part Two: Russia 109
    First Impressions 111
    Novgorod and Its Environs 119
    In the Trenches 125
    Main Headquarters 141
    At Division Headquarters 151
    The Russian Interpreters 153
    The Second Section and the '*Guardia Civil*' 157
    Hunting for Partisans 165
    Denouement 188

Endnotes 199
Index 251

List of Plates

1. With the red berets from the *Tercio de Navarra* on the Northern Front. From the album of Petr K. Odishariia. (*Private archive of military antique photography https://www.photo-war.com/*)
2. Georgian émigrés from the *Tercio de Navarra*. From the Nino Vachnadze-Koval'ski archive. (*National Parliamentary Library of Georgia*)
3. Nikolai V. Shinkarenko convalescing after a head wound. Previously unpublished. (*Private archive, Russian Federation*)
4. From Russian Major General to Spanish Lieutenant – Nikolai V. Shinkarenko. (*Private archive, Russian Federation*)
5. Russian officers in Spain. (*Private archive, Russian Federation*)
6. After the victory. (*Stanford University, Hoover Institution Archives*)
7. 'The dean' of Russian émigrés: Spanish Colonel Nikolai N. Boltin. (*Private archive, Russian Federation*)
8. Officers of the 3rd *tercio* of the Spanish Foreign Legion. (*Stanford University, Hoover Institution Archives*)
9. Konstantin A. Goncharenko. Previously unpublished. (*Gurskii family archive*)
10. Vladimir I. Kovalevskii's Blue Division enrolment card, 30 June 1941. (*Archivo General Militar de Ávila*)
11. Back on native soil. Ali (Sergei Konstantinovich) Gurskii-Magometov. (*Gurskii family archive*)
12. First Soviet POWs. (*Gurskii family archive*)
13–15. *Panikhida*. Orthodox memorial service at Konstantin A. Goncharenko's funeral and the funeral itself.
16. Ali Gurskii-Magometov and Igor Perchin. Grigorovo, winter 1942. (*Gurskii family archive*)
17. Zoning in on the enemy. (*Gurskii family archive*)
18–19. Russian reunion in Spain. (*Gurskii family archive*)

20. Despite losing both legs during his service with the Blue Division and having prosthetic limbs, Vadim A. Klimenko remained a staunch rider. (*Private archive, Russian Federation*)
21. The golden years. Georgii A. Staritskii. Palma de Mallorca, early 1960s. (*Staritskii family archive*)
22. Lost tales from the Russian past. Vladimir I. Kovalevskii's original manuscript. (*Central Museum of the Armed Forces of the Russian Federation*)
23. Made in America. Vladimir I. Kovalevskii's typescript from the Globus Publishers, San Francisco. (*Stanford University, Hoover Institution Archives*)

Preface

The book you are holding is a product of blind academic luck, along with professional tenacity and benevolent international cooperation. So far, this title has been published in Russia and Spain, and has had multiple print runs. It introduces an obscure, largely forgotten perspective on the Second World War and the German-Soviet front – that of a White Russian émigré, a nationalistic veteran, a sorrowful, spiteful, lonely witness to the war and to extreme cruelty.

Vladimir Ivanovich Kovalevskii was an officer of the Imperial Russian Army who lived a tumultuous and violence-ridden life, seeing service in five European wars. The trenches of the First World War merged almost seamlessly for him into those of the Russian Civil War. From an early stage, Kovalevskii took the side of the Russian anti-Bolsheviks. In 1920 he marched with the White Army along its road to defeat, embarking from Crimea for an exile that would last with only a short interruption until his death. A brief stint in the French Foreign Legion, under the African sun, was followed by semi-demobilized life in the Kingdom of Yugoslavia. Then in 1938 Kovalevskii took up arms again, this time travelling to Spain, where he fought in the Spanish Civil War on the side of General Francisco Franco.

With Hitler's invasion of the USSR in the summer of 1941, Kovalevskii enlisted in the Spanish Volunteer Division no. 250 of the Wehrmacht (also known as the Blue Division, *División Azul*) – a unit of Spanish volunteers in German service which, with enthusiastic support from the fascist Falange party, was sent by the dictator Franco to fight against the Red Army. Once Kovalevskii again set foot on his country's soil, his long-harboured desire for revenge and feelings of anti-Soviet Russian patriotism dissipated. What he encountered was a dark picture of desolation and endless civilian suffering, resulting in his own, crushing personal defeat. Confused, sick and depressed, he returned to Spain in the spring of 1942. After so many conflicts, it was this final war that shattered his last hopes for a better Russian future, and for his own private future as well. Kovalevskii began writing these memoirs in 1948. After his death in the 1980s the text crossed the ocean, only to be buried in an American and later a Russian archive.

Why would a Russian fight in so many wars, and eventually against his own countrymen? Who were the White Russian émigrés, and what is the story of their diaspora? What did they believe in? What was the Russians' role in the Spanish Civil War? What was the role of the Spaniards in the war of extermination conducted by the German army and its allies on Soviet soil? What was Kovalevskii's view of the German and Spanish occupation in the Novgorod region? What were the thought processes of such a person, an émigré volunteer? What was it like to be a Russian anti-Communist in foreign service?

All of these questions have been addressed in this book, which is made up of two parts. The Introduction takes up a multitude of intertwined topics. First, we paint a broad picture of Russians in exile, following the pulse of their hopes and struggles. Working through multiple contexts, we then introduce, reconstruct and analyse the experience of Russians in Spain's twentieth-century wars – the civil conflict of 1936–9, and the Spanish participation in the German-Soviet War. Only then do we introduce the biography of the protagonist, Vladimir Kovalevskii, and detail both his fate and that of his manuscript. Our introduction may be seen as an entrée to the main course, or perhaps as a map allowing one to confidently navigate the overlapping international histories that shaped Kovalevskii's life and ultimately shattered it. Our research is based on more than twenty-five archives, private collections and libraries in Australia, Andorra, Germany, Georgia, Finland, Spain, the Russian Federation, the USA and Ukraine.

Then follows the second part – Kovalevskii's memoirs of service in the Blue Division in 1941–2. We have commented meticulously on hundreds of individuals, locations, military and civilian phenomena, and events that he recounted, along with the conclusions he reached. Kovalevskii was not an objective observer by any means. He was a disgruntled old veteran, a nationalist who could find no understanding either in his own country or beyond its borders. Although he fought for Spain in two brutal wars and spent decades of his life on the Iberian Peninsula, he openly scorned the country, its culture, its army and even its people, which does not paint a favourable picture of him. Yet it is precisely his traumatized personality that explains why his account is so fiercely subjective, relentlessly critical, ardently ironic and unforgivingly spiteful in its treatment of almost everything he had seen and everyone he had known, including himself.

This text presents a contradictory, openly challenging view of the multifaceted war against the USSR and of the dark, complex episode of the German–Spanish occupation. While some may dismiss this account as the work of a single individual trying to depict enormous events, we regard the solitary and alien nature of the author as a feature of the source, not as a weakness. This is how Kovalevskii, a self-defined 'Russian without a fatherland', assessed his life, mused on his role, and remembered the last conflict he experienced. As a unique piece of historical writing, it stands on its own, offering *a very private version of the truth*. Whether you agree in full with Kovalevskii's version of the events, accept it only in part, or reject it altogether remains up to you, the reader.

Oleg Beyda, Xosé M. Núñez Seixas
December 2021

INTRODUCTION: 'WHITE, BLUE AND RED': RUSSIAN EMIGRANTS, THE SPANISH BLUE DIVISION AND THE USSR

'The Ongoing Defeat': Officers as Taxi Drivers

The process of destroying the Russian Empire and creating the new Soviet state was accompanied by a swath of violence: first the First World War and then the Revolution and Civil War of 1917–22, which cost millions of lives.[1] The Whites – or 'White Russians', this overall term covered a multitude of various political currents and ethnic and social groups – having lost to the Bolsheviks in the internal conflict, constituted an enormous diaspora. According to some estimates, following the October Revolution of 1917 around two million people left the former Russian Empire for Central Europe through Finland, Norway and the Baltic States. Yet another avenue of survival was the Black Sea. The final stage of this exodus was the evacuation of the Crimea by General Petr Nikolaevich Wrangel's army in November 1920. The Russian fleet gathered up 150,000 men, women and children. Upon departing, they set course for the unknown.[2]

Following the evacuation, part of the fleet remained in the Dardanelles, while at the same time other ships and 5,600 people ended up under French protection in the Tunisian port of Bizerte. Cossack units, numbering about 50,000 people, were maintained for the most part by French authorities on the Greek island of Lemnos until October 1921, when the I Army Corps (about 26,000 men) landed on the Gallipoli peninsula, where it essentially interned itself in an improvised camp. Civilians ended up in similar conditions in the suburbs of Istanbul.[3]

Despite the hardships and deprivations, the White Guards transformed their defeat and the internment camps into a symbol of military struggle and a prophecy of its renewal. Thus, was born the 'Gallipoli spirit' and the messianic consciousness of unbending warriors upon which it was based.[4] Many of these had left the camp as early as the end of 1920.[5]

Yesterday's soldiers and officers, along with thousands of Russian civilians, scattered throughout the world. A sizeable portion of them found refuge in Bulgaria and Yugoslavia, while others made it to Czechoslovakia, Western Europe and other points of the globe. The centre of this diaspora was France, where by 1930 from 100,000 to 200,000 former Russian subjects had settled, a significant number of whom resided in Paris.

The core of the White army, which managed to survive, became the basis for a unique organization – the Russian All-Military Union (*Russkii Obshchevoinskii Soiuz*, or ROVS). Founded by Wrangel himself in Yugoslavia in September 1924, the ROVS united groups of White Guards which had been created earlier (for example, the Union included the Society of Gallipolians, which had appeared three years before). The Union's goal was not only the preservation of the Whites' moral unity. The organization attempted to preserve troop cadres and their command element, although it was temporarily absorbed in civilian life, in order to once again call them to the colours in the future for war against the Soviet Union. Actually, behind the abbreviation there was hidden a temporarily demobilized volunteer host, linked by powerful ties of combat comradeship.[6]

As a system, the ROVS consisted of sections, which served as administrative subdivisions. Each section was broken up into subsections and each unit had its own command. A section usually embraced a country or group of countries where Russians had scattered: Section I included France, Italy, the Netherlands and North Africa; Section II included Germany; Section III operated in Bulgaria; Section IV in Yugoslavia; and Section V in Belgium. As the Russian émigré diaspora grew, subsections were created in Finland, the US, Australia, Brazil and Argentina.[7] Each section maintained close contact with local organizations founded by Russian soldiers.[8]

Unions and societies were not just circles for nostalgic veterans, but also mutual aid societies. While strengthening feelings of comradeship, these societies helped people find work or rendered financial assistance to soldiers and their families. While operating alongside religious, professional and educational establishments – including universities founded during the emigration – these organizations breathed life into the special micro-society that was the fellowship of patriots of a lost country. Celebrations, meetings and prayer services were conducted. They formed their own public sphere, independent of their country of residence, and woven from headlines in Russian newspapers, gatherings of young people in ethnic restaurants and their own calendar and ceremonies.[9] The Whites saw themselves as the last pillars of imperial Russia: it was precisely they, exiles without passport or a penny to their name, who were, in their opinion, the real Russians.[10] In comparing themselves with those who remained 'there', in the USSR, and who had been transformed into Soviet citizens, the emigrants considered themselves the spiritual source from which their motherland must draw hope for its own future.[11]

At the same time, the life that flowed on outside of the Russian microworld/parallel society was very prosaic and hard. The majority, including senior officers as well, was forced to look for work in the civilian economy. It was difficult to integrate oneself into local society: the emigrants suffered from limitations on their rights, and from the juridical point of view were seen as aliens, stateless persons who refused to become Soviet citizens. In order to legalize their status, in 1921 the Norwegian diplomat Fridtjof Nansen, who had become the High Commissioner on refugee affairs with the League of Nations, drew up a special identity document – the Nansen passport.[12]

In Paris, Berlin, Prague and Istanbul, where a large number of Slavic and Jewish émigrés from Eastern Europe lived at close quarters, the White Russians transformed certain areas into true ethnic enclaves. In the French capital they were concentrated in the 15th and 16th arrondisments, in the commune of Boulogne-Billancourt – where the Renault automobile factories were located – nearly 5,000 Russian workers were employed, as well as in Vinçennes and other places. Here they became carpenters, taxi drivers, waiters and factory workers: in the north of France and in Belgium many took up the miner's pick.[13] However, upon finishing the working day and in the company of their comrades-in-arms, many of them were once again transformed into Tsarist officers.

Little by little these people became typical residents of Berlin or Paris during the interwar era, while they caused both outbreaks of xenophobia amongst the locals as well as curiosity about the strange people from far away. If one is to believe one historical anecdote, Spanish general and future dictator Francisco Franco, who was passing through Paris in February 1935, flagged down a taxi, the driver of which turned out to be a Russian general. The encounter caused the Spanish officer to think long and hard about the communist threat.[14]

The endless ideological, cultural and even ethnic variety of the Russian emigration, which was split into a multitude of factions and groups, was not only the strength but also the Achilles heel of the émigré diaspora from the very beginning.[15] This layer remained heterogeneous. For the majority of military emigrants, the unifying motive became the cult of the memory of the Russian Civil War, which consolidated their nationalistic and imperial perceptions of the world. For at least 20 years no small part of the military emigrants considered their struggle unfinished. They lived on the hope of a 'spring campaign' – intervention in the USSR. But the years passed, and the Soviet state not only did not become decrepit following Lenin's death in 1924 but quite the opposite, grew in strength under Stalin.

The 1930s brought new and energetic disputes and a new schism regarding what strategy to choose. Two choices were offered: to cooperate with foreign powers which were pursuing the goal of destroying the Soviet state, or to follow one's own independent path. It was approximately at this time that two currents were noted: the 'defencists' and the 'defeatists'. The former saw cooperation with any interventionist foreign power as outright treason. The latter maintained that for the sake of crushing Bolshevism any means were acceptable, including just such cooperation.

Many officers, out of habit, were oriented toward the old Entente and dreamed of an alliance with Great Britain or France. Others considered joint work with the rising Fascist powers to be inevitable. The majority of military men, as well as adherents of monarchical and radical right-wing views, held to the 'defeatist' position.[16] The idea of some kind of 'defence of Russia' along with the Soviets was rejected by them as absurd, while fanatical anti-Bolshevism aroused them to take part in any conflict where the slightest hint of anti-communism and the fight against communists could be detected.[17] As we will see later, this sort of thinking brought some of them to Spain and later back their motherland, among the ranks of occupation troops.

Up until July 1936 the presence of Russians on Iberian soil was more likely episodic. Since 1917 the Spanish authorities had maintained a prohibitive position toward the subjects of the former Tsarist empire fleeing revolutions and wars. The Spaniards were afraid of the penetration of revolutionary elements, be these Bolsheviks, Mensheviks or anyone else. For this reason, the Spanish state refused to recognize the Nansen passports. According to census data for 1930, 171 Russians (84 men and 87 women) resided in Spain. They were concentrated, for the most part, in Barcelona and Madrid, as well as Valencia and Santa Cruz de Tenerife: the majority of emigrants were tradesmen, industrialists or members of the free professions, while a few were engaged in translating Russian literature. This geographical scattering did not make for the creation of a firm association. It was only in Barcelona that a few Russian aristocrats would gather to observe Orthodox services in a private chapel.[18] One may add to the Spanish diaspora no more than thirty or forty Russians who had earlier joined the Spanish Foreign Legion and who resided in the Spanish protectorate of Northern Morocco.

'It's Strangely the Same': General Franco's Russian Soldiers

Although many of the Russian officers took up civilian life, a decent share of them continued to see themselves only as experienced cadre soldiers. As did many demobilized military personnel in Germany and the former Austria-Hungary, some of the White Guards became military wanderers and adventurists, who accumulated military and civilian experience on various continents and in the most varied of conditions. In the break between the two world conflagrations some of them turned into truly unique soldiers.[1] Russian speech was heard in any number of military conflicts in which the White Guards had joined up as volunteers in foreign armies. Some fought by conviction, while others were content being a 'wild goose', a mercenary, and sometimes these two positions overlapped.

Let's take just the following examples. In December 1924 about 100 Russian émigrés, under the command of Major General Il'ia Mikhailovich Miklashevskii, took part in overthrowing the Albanian prime minister Fan Noli, the leader of the June revolution of that same year. Miklashevskii's troops came out on the side of his rival, Ahmet Zogu, who had secured the support of Yugoslavia.[2] In Manchuria hundreds of Whites hired themselves out to the variety of petty warlords with anti-communist views.[3] About seventy White Guards fought for Paraguay in 1932–5, during its war with Bolivia (the Chaco War); the most noted of these was Ivan (Juan) Timofeevich Beliaev.[4] Some made their military career in the armies of those independent countries formerly a part of Russia.[5] Finally, during 1920–40 nearly 10,000 Russians fought under the flag of the French Foreign Legion, while the first volunteers turned up in Gallipoli as early as 1921. Russians accounted for 12 per cent of the Legion's overall strength, becoming the second most-represented ethnic group after the Germans. They were quite dominant in some units: for example, in the 1st Foreign Cavalry Regiment (*1er régiment étranger de cavalerie*), which was created in 1921 from Cossacks.[6]

In 1922 the Spanish War Ministry sounded out the prospect of the large-scale recruitment of White Guards, living in Central Europe and the Balkans, for the Spanish Foreign Legion, which had been created in Morocco two years earlier. As early as 1921 several dozen Russians and some Ukrainians knocked at the doors of the Spanish embassies in Prague, Sofia and Tunis, wishing to be hired. However, the fear of the revolutionary infection, which had sunk deep roots amongst Madrid government officials, and the fear of the Russians' possible contacts with conscript soldiers arriving from the mother country, not to mention the shortage of means for transporting recruits to Spain, put an end to the plan, the realization of which was the desire of the army and the Legion command itself. Contacts with Wrangel and Beliaev yielded nothing. An attempt to resume negotiations in 1924 also failed, partly due to Wrangel's insistent wish not to scatter organized White units and to dispatch his men to the Moroccan protectorate, where they could have created semi-autonomous settlements. As a result, by the 1930s only thirty-two Russians had joined the Spanish Legion.[7]

Although the Spanish Civil War of 1936–9 did not attract a large number of White Guards, this event was filled with enormous symbolic significance for Russians abroad. It seemed as though the musical score of the Spanish conflict was warming up according to already familiar notes of the Russian socio-political schism.[8] All of this fitted into the picture of a pan-European civil war, in which the communists and anti-communists fought to the death in Hungary, Germany, Russia and Finland. In this the Russians were the symbol and messengers of fear of a Bolshevik revolution.[9] Nikolai Aleksandrovich Ragozin, who from the spring of 1922 served in the Spanish Air Force and who fought in Africa, told his fellow soldiers about what he had seen during the revolution: '. . . I hope that I acquired many supporters and introduced many waverers to the "right cause".'[10]

One leitmotif rapidly took shape in the speeches of those who rose against the Spanish Second Republic: everything revolved around the purported responsibility of the USSR for the beginning of the conflict and the Spanish Republicans' servile dependence on Stalin, who was interested in turning Spain into a colony. There was talk of a war of 'Spaniards against Russians', and a new Reconquest against a foreign communist invasion, supported by native traitors. These arguments essentially reminded one of those employed by the White Russians during 1917–20 and the Finnish Whites in the course of their brief civil war in 1918.[11] In the opinion of many ultra-rightists, militant Catholics and radical European conservatives, the defence of the Christian faith and European civilization itself was at stake in Spain.

Hundreds of Irish, French, Portuguese and Latin American volunteers came to defend these two principles. In these conditions was forged the peculiar experience of transnational fascism, which crossed state boundaries, while ultra-rightists of all stripes mutually influenced each other.[12]

The beginning of the Spanish Civil War in July 1936 greatly influenced the White diaspora. The combat wing of overseas Russians, hidden from the outside observer, became aroused. It was said that some emigrants sent Franco their St George crosses and medals 'as the dearest things remaining to them'.[13] Old disagreements continued with renewed heat. The 'defencists' and leftists (Mensheviks, Social Revolutionaries and others), starting with the former minister-chairman of the Provisional Government, Aleksandr Fedorovich Kerenskii, condemned the military uprising, comparing it with the Kornilov revolt of August 1917. On the other hand, on 19 July 1936 the ROVS expressed its support for the military rebels. News about the murder of priests and the desecration of churches in the Republican rear, it would seem, awoke a feeling of solidarity in the emigration's right wing.

All of this was interrelated: a victory for the Spanish generals presupposed the strengthening of Nazi Germany and Fascist Italy, which would have reinforced the radical right groups in France. The latter were campaigning intensely against Léon Blum's Popular Front government and its policies, while Blum, inspired by the American 'New Deal', had done quite a bit to defend the rights of Russian emigrants.[14] In spite of this, the ROVS and other rightist émigré groups looked upon what was happening in Spain with hope. All of this aside, they wish to 'cleanse' the Russian name by showing the entire world that this was not a conflict of Spaniards versus *Russians*, as the Francoist propaganda maintained, but of Spaniards against *Reds*.

But even among the rightists there could be heard the voices of those who favoured a policy of non-intervention. The monarchist-historian Anton Antonovich Kersnovskii, who was living in Paris, hewed to national egoism, believing that the war in Spain was someone else's war. The Russians should remember how during their civil war no Spaniards favoured the Whites with assistance.[15] Therefore, the diaspora should not be touched either by the blood of '"the Whites" on the pavement of Barcelona, nor the blood of the "Reds" on the walls of Seville'. 'The Spaniards, as did all foreigners, viewed with indifference our sufferings. Why should we feel sorry for them? Why should we play Don Quixote in favour of the descendants of Don Quixote?'[16] Major General Mikhail Fedorovich Skorodumov, who was living at the time in Belgrade, replied that, quite the opposite, the struggle in Spain corresponded to the knightly ideal of the Russian officer and anti-Bolshevism. No differences existed between national groups of Bolsheviks and, if nearly two decades had passed in pledges of irreconcilability, then it would not be consistent to give in before the newly-revealed opportunity to operate in an active fashion (that is, fight them). Kersnovskii riposted that there was no anti-Bolshevik International, within the confines of which one could 'operate', for each people fought against the Bolsheviks out of patriotic considerations, and the latter were always antagonistic toward each other; to put it simply, each nation was egoistic and therefore one should not get caught up in illusions and help outsiders.[17] Kersnovskii's articles met with a rebuff within the ROVS (and not just there) and the two sides had a falling out. This difference of opinion became the harbinger of the choices made by the sides in the coming world war.[18]

In the summer and autumn of 1936 individual Russian volunteers, on their own initiative, began to arrive in the Spanish conflagration. Only a few, more often already connected with the country, established themselves right away. The cuirassier, prince and member of the gentry Georgii Alekseevich Staritskii, who belonged to the party of monarchists-Alphonsists, 'Spanish Renewal' (*Renovación Española*), came out in favour of the insurgents as early as the end of July 1936.[19] A few more people arrived in the country in the autumn, but they got a cold reception. The Spaniards arrested Nikolai Petrovich Zotov and Grigorii Pavlovich Lamsdorf and threw them back across the border, after which the pair crossed it again. As early as October, Nikolai Vsevolodovich Shinkarenko crossed the border legally, but was sent back by the Spaniards to France.

Igor Konstantinovich Sakharov contrived to arrive from Germany, but not right away. The first steamship was detained in Spanish waters and returned to Hamburg; Sakharov secretly boarded another steamship at night and finally made it to Spain, where he joined the Foreign Legion. The battalion commander, a Spanish major, instead of gratitude, met him with shouts: 'You Russians, what are you doing here and what are our quarrels to you? You Russians, White and Red, have no business here.'[20]

The main flow began in 1937. Among those who illegally crossed the border were two major generals (Anatolii Vladimirovich Fok and Shinkarenko), two colonels (Nikolai Nikolaevich Boltin and Vladimir Abramovich Dvoichenko), and captains from various combat arms: Nikolai Evgen'evich

Krivosheia, Iakov Timofeevich Polukhin, Ali (Sergei Konstantinovich) Gurskii (Magometov) and Pavel Ivanovich Rashevskii. On 12 February 1937 Krivosheia, Polukhin, Fok and Shinkarenko crossed the Pyrenees together. Having finally reached his goal, Shinkarenko was inspired and wrote that everything in Spain reminded him of the civil war in Russia.[21] Fok was filled with even greater enthusiasm: 'Those of us who will be fighting for Nationalist Spain against the III International, as well as, in other words, against the Bolsheviks, will in this way carry out their duty to White Russia.'[22]

Insofar as many White Guards spoke French, the command proposed uniting them with French legitimist volunteers, but the Russians did not take to this idea. In the end, a significant portion of those newly-arrived received permission to join the Carlist traditionalist subunits – *Requetés* – whose religious fervour, traditionalism and extreme monarchism coincided to a great degree with what the emigrants believed. The most numerous group of Russians joined the *tercio* (regiment) of Aragonese Carlists *Doña María de Molina*, chiefly as part of Captain Emilio Vicente's 1st Company. In the middle of May 1937, the *tercio* included seventeen Russian volunteers, while another eight served in other units. A year later their number had grown to thirty-five.[23]

The command permitted them a special badge of identification – a white, blue and red chevron on the left pocket; the Russians sometimes sewed a small tricolored corner on the left sleeve in other *tercios*.[24] St. George cavaliers donned their crosses. The commander of the *Tercio Doña María de Molina* became acquainted with the Russians in March 1937 in Zaragoza:

> I then addressed them in French, explaining to them the goals and ideals of our struggle and that the slogan of our *requetés* was 'For God, the Motherland and the King' [*Dios, Patria, Rey*]. One of them replied on behalf of all the others that their ideal 'For the Faith, the Tsar and the Fatherland' was the traditional ideal of the Russian imperial army.[25]

Despite these individual signs of favour, the material situation of the newly-arrived Russians was awful. They could rely neither on help from their families nor a salary (with the exception of those who served in the Spanish Foreign Legion). Moreover, the Russians had to put up with serious humiliation in the form of their former ranks not being recognized, which meant a lack of respect to their great military experience – most of them were officers, but they were forced to serve as enlisted men.[26] There also was a difference in culture and experience: the old Russian officers noted their Spanish colleagues' absence of courtly manners and their low level of professional training.[27] According to Shinkarenko, the Russians serving in the *Tercio Doña María de Molina* did not get along and even quarrelled amongst themselves.[28]

Other Russians linked up with various subunits of the Francoist army on their own up until 1938. In July 1937 a dozen immigrants were fighting in the ranks of the Italian Expeditionary Corps (*Corpo Truppe Volontarie*, or CTV); some White volunteers asked to be taken into this formation's ranks, because they were dissatisfied with the cold reception they got in the Spanish units.[29] Some remained unknown. For example, in 1937 a propaganda leaflet was published in Russian, using the pre-revolutionary orthography, with an appeal to the soldiers of the International Brigades, promising to spare their lives and to repatriate them if they joined Franco's forces – evidently written by some exile.[30]

Various groups of non-Russian nationalists also supported the uprising against the Spanish Republic. The Armenian General Arsen Torkom proposed to Franco to recruit 300,000 (!) of his fellow countrymen in several countries. In his opinion Spain was fighting for the very same goals as had the first Armenian republic in 1918–20 – the 'rescue of Europe' from the 'Marxist gangrene'.[31] A similar position was also adopted by Georgian émigrés who believed that a victory by the rightist forces would weaken the Bolsheviks in Moscow and would hasten the independence of Georgia.[32] In September 1936 Mikhail Aleksandrovich (Pridon) Tsulukidze, a member of the 'White Georgii' organization (თეთრი გიორგი, 'Tetri Giorgi'), arrived in Spain and for the next five months observed the 'process of the rebirth of a great nation' at the front.[33] Six Georgians from the Union of Georgian Nobility, under the sponsorship of Colonel Aleksandr Vladimirovich Amilakhvari, left France and from November 1936 fought in the Carlist *Tercio de Navarra* in the north of Spain. Among them was the prince, the head of the union 'Those Who Swore an Oath of Fealty to Georgia', Lieutenant Elizbar Vachnadze, who fought as a partisan against the Red Army (RKKA) in the 1920s and who took part in the unsuccessful August uprising in 1924;[34] Captain Konstantin Aleksandrovich Gogidzhanov (Gogidzhanoshvili); Dmitrii Dzhordzhadze; and the naval cadet Petr Kirillovich Odishariia. There were also two or three

Ukrainian nationalists who fought against the Spanish Republic: for example, Volodymyr Belins'kyi, a former lieutenant in the Ukrainian National Republic's army.

From the very beginning the ROVS attempted to create a separate Russian subunit to take part in the fighting in Spain. Russian volunteers under Russian command would have become the first spark from which the flame of struggle and of a new and powerful army, capable of uniting the scattered national forces, should have arisen. For this purpose, in November 1936 the Union established contact with a representative of the Francoist side in Rome. The Spanish General Headquarters heard out the ROVS's proposals, which had been laid out by its chief – Lieutenant General Evgenii Karlovich Miller. At the end of December, the Spaniards received ROVS delegates in Salamanca, headed by General Pavel Nikolaevich Shatilov. The émigrés requested money for the hiring and passage of at least 2,000 soldiers. However, Franco himself declined these proposals, agreeing only to accept those Russian volunteers who possessed documentary proof of their membership in the ROVS into the ranks of the Spanish Legion. If there proved to be enough of these, then it might be possible to create their own subunits within the Legion. Both the Parisian leaders and those who had already left for the front wanted the Whites to have their own units or, at the very least, to be able to choose in which subunit they wished to serve.[35]

In January 1937 Miller and Shatilov dispatched memoranda to Franco.[36] These additional demands and proposals clearly seemed exhausting to the Spaniards, but their attitude did not cool the White émigrés' ardour. At the beginning of February the ROVS issued an appeal to its members to sign up as volunteers to fight in Spain. However, the results proved insignificant: no one responded to the appeal in Bulgaria, and only two in Yugoslavia, while Dvoichenko (who was Vladimir Kovalevskii's uncle[37]) later arrived from Romania, Aleksandr Esaulov-Obolenskii from Italy, and another two from Czechoslovakia. Whatever they might have wished, Russians living in Germany could not gather in large groups and be armed, for the Nazis had forbidden their recruitment for Spain and kept close track of their movements.[38]

France became the main 'supplier'. The volunteers would gather in groups of eight to ten men in the Society of Gallipoli Veterans in Paris, and from there would set out for the south, where they would cross the frontier, ending up in Irún. The first group organized by the ROVS consisted of seven men and left at the beginning of March, followed by another in the middle of the month.[39] The border along the Pyrenees was locked up tight and those Russian volunteers who did not possess French exit visas had to make their way across at their own peril, for example by swimming across the Bidasoa river or getting in touch with smugglers. Lieutenant General Boris Sergeevich Permikin volunteered to go and Prince Kirill Alekseevich Shirinskii-Shikhmatov helped him find some local guides who were supposed to take him across the Pyrenees by a secret and secure path. However, upon visiting their clandestine dwelling, Permikin smelled a rat and, afraid of falling into a trap, refused to go any further.[40]

Only a few émigrés made the journey comfortably and were greeted with respect. In mid-August 1937 Colonel Andrés Radzivill (Andrzej Radziwill) safely crossed the border at Irún. His arrival had been pre-emptively organized by Olga O'Donnell, a resident of Biarritz, and by Prince Mikhail Konstantinovich Gorchakov, one of the leaders of the Union of Russian Nobility (*Union de la Noblesse Russe*) in Paris. The local military mayor had issued him a 'passport' to go to the Castilian town of Burgos and present himself at Franco's headquarters. The colonel was received by Franco himself, and later was assigned to the VI Brigade of the 63rd Division of Navarre.[41]

Bolshevik intelligence found out about the ROVS's attempts to be of use to Franco.[42] The problem was not only the absence of money and the Spaniards' unwillingness to burden themselves with foreigners. A 'mole' had penetrated into the Union's leadership – Major General Nikolai Vladimirovich Skoblin, the several-times-wounded chief of Kornilov's Shock Troops, who had been working for the Bolsheviks for several years. It was in the Soviets' interest to disrupt any contacts between counterrevolutionaries, and Skoblin, who enjoyed absolute respect in the organization's higher echelons, was perfectly placed to carry out work to undermine the project. He was to have been at the Salamanca meeting in December 1936, but did not attend and disobeyed Miller's order; it was also most likely that he informed the French about the dispatch of volunteers.[43] On 16 April 1937 Captain Maksimovich's group was arrested while crossing the frontier, after which the ROVS cancelled the dispatch of volunteers. At this time only thirty-two officers from Section I of the ROVS had joined the Francoists' ranks.[44] Up until 1938 individual Russians continued to make their way to Spain.

Among the military emigration itself individual high-ranking officers did not approve of sending volunteers. Lieutenant General Anton Ivanovich Denikin, while wishing for a Francoist victory, considered the illegal crossings of the border along the Pyrenees a wasteful expenditure of Russian military strength, which should be saved for the cause of liberating Russia and not Spain.[45] Others sent parcels with warm clothes: officers and ladies in Berlin established an aid committee (for some reason, the Germans allowed this), in which the Grand Duchess Vera Konstantinova participated. She also petitioned for 'a good man from France', asking to help him make it to the war.[46] One of the Paris émigrés, an ethnic Kabardian Khokhondokova who became Comtesse du Loire through marriage, also helped the Russian volunteers.[47]

The Russian military émigrés' main journal, *Chasovoi*, which was published in Brussels, illuminated events in detail in its pages. The editorial board vigorously supported General Franco and his followers: the conflict was named the 'Spanish-Soviet War'; Franco's forces were the 'Whites' and the Republicans' the 'Reds', directed from Moscow. They printed letters from Russian volunteers in the Iberian peninsula, which emphasized the similarity in the experience between the old and new civil wars.[48] Shinkarenko, who took the pseudonym of Belogorskii, wrote an article entitled 'Greetings to the Spanish "Kornilovites"'.[49] The émigrés congratulated the defenders of the Alcázar de Toledo, the liberation of which had supposedly become possible thanks to divine intervention and the selflessness of the 'White heroes'.[50] Another officer wrote: 'This is the same thing, amazingly the same thing, as what we experienced in the Volunteer Army during the first months.'[51] One of the first to arrive agreed: 'We are conducting, in general, "The First Campaign", both in the sense of its difficulty, as well as the enemy's stubbornness . . . The war is incomparably more serious than ours and is being conducted according to all the latest rules of military art.'[52] Another time a village was captured and the population greeted the Carlists with church bells ringing, and 'all of this vividly reminded us of our long-ago victorious march on Moscow [1919]'.[53] A Russian serving in the Legion ascribed to Stalin the overall leadership of the Republican side and assumed that the same disciplinary measures were employed as in the Red Army 15 years earlier, including mass firing squads; he also believed that in Spain the battle was for 'the faith, culture and all of Europe'.[54] Anti-Semitic notes were also heard: 'There's no speculation, because there are no Jews . . . Here you truly feel yourself a fully-enfranchised citizen and our [Nansen] Rubenstein citizenship has disappeared without a trace.'[55]

The extreme right activists of the Russian National Union of War Participants (RNSUV), who saw themselves as rivals of the ROVS, hewed to a similar line here: 'The Spanish war is continuing in our time the pictures of that which we observed in Russia during the Kornilov campaign and the sinister flame of burning cathedrals is lit by the hammer and sickle of "popular fronts".'[56] It is amazing just how the tone of the ultra-right émigrés coincided with the émigrés of other nationalities, although politically speaking these groups were diametrically opposed. In March 1937 the previously mentioned Amilakhvari wrote a letter from the Bilbao area to the Parisian journal *Kartlossi*, which was the mouthpiece for a very small organization, the 'Fascist Union of Georgia'.

> We Georgians, who now serve within the ranks of the Carlists, are happy in that we are granted the opportunity, if only here in Spain, in the mountains of Navarre, to do battle with the bearers of ideas that destroyed our Motherland. The hour is not far off, when the bell of liberty for our country will ring out. At that time, we want to be and will be together with the Georgian people in the first ranks of warriors.[57]

Soviet propaganda, which employed terms from the Russian Civil War, did not lag behind: the Francoists were 'White bandits', carrying out a 'White terror' in the areas under their control.[58] They went so far as to make direct comparisons: 'The atrocities of the fascist executioners in Spain remind one of the violence of the White Generals in the Crimea.'[59] These same designations also remained in some memoirs after the war: Ragozin, who scoured the skies of Spain, recalled 'the main White forces (the Spaniards called them 'blue')' and the 'Hispano-Bolshevik war'.[60]

The Whites were distinguished by a high degree of motivation and displayed self-abnegation in the fighting, despite their often advanced age. Some of them, for example Rashevskii, left their families in France; others were not weighed down by obligations and took part in this military adventure on their own. In April 1937 Shinkarenko received a serious head wound and this put him out of action for a long time.[61] The repeatedly wounded

Gogidzhanoshvili, who lost his left eye in battle, also distinguished himself and within a few months he was promoted to the rank of lieutenant.[62]

In April 1937 Franco's General Staff once again reviewed the question of creating a separate Russian unit. It was not a major problem, as there were only about 100 volunteers, which quashed the idea. Within three months Fok, Shatilov and Shinkarenko once again approached Franco with a request to move the proposal forward. Such a formation, they maintained, could become a magnet attracting to Spain hundreds of White Guards from all over the world. Upon the conclusion of the struggle in Spain, they would become the core of a new force, which would carry out a *Reconquista*, this time in Russia. The Francoists were unenthusiastic about the Russians' dreams, probably having reached a conclusion from the low effectiveness of the other foreign volunteer units, or simply from fear that the Russians would slip out of effective control. Shinkarenko managed to meet the Spanish *Caudillo* following his wounding, but the sole result of this audience was his appointment to the Spanish Legion.[63] The wounded Rashevskii wrote Franco from hospital, requesting that he form a separate Russian unit, but this was ignored.[64]

The arid Spanish land drank up Russian blood. On 24 August 1937, during the course of the Republicans' offensive in the Belchite and Quinto de Ebro sector, the Francoist troops suffered heavy losses. On the Republican side, the XV Abraham Lincoln International Brigade, consisting of North American volunteers, particularly distinguished itself. Among those defending Quinto de Ebro was the 2nd Company of the *Doña María de Molina tercio*, in which Lieutenants Polukhin and Fok fought, who had been promoted in rank for their successes in service.[65] Polukhin died on that day; wounded in the neck, he was carried into a church, into the St. Anne side-altar, which was later hit by a shell which buried the wounded alive.[66]

The officers in charge of the defence ended up blocked in on a neighbouring hill (Purubell Hill) and held out for another two days, cut off from drinking water. They refused to surrender. At dawn on 26 August the Americans attempted to storm the position. Fok was among the last of the defenders. An American veteran of the International Brigade recalled:

> At one point we see a White Russian officer. Larry O'Toole and I approach him. He is screaming in Russian: 'Red pigs! Red pigs'. Then in Spanish: 'If you come any closer, I'll shoot'. O'Toole yells

back, 'Go ahead and shoot, you bastard. If you don't, I will'. He has his gun in his hand and he blows his brains out, and I take his gun and a sword and a Russian Bible from his body.[67]

Another American bragged that they had taken 1,200 prisoners and 'as many chickens. Executed 32 officers and a Russian White Guard and a Nazi officer committed suicide.'[68] The Republicans turned over Fok's personal correspondence to the Soviet spy Mikhail Efimovich Kol'tsov. The defenders of Quinto were highly praised by Francoist propaganda and were bestowed the highest award – the collective cross of the Order of St. Ferdinand. The two Russians, Fok and Polukhin, were also remembered and venerated in the diaspora.[69]

It was as if the Spanish war had taken to its bosom the interwoven scripts of the Russian past. Everything was intertwined and everything was in it – personal tragedies, echoes of the collapse of the Russian Empire, old grudges, and the different choices of Russian people. The British volunteer, Peter Kemp, met old Russian officers in Spain:

> He shook his head sadly when I told him I was English. Later I heard that, like many of his countrymen, he had little love for the English. I met another like him, nearly two years later, in San Sebastián, who informed me that he was so disgusted with the British for the way they had let down his Tsar that he had ceased altogether to drink whisky.[70]

Exactly as if in a distorted mirror, the Russian discord of 20 years' standing was fleetingly glimpsed on the crest of a new war. Igor Sakharov recalled an incident when they captured a quite young pilot from among the Soviet specialists, who had been shot down. To no avail the émigrés who were fighting for Franco begged him to answer the Spanish officers' questions and save his life. The young Soviet pilot absolutely refused to do so and was shot, 'without even having given us his name'.[71] Another emigrant recalled:

> In our battles, quick and cruel, we once met the inspirers of the entire Spanish conflagration – Russian communists. One of them was a tank crewman from a tank that we had knocked out. Slightly concussed by a grenade explosion, he humbly walked ahead of me

to Legion headquarters. I can't put into words everything I was thinking, while leading my own Russian to death . . . An inadvertent curse word, which I let out when I tripped, gave me away . . . He understood that I was Russian and that we were both sons of a great Motherland, and in mortal sorrow he begged: 'Save me, I'm not a Bolshevik, not a communist, brother, save me . . . ' I vouched for him and he became my combat comrade and hates the Reds just as much as I do.[72]

Franco won in the spring of 1939.[73] Riding the wave of this victory, the Russian exiles sought to make sense of what they had witnessed, while comparing it with the White Army's past, and by no means in the latter's favour. Baron Boris Sergeevich von Lüdinghausen-Wolff, who had fought in the Carlist *Montejurra tercio*, following a comprehensive analysis of the new Spain, concluded that the entire matter lay in unity of command. His recipe was as follows: 'There should also be one political party in Russia, which takes everything healthy from Italian, Spanish and German fascism and all that is applicable to the country. The task facing Russia is to unite the monarchical past with contemporary fascism.'[74]

On 3 May 1939 the Russian volunteers marched in the victory parade (*Desfile de la Victoria*) in Valencia. On 22 May they received a gift from Germany, where at the beginning of the month the local émigrés had drawn up a two-class medal for participants in the war, with a sword for combatants and on without for civilians.[75] At the end of June all the Russians were officially demobilized. On 25 October a group, led by Colonel Nikolai Boltin, an aristocrat who appeared as the unofficial leader of the émigrés, met with the hero of the defence of the Alcázar, General José Moscardó, and on 29 October with Franco himself. During the meeting with the latter, Boltin declared that the Russians would like to join the Spanish Legion as officers, that is, to remain in military service and receive a salary.[76]

Boltin subsequently received the rank of honorary Colonel in the national militia, dependent on the Spanish Fascist Falange (*FET de las JONS*), and enjoyed the patronage of Raimundo Fernández-Cuesta, a leading member of the party. This enabled Boltin the opportunity to solicit in the army ministry for the Russian soldiers, demanding for them the rank of junior or honorary lieutenant, which would have offered them a small salary while they were looking for work.[77]

What were the results? The Russians became an exotic but non-influential part of the international contingent of Franco partisans. There were fewer than 200 White Guards, while the Italians numbered 79,000 and the Germans 25,000 (mostly non-combat troops), nearly 10,000 Portuguese, 2,000 Frenchmen, 700 Irish, and 200 or 300 Latin Americans.[78] According to the highest estimate, from 150 to 170 White Russians fought for Franco, of whom 19 perished and many more were wounded.[79] Other sources speak of only fifty soldiers, of whom seven perished.[80] Boltin, in approaching the army ministry in April 1940 and standing up for his own, mentioned that seventy-two men arrived in the country, 'almost all of whom were Russian army officers', of whom thirty-four perished in battle.[81] On the other side, there were also Russians who came to fight for the Republic from various countries, from Canada to France. Their number is estimated at 285, although it is worth remembering that not all of them were part of the Russian migrant diaspora.[82] According to data from ROVS, only about forty former officers from the White armies served in the Republican army.[83]

For the right-wing Russian émigrés, who had been oppressed by the years of wars and wanderings, participation in the Spanish conflict played an important symbolic role. The victory of the Francoists raised their fallen spirits and hopes for a triumphant return home. At the same time, some veterans complained bitterly about their overseas brethren, who had put forward such a ridiculously small number of volunteers.[84]

The diaspora's enthusiasm was palpable; however, it proved to be fettered by a multitude of factors that brought this to nothing. The ROVS which tried to take part in the conflict as an organization ended up being weakened for external and internal reasons. The external reason was that the Russian Whites and their desire to assist Russia through Spain proved to be unneeded by the right-wing Spaniards. The latter sought to solve questions of internal politics through civil war, hence any other non-Spanish nationalist agenda remained irrelevant to them, or at least too far removed from the fate of Spain, and not Russia, which was at stake. Secondly, there were quarrels enough within the ROVS and unity was lacking, exacerbated by moles such as Skoblin in the highest echelon of the organization. Thirdly, and the most important, any recruitment of volunteers required funnelling large sums of money, and the ROVS simply did not have any considerable amount of funds to spend on dispatching a large number of soldiers. Thus, a European-wide mobilization through the sections of the ROVS simply did not happen, since volunteering remained too complicated an endeavour, both logistically and economically.

Matters stood roughly the same in the other émigré organizations. In Bulgaria the émigrés wrote to the newspaper *Russia's Voice* (*Golos Rossii*), asking them for assistance in reaching Franco's army, but the newspaper replied regretfully that it lacked the means to help.[85] This stood in sharp contrast with the Whites' enemy, the III International, which was superior to them both financially and organizationally, and was able to successfully organize support for the Republic, to the point where thousands of volunteers arrived from all over the world, among whom were several thousand from the US, Canada, France, Italian and German antifascist diasporas, several hundred from countries ranging from Denmark to the Netherlands, and several dozen from Australia and Ireland.[86]

Finally, Spain and its problems were too far from Russia and the sufferings of the émigrés themselves: old White Guards were ready to manifest 'activism' for Russia's sake, but not for a country that was completely foreign to them.[87] Only a minority of exiles were ready to fight against communism at any place on the planet and under any conditions. Rifle fire soothed the ears of the majority only on the pages of newspapers. Having lulled themselves with published stories about 'sticking it to the Reds', they could refrain from doing anything.

Veterans of Spain were covered with glory and acclaimed within the diaspora as worthy continuers of the anti-Bolshevik cause. The problem of the cooling of ardour was a serious one. As early as March 1937 they were speaking of a group of Parisian drivers who had ended up in Alicante and who had already gone through the various stages of personal evolution: disillusionment with the anti-communist struggle and a retreat into private life, the renunciation of the right-wing nationalist world view, an ideological collapse as such, the status of a refugee without ideals, recognition of Soviet power, and as a result – to fight for the Spanish Republic for the purpose of earning 'forgiveness' from the Bolsheviks.[88] There were other examples as well.[89] In 1938 the false memoirs of 'Count Ivan Petrov', written by the Francoist journalist José Cirre Jiménez, were published in the Francoist rear. In the book, the 'penitent' émigré recalled how he had left Paris and ended up on the side of the Spanish Republicans, who are pictured as bloodthirsty creatures.[90]

Russian volunteers of the *requeté* units were the 'antidote'.[91] The leaders of military organizations saw in the 'old-new' soldiers miracle-workers, with whose help they could cure the cadres of the ROVS itself of disappointment and boost their spirits.[92] In fact, the same narrative worked for civilian exiles as well. In late May 1939, Archbishop Nikon (de Grève) had paid the Russians in Spain a short visit. Once back in Paris, Nikon held a public speech at the Alexander Nevsky Cathedral. The place was packed with émigrés, including parents of Russian volunteers, ardently listening to Nikon's account of exceptional valour on Spanish soil.[93] '[The Russian volunteers] are happy, they are proud of their heroic struggle against communism, full of hardship and sacrifice, the one they carry out among foreign people in an alien land. Bound by blood spilt together, Russians and Spaniards are not foreign to each other anymore – they are brothers!'[94]

In the diaspora, the Russian veterans' fate and their participation in the Spanish conflict were portrayed in the most exalted terms. The Paris section of the ROVS reported in the spring of 1940:

> They have all been awarded with the three existing combat crosses and medals and the high command's treatment of them leaves nothing to be desired. Our heroes not only maintained the reputation of the brave Russian officer, but also did everything they could so that the Spaniards learned the truth about Russia, about the White struggle, and not to confuse Russians with communists.[95]

Even in 1944 some émigrés praised those who had fallen in Spain and put them forth as an example.[96] It was considered normal to be a simultaneous member of several organizations, so other political organizations also got the opportunity to declare that they had taken part in the Spanish conflict. For example, since 1934 Polukhin had been a member of the Russian Imperial Union-Order (RISO) and was the secretary of the RISO's 2nd Parisian Detachment; Nikolai Ivanov, who was killed on the Catalonia front 15 days before the end of the war, was a member of the same monarchist group. The members of the RISO drew up a special greeting in their honour, which is used by members of the organization to this day.[97] And the non-Russian émigrés also took pride in their Spanish mission: according to a prominent nationalist, General Shalva Maglakelidze, the Georgian returnees arrived in Paris 'sporting the Spanish berets'.[98]

The Francoists' victory influenced the Russian diaspora in the following manner. First of all, it brought a rare feeling of long-awaited revenge for their own defeat of 1920 ('We couldn't make it happen, but we at least got it right somewhere'). Secondly, it became the stimulus for the unification of the 'defeatists', who wished to crush the USSR at any price ('Maybe this time we'll get it right at home'). This is what Staff Captain Anton Prokof'evich Iaremchuk II wrote in June 1939 about the opportunity to once again take up arms against sworn enemies:

> But we came to know the soldier's highest joy: the incomparable consciousness of victory over the enemy, who is the enemy of our Motherland too. And we, Russian volunteers in the Spanish National Army, have fulfilled our duty. For it is we who put forth our efforts in the struggle of the forces of light against the common enemy and assisted in the struggle against communism, which has been reduced to dust here in Spain. This gives us the right to believe that communism, which has enslaved our great and beautiful Motherland – Russia – will fall and that the Russian tricolor will once again wave over the Russian land. We believe that we do not have long to wait.[99]

Pavel Rashevskii, in his turn, revealed his own plans to one Carlist volunteer: 'As soon as we end the war in Spain, we will move against the French Reds . . . . And then all together – Italy, Germany, Portugal, Spain, and France, as brothers in civilization – will take on the cursed tyrants of my country, my native Russia, from where I constantly hear groaning.'[100]

Undoubtedly, Iaremchuk and Rashevskii, and the entire Russian military emigration, were incapable of recognizing their own political and military impotence. In 1939 there was not the slightest reason to think that the road from sunny Madrid would lead to the red stars of Moscow. However, the opportunity to cross swords with the old enemy on one's native soil soon became available – to be sure, in completely different conditions and in a different situation.

'Sandcastles': Russian Émigrés and Operation Barbarossa

As early as the 1920s, during the Munich period in the history of German National Socialism, the Nazis and Russian émigrés maintained contact and even worked together. Before Adolf Hitler and General Erich Ludendorff's 'Beer Hall Putsch' in November 1923, there was a certain amount of cooperation between the Nazi Party and individual groups of Russian rightists, which was conducted through the 'Reconstruction' (*Aufbau*) organization. A central figure in these contacts was Max von Scheubner-Richter, a Baltic German from Russia and a close comrade-in-arms of Hitler, who had established a bridge with those émigrés among the Russian extreme monarchists and nationalists, and who also enjoyed their financial support. In those early years some Brownshirts supported Grand Duke Kirill Vladimirovich Romanov, who resided in Coburg, as a candidate for the Tsarist throne. Individual émigrés in Munich, who shared anti-Semitic and anti-democratic views, were close to the Nazi Party (NSDAP).[1] Some of these Russian émigrés later had an impressive career.[2]

It was precisely they who to some degree shaped in Hitler the perception that there was supposedly a close connection between Judaism and Bolshevism. Nikolai Vasil'evich Snesarev, a journalist and former deputy in the State Duma, who adhered to radical-right views in exile, closely cooperated with the future *Führer* for a certain period of time. One might surmise that during the period up to 1924 Adolf Hitler, who was under the clear influence of Scheubner-Richter, himself allowed for a certain variation on a theoretical alliance between national Germany and a reborn monarchist Russia, which together would erect a 'barrier' to communism. However, these ideas, if they existed, evaporated quite quickly, and in the end Hitler himself polished his world view, having gotten rid of Russian fellow travellers who had become unnecessary. No one spoke any more about any kind of potential German-Russian cooperation or anti-Bolshevik Russians as allies: anti-Semitism, the hierarchy of genetically defined racial origin and the idea of expanding 'living space' towards the European East became the basic lines in *Mein Kampf*.[3]

If one were to break down National Socialism into its component parts, then this idea was based upon a combination of the following principles: radical anti-Semitism and biological racism; anti-communism and anti-democracy; German nationalism and the idea of 'living space' (racist colonialism), which legitimized German territorial expansion. The Russian 'defeatists' were people of, at a minimum, rightist convictions, and often far right. Anti-communism, anti-democracy and cultural-religious anti-Semitism (sometimes though with a racial component) were their common ground with the Nazis. However, the racial-biological worldview was fully adopted by only a small group of émigrés, while very few of them were ready to give up Russian territory to German settlers or simply the German state. More often than not the Russian exiles, who lacked the strength or did not wish to admit that they were confusing wishes with reality, simply closed their eyes to the unambiguously detailed German expansionist aspirations.

Many of them read Hitler's popular book *Mein Kampf*, but decided not to take his words seriously. As Lieutenant General Aleksandr Sergeevich Lukomskii wrote in February 1939, these were only 'terrible words'.[4] Besides, the spirit always predominated over matter among the émigrés, and 'land', as such, did not have any significance. Nikolai Aleksandrovich Tsurikov, philosopher and ideologist of the ROVS, called the blind following of geographical borders 'territorial fetishism', as a result of which the main task was lost – 'the preservation of one's nation's living strength'. For the 'defeatists' the loss of the 'people's soul and culture' was more terrible than any loss of land. Correspondingly, in comparison with the existence of the Bolshevik regime, even German Nazism appeared as a sort of 'alternative' in their consciousness. This obvious discomfort was explained away by means of an unusual patriotic reverse: the Germans had their own claims, to be sure, but they were the only ones capable of destroying Stalin; besides, Germany supposedly would not be able 'to swallow and digest' Russia, insofar as 'the biological strength of the Russian people was unconquerable'.[5]

Of course, this was just internal discourse. All of this talk was confined to the White diaspora, which was searching for its place. The German leadership was quite consistent and was sharply negative toward the idea of Russian émigrés serving in its armed forces; the idea of appointing émigrés to any kind of leading positions seemed all the more absurd. They did not bring in the émigrés as experts while they were drawing up plans for the future of the Russian territories.[6] Their role, if they got that far, was a nominally functional one. Nonetheless, the struggle between diverse offices and institutions, which in the Nazi state's polyarchy actively competed for the attention of the leader while taking the form of a single bureaucratic mechanism, created some 'windows of opportunity' and niches. The émigrés managed to find go-betweens and even interlocutors among them, which made it possible to satisfy some requests. It was precisely in this sphere, where the German state's concrete and urgent interests coincided with the readiness of the exiles (even if for another reason) to serve that system, they managed to achieve their goals. In this fashion many managed to get around the clear taboos against émigrés serving in the army and joined the ranks of the Wehrmacht as interpreters, drivers and construction workers.[7]

Nazi Germany's war against Stalinist Russia unleashed in June 1941 was not an ordinary conflict. It was a campaign for the complete and systematic extermination of the enemy and his political worldview. According to the National Socialists' convictions, the Slavic peoples were not entitled to their own state system and their lands were to be completely colonized. The war's principles and nature were outlined by Hitler and his Nazi comrades-in-arms, but a large part of the Wehrmacht's generals shared these basic ideas.[8]

As early as March 1941 the rulers of the Third Reich excluded any possibility of including émigrés in the planned invasion. The German state derived no benefit from Russian intellectuals who arrived with the Wehrmacht in the occupied territories. As the Germans themselves believed, it was unlikely that following 20 years away from their Motherland they would be in any way accepted by the Russian population. Of course, it was obvious to the Wehrmacht that the émigrés were playing their own game, being Russian nationalists, that is, latent opponents of the new German 'teaching'. The Wehrmacht High Command (*Oberkommando der Wehrmacht*, OKW) openly wrote: 'Also, we must in no way allow the Bolshevik state to be replaced by a nationalist Russia, which in the final analysis (as history shows), will once again oppose Germany.'[9]

Unaware of these secret documents and being convinced that war was close and inevitable, the ROVS chiefs attempted to offer their services to the Wehrmacht. The most famous attempt was the appeal of the chief of the semi-autonomous ORVS,[10] Major General Aleksei Aleksandrovich von Lampe, which he sent on 21 May 1941 to the commander-in-chief of the Army High Command (*Oberkommando des Heeres*, OKH), General Field Marshal Walther von Brauchitsch.[11] Lampe placed his organization at the

German army's disposal and requested that it be given the opportunity to participate in the approaching conflict. The Germans did not even bother to reply.

On 18 June the Gestapo (the secret police) forbade Russian émigrés residing in the territory of the Reich to enter their native land without prior authorization. Leaving one's workplace without a permit was a reason for arrest.[12] Within four days Operation Barbarossa began and the Fascists, ultra-rightists, Catholics and radical anti-communists of Europe believed that the German divisions were the force which would finish off Soviet power. Various proposals to create foreign units rained down. On 30 June a conference of representatives from the Nazi Party, the Foreign Ministry, the OKW and the SS (*Schutzstaffeln*, the Nazi Party's security detachments) took place in Berlin. Here were confirmed the general directives for dealing with foreign volunteers against the Soviet Union, in accordance with a strictly observed ethnic hierarchy. Exception was made only for Russian émigrés and Czech collaborators – their proposals to volunteer were to be rejected, and they were not to be accepted into service. German embassies all over Europe received from Berlin precise instructions to refuse Russian émigré requests that they be sent to the ranks of the invading army.[13]

Once again, not knowing of these decisions, the 'defeatists' in the ROVS (and not just there) were full of incomparable joy. The Russian military émigrés flooded their chiefs with correspondence. Prayer services of thanks were held. Meetings were held in the chief cities of Europe, attended by thousands of Russian exiles. Hosannas were sung to the German 'liberators', and absurdly grandiose plans were proclaimed for the return to some kind of 'national life' and an eternal 'union' between Germany and (the future) Russia, based on the principles of mutual respect. All of these people believed that the occupiers would meet them halfway by putting the reins of power in their hands, and that 21 years of expectations and wanderings were behind them. The patriotic dreams they had held in their exile had become reality.[14]

'German Prohibitions, Spanish Needs': Émigrés in the Blue Division

On 22 June 1941 Francoist Spain formally abstained from participation in the war against the Soviet Union, and maintained its non-belligerent status. The Falangists and radical Fascists who passionately wished to make their contribution to the imposition of a 'New Order' in Europe and to support National Socialist hegemony, organized an initiative to create a voluntary expeditionary corps. A good portion of the Spanish army, the mass of Catholics and anti-communists shared this Germanophilia. All of these groups saw God's hand in the German *Drang nach Osten*, which would supposedly put an end to Bolshevism, and, possibly, would return the Russia that had 'forgotten God' back to the bosom of Christianity. However, the dictator Franco made a Solomonic decision: to dispatch to the Russian front – from which they expected no more than an easy 'tank walk' – a division of volunteers made up of officers, sergeants and NCOs provided by the Spanish army, and rank-and-file soldiers recruited by the Falange. The division was to become part of the Wehrmacht on equal terms, although with its own juridical norms.

In less than three weeks the first group of volunteers had been gathered. In spite of this, the level of enthusiasm varied in the diverse regions of the country. 17,000 men departed for the front in the beginning of July. The first group consisted heavily of Falangists, anti-communist Catholics, everyday opportunists, time-serving sergeants and NCOs hoping to move up the career ladder, and professional army officers with similar motives. Among the first volunteers was no small number of former prisoners and people who had undergone political persecution in the Republican zone: they had been unable to take part in the recently concluded war on the side of the Francoists. Similar in orientation were numerous Falangist university students, who due to their young age had not taken part in combat operations earlier.[1]

The opening of recruiting stations by the Falange became for the handful of White émigrés that had remained in Spain after 1939 that very cherished opportunity to get a ticket home and to finally carry out their long-held dream to cross swords with the 'main enemy'. There were similar groups, which put forth their military contingent for the Germans, in almost every occupied European country. One large group of exiles enrolled in the Legion of French Volunteers against Bolshevism (*Légion des Volontaires Français contre le Bolchévisme*, LVF),[2] some joined the Wehrmacht's Walloon Legion (*Légion Wallonie*), while others enrolled in the Italian Expeditionary Corps (*Corpo di Spedizione Italiano in Russia*, CSIR). After the 638th French Regiment, it was precisely the Wehrmacht's 250th Division, otherwise known as the Blue Division (*División Azul*), for the colour of the Falangist shirts, that numbered the greatest number of White émigrés.[3]

Not long after the attack on the Soviet Union, some Russian Whites approached the German embassy in Madrid. The already familiar Nikolai Boltin declared himself a volunteer and handed over a memorandum on behalf of twenty-nine émigrés. All the signatories were veterans of the Spanish Civil War and had been awarded Spanish citizenship. However, the embassy quickly informed the petitioners that Berlin, with the exception of special cases, did not wish to see such gentlemen in its army. Perhaps in the future exceptions would be made for citizens of the Baltic States annexed by the Bolsheviks in 1940. Boltin then proposed to procure his comrades-in-arms as propagandists, but this latest proposal went unanswered.[4]

Iaremchuk recalled this episode in the following way:

> In the morning the Spanish leadership summoned us and informed us that a Colonel, the German embassy's military attaché, wished to see us. Several men went to see him and he informed us, with an embarrassed expression on his face, that there was an order by Hitler prohibiting White Russians to serve in the ranks of the German army in the war against the USSR. It was like they had poured a bucket of cold water on our heads . . . An exception had been made for a few Russians who had served as officers in the Foreign Legion . . . It was later discovered that the Germans had approved these officers' participation, because some of them were born in Ukraine, and the thickheaded Germans imagined that they must automatically be Ukrainian independence fighters and later demanded that they be sent back to Spain, but the commander of the 'Blue Division', General Muñoz Grandes, replied that 'I have

no Russian officers, but only Spanish officers' . . . The Germans were forced to swallow the pill.[5]

The Russians came by two paths. On 28 June Boltin, at the same time as the trip to the embassy, sent a letter to the ministry of the Spanish army with a list of eighteen 'volunteers of Russian descent, who have fought in the ranks of the glorious Spanish army and who have continued to serve', who very much wished to attach themselves to the 'Crusade for the liberation of Russia from the common enemy – Communism'. Five days later Boltin sent a new list, adding the ranks of the volunteers in the Russian army and the ranks awarded in the war years in Spain, as well as increasing the number of names to twenty-eight.[6] At the same time the press was reporting that some Russians had already signed up as volunteers. Spanish correspondents in Berlin noted the enthusiasm of the Russian émigrés who wished to return to their Motherland alongside the Wehrmacht.

As Iaremchuk recalled, the Spanish military did everything possible to get around the Germans' instructions. Lieutenant Colonel Joaquín Romero got in touch with Berlin, from where they once again explained to him that White Russians could not be accepted into service, with the exception of those who had a Spanish passport. There were eighteen such in Boltin's list, while there was simply no data on the others. The Army General Staff sent the lists to General Agustín Muñoz Grandes, the recently appointed commander-in-chief of the expeditionary corps, asking to know 'whether he finds it necessary to assign them some functions or another'.[7] Viktor Voronin also wanted to serve on the German-Soviet front. Everything points to the fact that Muñoz Grandes made the decision to ignore the German prohibition. Therefore, he accepted all Russian émigrés who wished to serve, and who obviously were bound to be extremely useful for the Spaniards when the division reached the unknown country.

With the exception of a polyglot translator with a Nansen passport, who had grown up in a family of Russian Germans living in Estonia and Buenos Aires, practically no one in the Spanish corps had knowledge of the Russian language. The hunger for interpreters was great. In summer 1941, Demetrius Dvoichenko-Markov, who was naturalized together with his father Vladimir Dvoichenko and later became an officer in the US Army, was passing through Spain to join his mother in America:

In fact, when I arrived in Spain, there was a Spanish Colonel, who said 'Oh, we need you as an interpreter! We are sending a division to the Eastern Front, [and] with the Blue Division we need an interpreter. Would you volunteer?' I said 'No, I have to join my mother, I cannot do that'. And he said 'Well, we will wait until you are 21. According to Spanish law, we can draft you at 21'. Oh boy, was I praying to get the American visa [laughs], because they wanted me to go as an interpreter with the Blue Division.[8]

The White Guards, although no longer young, and in some cases not yet recovered from their wounds, demonstrated enormous enthusiasm. Georgii Staritskii, who knew five languages, volunteered for the division and was subsequently sent as a translator to the 269th Infantry Regiment's second section. Two Russians, Aleksandr Vladimirovich Bibikov and Vladimir Ivanovich Kovalevskii, served in the Falangist militia headquarters in Guipúzcoa: both volunteered for the division. One of them wrote in the Falangist local daily *Unity* (*Unidad*), that the White Russians were leaving 'with suitcases packed, on their way to the great return . . . about which they had been mad about for so many years'; they were also ready to sing the Falangist hymn, 'Facing the Sun' (*Cara al sol*) and to continue 'on our steppes' the campaign begun in 1936 'in the fightings of the Alto de los Leones [literally, Hill of the Lions]', a disputed position in the north of the Madrid front. The author finished his tirade with the slogans 'Long live national Russia!' and 'Up with Spain! (*Arriba España!*)'.[9]

The Spanish Legion's 46-year-old Lieutenant Ali (Sergei Konstantinovich) Gurskii (Magometov) had managed to serve in two Carlist *tercios* – *Doña María de Molina* and *Montejurra*. Gurskii was repeatedly wounded and in 1941 worked in the Higher Army School: he approached Franco in a letter for permission to join the German army. His motives were an explosive mix of anti-communism, nationalism and a certain dollop of anti-Semitism:

When the Fuhrer [*sic*], Hitler, declared war on the communists, Bolsheviks and Jews, who defeated my Motherland, and who stepped foot on Russian soil, I considered it my holy duty as a former Russian officer and patriot to immediately leave for there in order to once again assist, with my strength and knowledge, the liberation of my former Motherland from the horrible terror of communism.[10]

Gurskii was not alone in his views: the Russian émigrés naively believed in the political goodwill of the Nazis and their allies and not in their desire to pick up land and slaves from among the 'Eastern peoples'. Nor did Boltin and Dvoichenko among the veteran Francoist fighters, who were too old, depart. The first, although he had tried to volunteer in the first days, finally decided not to get involved in an adventure and believed that the Nazis would lose. Dvoichenko did not wish to help Hitler conquer Russia and during the war was engaged in basic training for the Spaniards. Once the Falangist leadership demanded that he give the Nazi salute, to which he curtly replied that he served Spain and was ready to pronounce its slogans, but not German ones, after which they left him alone. At home he carefully traced the movement of the front line on a map hanging from the wall. Shinkarenko also took a decisive anti-Hitler stance.[11] Following the war he did not hide the facts and recalled that the overwhelming majority of their comrades-in-arms, 'made their decision', as he called it: they took the Germans' side.

From this moment their paths went separate ways. In Pavel Rashevskii's file the Spaniards discovered unclear areas, as a result of which after enrolling him in the division they left him in Spain. Another two White émigrés, who had lived in Spain before 1936, were also included in this small group of Russians: Igor Perchin and Sergei Ponomarev. The first was the son of Russian émigrés and grew up in Madrid, spoke excellent Spanish, was loyal to the Spanish authorities and worked as a translator and censor. Ponomarev settled down in Barcelona and, while maintaining that he had been a member of the Falange since 1934, made the rounds of the local Falangist headquarters and the German consulate for the opportunity to join the 'Russian imperial forces fighting on Germany's side'. On 26 June he left for the border town of Irún and was enrolled in the division. There remain another two requests to join the division, sent from two Russians from Bucharest and Morocco: both were turned down in September 1941 by the Army General Staff.[12] Finally, there was a small group of those officers who were turned down – they left for the Russian front much later as translators for the Italian army.[13]

Those who left with the Blue Division wrote letters to their comrades-in-arms in the ROVS, thus facilitating the strengthening of the illusions of the émigrés in the rear, as well as their own. Mikhail Nikolaevich Iureninskii reported from Madrid that all those Russians who had fought in Spain had been taken into the division: many of them had already left, while others, including himself, were waiting for a rapid departure for the front.[14] Of course, this was not the truth, if only because the Spaniards did not take everyone. In September 1941 Major General Mikhail Mikhailovich Zinkevich reported to Prague: 'In the letters of our "Spaniards" (half are already in the Legion or on the way) they write "Christ has risen" to our Motherland and to all of us. I feel this with all my heart.'[15] All of these optimistic hopes later faded. In 1943 there was an attempt to somehow present the émigrés in Madrid with General Andreii Vlasov's project for creating the ROA (Russian Liberation Army), although it does not appear that this had serious consequences.[16] But the Germans' refusals and prohibitions were remembered for a long time. At the end of April 1944 the chief of the ROVS, Lieutenant General Aleksei Petrovich Arkhangel'skii, grieved: 'White Russians were not even allowed to join the "Spanish Blue Division" . . . This was bitter and insulting for us.'[17]

In the USSR the Spaniards had already gathered up during their deployment at the front a small number of Soviet citizens who knew the language and who performed the role of translators. Some of these people left with the division for Spain in late 1943.[18] Three children were known to have been in the 263rd Infantry Regiment: the Spanish dressed the boys in uniform, they lived with the unit and carried out small tasks; dissatisfied with this Spanish bending of the rules, the Germans ordered them to move the kids out of the division.[19] With the division there were even (one cannot say that they 'served') captured Red Army soldiers, who did the grunt work. The division staff's second section allocated most of them to the supply section (*Intendencia*), broken up into groups of eight men each. Judging from Spanish and German documents and photographs, these people's situation was mournful; although it seems that the Spaniards treated their prisoners better than the Germans did, they also fed their forced labourers poorly and beat them. The German high command – not out of humanitarian concerns, but for the purpose of effectively employing this human resource – recommended in July 1942 that the Spaniards treat the prisoners working within the division better, while urging the Spanish officers to watch them strictly.[20] In the spring and summer of 1943 an attempt was made to transfer them to the 1st Guards Brigade of the ROA (Russian Liberation Army of

General Vlasov), which was undergoing formation, in which a veteran of Spain, Captain Grigorii Pavlovich Lamsdorf, served in one of the important posts. The attempt was not crowned with success and was blocked by the Germans.[21] In exceptional instances, Soviet prisoners remained with the Blue Legion, the smaller successor unit that stayed at the Russian front until March 1944.[22] It is not known what became of the others.

'The Young Lady is *Mucho* Beautiful!': Spaniards on the Russians, Russians on the Spaniards

At the end of August 1941, after only six weeks of training at the camp at Grafenwöhr, the Blue Division left for the front. Following an exhaustingly long 900km march on foot through occupied Eastern Poland, Lithuania and Russia, the first Spanish units arrived at the beginning of October within the confines of Army Group North, on the Volkhov and Lake Il'men. They took up their positions north and south of Novgorod, where they took part in an offensive in October and November 1941, crossing the Volkhov river and holding a bridgehead on its eastern bank for several weeks.

The German command did not have a very high opinion of the Spaniards' combat capabilities, and from January 1942 they mostly employed them to hold the defence line. There were a few exceptional episodes when sub-units were engaged; for example, the Spaniards' participation in the operations to encircle and smash the 'Volkhov Pocket' in May–June 1942. From August 1942 through November 1943 the Blue Division was on the southern approaches to Leningrad and was engaged in positional fighting. The Spanish units only undertook combat operations a few times with the forces of individual battalions. When the Red Army attempted to launch an offensive to break the Leningrad blockade in February 1943, the Spaniards suffered heavy casualties at Krasnyi Bor; yet, alongside the Germans and other foreign units, they managed to stop the Soviet advance.

Reinforcements arrived from Spain in order to make up for their losses, although these no longer had the same level of motivation as the first volunteers. In all, 47,000 Spaniards served on the Russian front, of which 5,000 remained there forever. There were far more wounded who returned home: the number of maimed alone was 2,200 men. Around 400 Spaniards were captured, of whom 115 died in Soviet camps.

Soviet citizens who lived through the occupation in the Volkhov area and around Leningrad recalled the Spaniards as the more 'decent' of the occupiers, if one compares them with the German soldiers or local collaborators. Such a 'more advantageous' portrait of the Spaniards is somewhat similar to the collective memory of the Italians along the Don front, and it was just this picture that was cultivated by the Blue Division veterans themselves in their innumerable memoirs. Building on this benevolent image, and stressing the 'heroic deeds' of Spanish soldiers at the front, the Francoist regime built in the 1950s and 1960s a culture of memory, in which the noble-professional image of the Spanish volunteers, alongside the mourning of the fallen, 'those who are in Russia', became a component part.[1] The heroically presented past was not supposed to cause embarrassment: one had to concentrate on the victories and details of the fighting ('Our *guripas* [soldiers] halted the offensive by the 55th Army at Krasnyi Bor in February 1943') and not on that which all of these operational achievements led to (the Spanish defence interfered with removing the chokehold from the neck of blockaded Leningrad, which was dying from hunger). The idea of the 'other occupiers' was and remains very popular in Spain itself, as well as elsewhere, even after the transition from dictatorship to democracy: this version is supported by dozens of historical books penned by amateur historians and propagandists and several movies, as well as no small part of the publications of the associations of the division's former soldiers.

Academic and empirical studies paint, if not another, then a far more nuanced picture than that of the veterans' stories. Yes, on the whole, the Blue Division's occupation policy was less cruel than that which was carried out in the zones controlled by German units. This is obvious, judging by their treatment of Soviet prisoners, although even here there are definite doubts as to the (non)fulfilment by Spanish officers of the Commissar Order.[2] Compared to other units, the Spaniards' behaviour toward the civilian population proved to be better than that of the Hungarians, Germans or Romanians. There are several reasons for this: the stable situation at the front, which meant a relatively quiet rear with a less intensive partisan movement; less time spent at the front than the Germans (from nine to twelve months, followed by rotation); finally, the absence of the systematic propaganda of biological racism in the preceding years. In the case of the Spaniards, there was no intensive exacerbation of combat operations and the subsequent escalating brutalization of warfare, as was the case with other formations elsewhere on the German-Soviet front. There was also the absence of ideological doping, which drove the soldiers to the compulsory physical extermination of the enemy.[3]

Nevertheless, it is hard to call the Spanish *divisionarios* an undisputed model of exemplary behaviour. Spanish soldiers were often involved in marauding. Reports by German liaison officers with the Blue Division (*Verbindungsstab*) and various army corps of the Wehrmacht, to which the Blue Division was attached, unanimously note the Spaniards' burning passion for chaotic thievery and stealing, just as did the Russian population.[4] Cases of sexual assault were noted while marauding; Spanish soldiers often beat their victims, and in some cases killed them.[5] However, as opposed to many Hungarian, German, Romanian or collaborator units, the Spanish soldiers almost never resorted to indiscriminate and mass repressions, that is, to the execution of civilians and hostages as 'revenge' for partisan actions. Certainly, the Spaniards killed some civilians suspected of helping the partisans.[6] Nevertheless, we have so far been unable to unearth incidents of mass military sadism in the history of the Blue Division, or of collective reprisals or mass murders. Spaniards did not take part in 'dead zone' operations, when villages, their inhabitants, crops and livestock would be put to the torch. The Spaniards' lesser cruelty during the course of anti-partisan operations may be partially explained by the fact that the Blue Division took little part in punitive expeditions, its tenure in the rear was relatively short, and therefore its occupation practices lacked coherence. Therefore, the efficiency of the Spanish counter-partisan subunits was quite reduced.[7] In this regard Kovalevskii's testimony confirms, but also refines, a good portion of the claims made by some uncritical or apologetic Spanish authors.

Within the memory of Soviet citizens who lived under the Spanish rule or worked for the Iberians in some way, the reigning image is one of wild but not cruel occupants, often gripped by kleptomania. A feature of theirs, very important under conditions of occupation, was that they were much less disciplined and less predictable than the Germans.[8] It was the latter who were quite predictable in their mechanical ruthlessness and they ruled with the aid of the whip, as did their auxiliary formations. As Viktor Mikhailovich Ivanov, who lived under the occupation, recalled: 'I don't recall the Spaniards ever mistreating somebody, as, for example, the Latvians did. The latter didn't have any problem with simply beating someone with sticks and shooting them.'[9]

A doctor, Evdokiia Vasil'evna Bogacheva-Baskakova, who spent the entire occupation in the town of Pushkin, recalled that the Spaniards who came had much better food than the Germans and even fed the local population with bean soup and pig fat. 'My God! What a golden time for us starving civilians, of whom, unfortunately, there remained very few in Pushkin.'[10] However, in spite of being treated like royalty, she was always afraid of running into the occupiers face to face.

> After all, the Spanish soldier is the same sort of rapist as the German one, with the only difference being that the former will give up if faced with the slightest bit of resistance from his victim, without doing her any harm, while the German soldier is a one-hundred percent rapist, so that once he's caught his victim he won't let her go and afterwards will shoot her. This is explained by the fact that the German soldier is highly disciplined and could face military justice. The Spanish army is very undisciplined and does not fear its commanders.[11]

The threat was quite real. Two Spaniards tried to rape an acquaintance of hers and only a German was able to chase them away. In another incident, three Spaniards raped an elderly woman from a neighbouring village. 'They didn't shoot her and she later recovered', which was how Bogacheva-Baskakova put it casually.[12] At the same time, there were exceptions even in such conditions: Bogacheva-Baskakova wrote that young girls would shack up more readily with Spaniards than with the Germans.

Yet another aspect of the post-war myth depicts the Spaniards as true believers in God and pious people, meaning that they respected the Orthodox branch of the Christian faith and its sacred places that had suffered during Bolshevik rule. Once again there exists the testimony of those under occupation, which runs directly counter to the created image of 'armed Christians'. In February 1944 Archpriest Nikolai Ivanovich Lomakin complained that the Germans and Spaniards had turned the churches into 'barracks, public toilets, storage sites for vegetables, cabarets, and in a few cases dirty field hospitals, observation posts, stables, garages, pillboxes and unit headquarters', and they also drew all over the walls and scattered pornographic pictures.[13] A famous medievalist Dmitrii Sergeevich Ligachev visited Novgorod in the spring of 1944 and found similar traces of the Spaniards and Germans' stay in the city. The churches and monasteries had been robbed and bore the signs of having been bombarded. If the Germans buried their dead in modest graves, then the Spaniards loved pompous graves made of stolen stones. In the St. George's (Yuriev) Monastery 'Spanish lovers of art drew naked women right on the remains of frescos dating from the XII century'.[14] There exists other testimony that the Spaniards stole icons from the civilian population.

On the other hand, Soviet collaborators painted the Spaniards as being sharply distinct from the other soldiers of the German army. In such memoirs the *divisionarios* are portrayed as nearly being 'anti-Germans', believing Christians, emotional and quick-tempered but not ones to hold grudges, and at times even generous and capable of sharing part of their rations with an unknown Russian peasant. Daniil Fedorovich Petrov (better known by his later journalist penname 'Vladimir Rudinskii'), a Soviet citizen who worked as a translator in the Blue Division from May through November 1942, wrote quite a bit about them.[15] His Spaniards were fearless anti-communists, serving in the Wehrmacht but not approving the Germans' haughty racism and stupid cruelty and tracing their lineage to the soldiers of old imperial Spain of the sixteenth century. These life-loving Spaniards despised the Germans, those 'automatons without heart or soul', and persistently tried to gain the favour of women with phrases like 'The young lady is *mucho* beautiful! Very much beautiful!'[16]

Among the Spaniards were also those who said these words in perfect Russian.

'Bygone Natures': Russians on Russians and About Themselves

White émigrés were an absolute minority in the Blue Division.[1] The majority of them served with the division, regimental and battalion staffs, so that their relations with private soldiers at the front were not always particularly close. The exiles' average age was over 40 and there was simply nothing for these people to talk about with young Spaniards who had grown up amid the ruins of the Civil War. The veterans of the Spanish campaign in Soviet Russia themselves only mentioned their Russian comrades-in-arms occasionally and the latter never did occupy a noticeable place in their own memoirs. Only individual White Guards were worthy of mention in various sources. In the autumn of 1941 the Falangist Dionisio Ridruejo made the following entry about his Russian colleague, Aleksandr Bibikov (who acted as translator for Colonel Martínez Esparza), in his diary:

> Prince Bibikov, a former lieutenant in the Tsarist army and son of a major landowner (Starinskii [Staritskii] confirmed this to me) under the old regime, arrived with us. He is now serving as a translator in the group. I sometimes notice how he, taciturn and sad, would go out for a long walk. Although I don't like those Russians who are fighting against their own people (no matter who they are today), I understand, or at least can well imagine the feelings of this man regarding his Motherland, her suffering cities and fields. Or it only seems to me that he is upset?[2]

In February 1942 one of the Spaniards' strongpoints was the monastery in Khutyn', where one night Konstantin Andreevich Goncharenko sang Russian songs, accompanied by a guitar. The vaults of the half-destroyed monastery, the candles burning in the darkness, the atmosphere and the songs themselves, which were amplified by the acoustics of the place, impressed the Spaniards and some of the officers wrote about this in their letters home.[3]

The few testimonies of those under occupation described the White émigrés who arrived with the Spaniards in an entirely different light. Official Soviet authors rarely mentioned Russians who in one way or another wormed their way into the Spanish units. The journalist Pavel Nikolaevich Luknitskii wrote in his diary the testimony of one of the eyewitnesses: the exiles served in the gendarmerie's subunits and took bribes and one of them, a certain 'Nikolai Anastas'evich', would 'beat prisoners'.[4] At least one émigré writer, Lev Fabritsius, mentions in his work Russian translators working for the Spaniards. In his novel, *The Belago Family*, the main hero is the Soviet prisoner Anton, who is interrogated by a former captain in the White army and who was now serving the Spaniards as a translator. Anton's initial contempt is replaced by interest and then by sympathy for the émigré, with whom he argues and discusses the past.[5]

The role of only about twenty Russian translators in relations between the occupiers and those occupied made them noticeable figures in the eyes of the population torn by the war. The rare unofficial testimony available to us emerged, for the most part, from the pens of Soviet collaborators serving either the Spaniards or Germans. Such are, for example, the notes of Boris Andreevich Filistinskii, a Novgorod resident and participant in mass killings, who at the end of 1941 became acquainted with Goncharenko. Years later Filistinskii reproduced their conversations in his memoirs. To judge from this source, Goncharenko told him that he did not expect to see Russian peasants in such a condition in which he found them. As we will see later, just like Kovalevskii, he had imagined before returning in 1941 that the peasants 'must be some kind of special, completely brutalized Bolsheviks or either complete martyrs, as they portray on old icons, and that the women and girls, if you'll forgive me, have been hopelessly debauched'. The picture he gave now was different:

> However, they [Russian peasants] proved to be just people: they sing songs, jolly, carefree and simple. Of course, they use cunning and try to trick you, but this is all the good: they see us as foreigners, as enemies. As for the women and girls, I'd like to see how the French and German women meet their conquerors! These are just amazing . . . No, I can't get enough of Russia!

Goncharenko had a heart-to-heart talk with Filistinskii about the civil war. According to the latter's version, the leitmotif of his decision to continue the struggle was revenge: when he was 17 Goncharenko witnessed the execution of his father and uncle by the Bolsheviks.[6]

Another example of the Soviet citizens' observations of the Spaniards is the diary of Olimpiada Georgievna Poliakova ('Lidiia Osipova'), an excitable woman living in Pavlovsk, who passionately awaited the arrival of the Germans. Hardly had the 'liberators' from the Stalin regime descended upon them that she began to cooperate with them. From August 1942 passages appear in her diary about the coexistence between Soviet people and the Spaniards who arrived in the town. They quartered the latter in the town and Osipova went to the gendarme headquarters to discuss the matter of finding work in the Blue Division's laundry section.

She often encountered the translators and singled out in particular two from the many émigrés she came across. The first was Aleksandr Aleksandrovich Tringam (she distorted the name as 'Trikdan'), who won her over with his manners. His complete opposite was Lev Georgievich Totskii (again, distorted as 'Dotskii'), 'a vulgar thief in no way like Trikdan'. Totskii lacked education, principles and morals. He set her up as a laundress for a bribe. During interrogations Totskii purposely translated incorrectly the statements by civilians and set up those whom he did not like. The Spaniards who worked with him recalled this habit: even though they did not know Russian it was obvious to them that the interpreter would distort and summarize what was said.[7] He was not averse to taking the last of his impoverished fellow countrymen's things. In order to curry favour with the Spanish officers, Totskii would resell icons that he had bought for a song: 'Sometimes he would not pay at all and simply took the icon. Should anyone protest, he would threaten them with his revolver. To whom are you going to complain?'[8]

The complexity of the relations between the White émigrés and the Soviet population is described by Ivan Efimovich Bratyshenko, who lived near Novgorod in the village of Grigorovo. Although he called Ali Gurskii-Magometov an 'unfinished-off' White Guard and took notice of his manner of lying and embellishing when speaking of himself, he did save Bratyshenko's family by driving off drunken German soldiers who tried to break into his hut one night. However, Georgii Staritskii had a negative impression of him:

He sits on the seat of a transport vehicle that was somehow procured by my daughter, imagining that he is sitting on a soft sofa, shaven and scented, and carrying on a conversation with me. He said that he knows that his buildings in Kursk are in one piece and that he will soon once again be their owner. I asked him where he was born. He replied: 'You know my surname? I am Prince Staritskii. All of the Tver' province's Staritskii district is our home estate and I, of course, will receive ownership'. I wanted to reply to this monologue, but . . . let him swagger a bit. He added that he was a big liberal and his father's and his peasants worked readily and lived well.[9]

The Russian exiles of the Blue Division left an extremely small number (less than five) of sources and notes. Kovalevskii therefore is the most detailed and contradictory of them. Aleksandr Tringam occupies second place: his letters from the front and memoirs have been preserved. In a letter of 4 September he wrote of his shock upon entering Russia: 'This is a simply indescribable impression that seized me upon crossing the Russian frontier, when I saw Russian signs everywhere and I could talk with everyone without making mistakes, and when everyone understands you.' To this national feeling was attached religion: in November 1941 Tringam visited the cathedral in Grodno, where he confessed and took communion.

In the group of sources created by the émigrés themselves, relations with the local population are more often portrayed as practically beyond reproach and unconditionally heartfelt. In November 1941 Tringam was quartered in the home of a woman with two children. According to him, in the spring of 1942 he saved her life during a bombing raid. Sometimes these evaluations intersect: according to Rudinskii's memoirs, Tringam tried to help the peasants in the village and saved a captured Red Army soldier from a camp and the latter became his orderly. A convinced monarchist, Tringam was 'precisely that man, from which, in our imagination, the emigration must consist of'.[10] As you will read further on, Kovalevskii was a witness to the quite different, much less attractive, conduct of his comrade.

There was also love. We will note that the division command followed the German prohibition and did not recognize marriages between Spanish soldiers and local women, who were also forbidden to follow their husbands back to Spain. An exception was made only for the group of émigré translators.

In November 1943 Tringam married the opera singer Tat'iana G. Shitnikova (Filonova), the widow of a captain in the Tsarist army who died in 1936 and who resided near Tallinn, where she served in a Wehrmacht propaganda company. Following a good deal of jumping through various hoops, including gathering positive recommendations from other translators, the Spanish Army Ministry gave him permission to marry. In February 1944 Tringam returned to Spain together with his wife.[11] According to Osipov, in 1942 Totskii the translator 'found precisely that about which he had dreamed in all the years of exile' – a doctor's daughter, Irina Stepanovna Parysheva, a young and well-educated worker in the Pavlovsk pharmacy who loved to gossip, with whom he left for Spain. In January 1943 the émigré Nikolai Evgen'evich Krivosheia married Mariia Bondina, who was born in Nikol'skoe and who also left for Spain with her husband.[12] In rare instances the Spaniards themselves tried to get around the prohibition. Colonel Ramón Robles Pazos suggested to his Russian lover that she marry one of the émigré translators so that she could leave with him for Spain, where the pair would be reunited.[13]

The Allies' pressure on the Franco regime and the gradual shifting of the *Caudillo*'s strategic orientation in foreign policy, accompanied by the decreasing influence of Falangists on the dictatorship, led to a new situation. In September 1943 Madrid ordered the withdrawal of the Blue Division, and during October-November its formations departed. As a consolation prize for Hitler, they left a formation several times smaller, which also theoretically consisted of volunteers – the Spanish Volunteer Legion, more famous as the Blue Legion; this consisted of three battalions with an overall strength of 2,269 men. The performance of this simultaneous game did not suit the Allies: new demands followed, and Franco was forced to recall the Legion as early as March 1944. Only a few hundred Spaniards continued to fight as individual soldiers as part of Wehrmacht and SS units. For the fanatics among them the war ended only in the beginning of May 1945, in Berlin.

The Russian translators returned to Spain along with the bulk of the Blue Division. The exceptions were three men: two (Goncharenko and Shebeko),[14] and the Georgian Gogidzhanoshvili, who remained in the Blue Legion with the rank of lieutenant. A small group of demobilized émigrés who had served in the Italian army on the Russian front met their comrades-in-arms from Spain in the German town of Hof (Upper Franconia), a staging post from where the Blue Division travelled to Spain. According to Iaremchuk's memoirs, all the Russian translators enjoyed the respect and goodwill of their comrades, with the exception of Gogidzhanovshvili, who had a repulsive reputation, which Kovalevskii himself spoke about.[15]

For at least the first 20 years of the Cold War the Russian exiles stoutly cultivated their nostalgic view of past wars. The myth of Gallipoli, and its spirit, was preserved for decades.[16] At the same time, the Whites bitterly recognized that as opposed to the anti-communists in Spain or Finland, their side lost absolutely everything in the war against the USSR: 'Fate smiled upon the Spanish Whites: they triumphed. It was cruel to us: we have only recollections of past valour and . . . innumerable and unknown graves scattered across all the countries of the earth . . . While we are alive, while there remain if only a few Gallipoli veterans, the idea of Gallipoli will not die.'[17] Many years later the withdrawal from the Crimea was no longer interpreted as a personal or Russian defeat by some White Guards, but as a defeat for those who fought 'for all of mankind'. Having lived through several wars, decades of poverty and an unsettled existence, the military émigrés did not give up their ideals of a specific patriotism, a spirit of self-sacrifice and combat brotherhood.[18]

The Russian veterans of Spanish wars received no symbolic thanks from the Franco dictatorship. Those foreigners who fought for the Spanish Republic have dozens of monuments and memorials erected to them all over the world: 102 Luxembourgers, 70 Australians and even 20 New Zealanders, who served in numbers comparable to those of the Whites, were worthy of memorials in Dudelange and Canberra and plaques in Wellington.[19] While possessing absolute power, the regime did not design to award the Russians who fell for it with even a road sign, while post-Franco Spain was indifferent to these people. The diaspora itself grew weaker with each year and proved to be incapable of perpetuating its memory in granite. It was only in June 2012, on the personal initiative of the Very Reverend Andrei Kordochkin, and with the support of the mayor Jesús Alba Mansilla (a Socialist, by the way), that an Orthodox cross was erected and consecrated to their memory on the top of the hill of Cerro del Contadero, near the village of Checa. Apart from that, only sporadic mentions of the émigrés remain in Spanish culture. In 1961 the novel *La soledad de Alcuneza* (*Alcuneza's Solitude*), written by the diplomat and Francoist war veteran Salvador García de Pruneda, was published. The main hero loses his entire family and fights in Franco's cavalry, but cannot find himself in post-war life. One of the secondary characters is a Russian cavalry officer, who pronounces lengthy monologues.[20]

The fates of the White Russian war veterans after 1945 were variable. Some, including Kovalevskii, withdrew into private life. Only a few managed to live to their heart's content during their sunset years. Staritskii returned to Palma de Mallorca in June 1942. Within a year he received citizenship and attempted once again to leave for the front, but did not succeed. Following the war he was engaged in the antiques trade. While living in an elegant apartment and impeccably dressed and holding himself well, this aristocrat, who was well-known in Barcelona and France, concluded deals at a reserved table in a café.

Others continued to live according to the ideals of soldierly honour. Vadim Aleksandrovich Klimenko became a graduate of an officer's cavalry school after 1939, although during his service with the Blue Division he suffered frostbite and lost both legs. Despite this, following the war he managed to become a graduate of the Higher Army School and rose to the rank of major, married a Spanish woman, and remained politically active. Others, like Gurskii-Magometov, broadcast on anti-communist radio, which had been created under the aegis of the Spanish government. By the way, the Spanish wrapped up the Russian section in the 1960s, while at the same time retaining programmes on other Eastern European languages.[21]

Shinkarenko begrudgingly accepted the collapse of his personal hopes of promotion to higher rank and widespread recognition of his talents as an author.[22] Living modestly on the pension of a lieutenant in the Spanish Legion, he left detailed memoirs about his fate, which took up six archival boxes. In 1957 he summed up the results:

> Both Fok and I assumed that in Spain there would finally accumulate a great number, as many as a thousand or fifteen hundred of our volunteers. From then we could form at least a Russian brigade and this brigade, which was combat ready, would later serve as the basis of the war for Russia. A necessary basis, for all of the unions and organizations proved to be good for nothing. Fok was older than me and I reported to him that the command of all Russians in Spain must by right belong to him; I would be his deputy. Thus it was agreed. A thousand or fifteen hundred of our White Russians . . . What an illusion and self deception . . . About 50 men gathered in Spain . . . . As a result, General Fok shot himself in order not to be captured; Polukhin was killed in

the same battle near Quinto de Ebro; and I am simply nothing, just like before. The result was zero. And now, in the present, all of this is meaningless. Meaningless, for life has changed and our 'White' cause has proven good for nothing. Time has passed.[23]

Within ten years his life ended under the wheels of a truck.

Three dates were burned into the emigres' memory. The Russian 1920, the Spanish 1939 and the German 1945, and for those exiles who crossed all three Rubicons these individual events became complexly intertwined. The bell, which tolled the Crimean defeat, awoke in Spain: this time its peal was transformed into a hymn of the exiles' determination and merged with the Francoist victory marches. If in 1939 the exiled White *requetés* 'saved the name of Russia from contempt and hatred', then in 1941–5 'their hope that Russia would be reborn in the flame of unprecedented war was not justified'.[24] 1939 remained the sole bright spot which enabled them to draw a veil over the collapse of the anti-Russian side on which the Blue Division fought and the cruelty of the occupation in which the division took part, and Franco's tepid gratitude. Thus the Spanish year of hope softened the unforgettable failures and exodus from the Crimea.

To this was added and created the myth of the Spanish past. At a minimum, Gurskii-Magometov, Klimenko, Krivosheia and Tringam associated with their fellow soldiers from the 250th Division and Staritskii became one of the founders of the 'Brotherhood of Former Combatants of the Blue Division' (*Hermanadad de Excombatientes de la Division Azul*) on the Balearic Islands. At the end of March 1962 nine officers celebrated 25 years of the Russian detachment from the *Doña María de Molina tercio*. They were received by the first commander of the Blue Division, General Muñoz Grandes, who was then serving as the Chief of the General Staff.[25]

As has already been mentioned, in the Spanish memory of 1941–5 a key fact – that the division fought on the defeated side that was not noted for its humanity – was pushed into the background; quite the opposite, the Spaniards battle prowess and heartbreak were emphasized. The memory of the émigré legionnaires took shape in a similar way. Their motives were different from those of the defeated Germans, which enabled them to evaluate their actions as 'independent' ones. Thus was removed the problem of the oath and uniform, which linked any serviceman from the German army, even of the Spanish division, with Nazism. Tringam wrote in 1968:

Russians joined this division not in order to kill their fellow Russians, but in order to help Russians in their fight against both the Germans and the Communist-Bolsheviks. And all of those who were there, with the exception of a very few, sought to ease the sufferings of their fellow Russians, who stood between two fires . . . . This is what we did and, yes, it could not be otherwise. If we came to Spain to fight the enslavers of our Motherland, then how could we remain in Spain when the Spanish division was going to Russia to fight against our common enemy in our land?[26]

The political metamorphoses and recreation of memory that began after Franco's death in 1975 did not gratify the Russians.[27] A harbour of consolation was nevertheless found in the combination of various meanings – one's own life, the Spanish victory and in military history. In the spring of 1950, von Lampe made a trip to Madrid, where he met with members of the ROVS residing there. 'They, just like us, who were not victorious on the White front of the civil war in Russia, were the victors on the White side of the Spanish front of the civil war. And they quite rightfully feel themselves to be victors . . . ; that is their service, and they are aware of it.'[28] Two years later, Leonid Nikolaevich Kutukov ('Nikolai Kremnev') visited the army museum (*Museo del Ejército*) in Madrid and left an exultant remark about this excursion. The officer viewed the history of a foreign people just as if the history had been his own, and it was namely the Russian volunteers in two wars who were for him that symbol, that link and filter through which one evaluated the successes of a foreign power and its past.[29] And in the 1980s, and even at the very end of the 1990s, the last of the ROVS veterans continued to recall with a kind word the White volunteers who fought in Spain.[30]

For the émigrés it was precisely the volunteers from their number who helped Spain defeat the communists and to come to life again, and thus this page from the *Spanish* past was for them a part of Russian life, and thus of Russian history. In the end it was, *only in this* version of the past that the Whites emerged as victors.

'The Riddle of a Life': Vladimir Ivanovich Kovalevskii

The author of the memoirs presented here differs little from the average Russian volunteer in the Spanish Civil War and who later joined the Blue Division. Relatively little is known of his biography before 1936, particularly about the first 15 years of his life in emigration. His life following the Second World War is hidden behind a curtain of secrecy – we cannot even state the date of his death and place of burial. Only in January 2022 a decisive event took place – we have obtained photographs with Kovalevskii in them. Previously, Vladimir Ivanovich had stayed thoroughly beyond the reach of any émigré camera and was not to be found in any of the photographs we had analysed. The fateful discovery was made possible thanks to the kindness of Ali Gurskii-Magometov's descendants who allowed us to use their father's private archive.

According to the information presented by him upon being enrolled into the Blue Division, as well as data for 1944, Vladimir Kovalevskii was the son of Ivan and Margarita (an ethnic Swede) and was born in Khar'kov on 30 March 1892. His sister Galina resided in the same city. His native language was Russian. He was a bachelor in 1941, had a military bearing and height of 180cm, with light-coloured hair, blue eyes and a dark complexion.

Kovalevskii was a graduate of the 1st Kiev Konstantin Military School and took part in the First World War from 1914. The Spaniards would many years later write that he had been an infantry lieutenant (*poruchik*) and knew automatic weaponry very well. According to Boltin's memorandum, Kovalevskii served in the St George's Company – one of the first nucleus units in General Lavr Georgievich Kornilov's Volunteer Army. In February 1918 the Company was merged into the Kornilov Shock Regiment. Later, although it is not known when, Kovalevskii commanded a machine-gun crew in the 1st Kuban' Rifle Regiment, which had been created in March 1918. In any event, he went through the First Kuban' ('Ice') March.

In 1920 Kovalevskii left the Crimea together with Wrangel and ended up in the camp at Gallipoli. How did his fate unfold further? In 1944 he claimed that he had served as an ensign in the British army and as a sergeant in the French Foreign Legion.¹ Some authors mention that he fought in the Chaco War of 1932–5, although this is highly unlikely.² According to Iaremchuk, 'in Gallipoli Kovalevskii was a cadet from some kind of military school and joined the French Foreign Legion in Africa for five years, deserted and came to Yugoslavia, where he completed university in the department of Romance languages, and then came to the French consul in Belgrade with an acknowledgement of guilt, as if to say, convict me, but they only laughed and let him go'.³ In Belgrade he was the champion of the Russian chess club.

At the beginning of the summer of 1938 Kovalevskii and Tringam left for Spain. This was not so easy. First of all, the sole representative of the Franco government in the Balkans, Pedro de Prat y Soutzo, resided in Bucharest and thus the obtaining of exit documents stretched out for a long time. Secondly, Tringam, a former member of the RNSUV, was forced to fill out his visa almost in secret: for some reason the head of the union, Major General Anton Vasil'evich Turkul, gave orders not to let any of the union's members into Spain, although his organization supported Franco, at least in words. In Belgrade they organized a send-off and blessed them with an Orthodox icon on their way to the station.⁴ The two Russians left for Italy on a tourist visa, where they appeared before the Francoist military representative, who supplied them with a complete set of Spanish documents, a ticket on a steamship and a small amount of money. Having spent five days in Genoa, they boarded the steamship for Seville and from there made their way to Pamplona.⁵

On 1 July both émigrés joined up with the *Tercio de Navarra*, which was subordinated to the 11th Division. Kovalevskii was assigned to a machine-gun company, while Tringam remained with the headquarters.⁶ The 11th Division was constantly being thrown from one hotspot to another. On 21–22 August it broke through the front near the village of Azután, capturing the villages of Aldenueva de Barbarroya and La Nava de Ricomalillo without a struggle. The Republicans undertook an unsuccessful counter-attack from the rear and lost 300 men captured. Thus Kovalevskii received his Spanish baptism of fire. In the beginning of October 1938, he went to Cerro del Contadero (height 1639) to the Russian detachment of the *Doña María de Molina tercio* in order to observe John the Theologian's day.⁷

Particularly bloody was the fighting of 7–8 January in the Monterrubio–Extremadura sector, about which Kovalevskii recalled separately:

At first a rifle shot sounded mournfully somewhere to the left, and then all around, in front, to the right and left there reigned some kind of hell: these were not the individual explosions of single grenades, but a sort of all-embracing howl, clanking and noise. At times it was so light that the distorted faces of my comrades were visible, but the main thing was the hands—dozens of hands throwing grenades somewhere into space. A machine gun began to bang away, but jammed up as early as the first belt, but to tell the truth, it could do little good. Cries of 'Viva España' and 'Viva República' merged with the howls of the wounded. . . . At dawn the Reds launched a new attack against the 1st Company. Turning its undefended left flank, which was hanging in the air, from three sides, the Reds threw a hail of grenades against the remnants of the Company, which was hanging on to the cliffs. This battle made an eerie impression by the light of day. It was as if people were playing baskenball [sic] or throwing snowballs. Heavy grenades flew into the air, unwinding behind them a long, white trail. They blew up with a terrible crash, laying waste to what was around. If a grenade exploded too close to a man, his skull would burst like a shell. The picture of the battlefield is terrible after such a fight. The unfortunate surrounded red berets of the 1st Company rushed about the cliffs, hiding on either one or the other side, depending on from where the enemy was approaching. Often not everyone managed to run to the other side, and I saw myself how one red beret fell with a howl, killed by a grenade thrown by his own comrades. It was terrible to witness such a battle. Not having the opportunity to come and save our own, we sprinkled the attacking enemy with rifle and machine gun fire. The 'Melilla' Battalion came to our support from brigade headquarters. The attack was beaten off. We breathed a sigh of relief.[8]

In January 1939 he was sent to the Badajoz front and at the end of February transferred to the Toledo–Talavera sector. On 23 March Kovalevskii was transferred to the *Doña María de Molina tercio*, where he served in a machine-gun company until the end of the war. He carried out garrison duty for a short time and trained soldiers in Llíria, in the province of Valencia. On 3 May 1939 he took part in the victory parade in Valencia.[9]

In a similar way to the majority of his comrades-in-arms, following demobilization on 1 June Kovalevskii ended up without means of subsistence. He received a two-month furlough with funds, which he spent on an artistic troupe of Russian red berets, which had been created by Boltin and which toured Spain and entertained the public by performing Russian folk songs and dances. During this short summer tour, the actor-veterans managed to gather funds in support of the Society for War Orphans (*Colegio de Huérfanos de Guerra*), an organization under the personal patronage of Franco's wife, Carmen Polo, who met with the Russian troupe. The Spaniards greeted the Russians well wherever they went, in which many saw as yet another sign of the political ties between the Whites and the Spanish anti-communists. As Tringam recalled of that unemployed time, 'During those blessed times they made a fuss over us as victors; they dressed us up in civilian dress, even with ties, and surrounded us with attention'.[10]

Then the Second World War began. The reigning opinion among the troupe was that it was stupid to get mixed up in a foreign conflict between France and Germany and that they should wait it out. According to Iaremchuk, on 18 September Kovalevskii had a falling-out with his comrades-in-arms on this issue, called everyone a coward and left for San Sebastián, from where he got ready to depart to fight for the French. He evidently was not able to do this and remained in Spain. In the beginning of October 1939 Kovalevskii, along with several émigrés, was awarded Spanish citizenship.[11] Only after this was he able to take advantage of the fruits reaped by Boltin, who requested allowing Russian soldiers to return to military service at the rank of junior and mid-level officers. Kovalevskii received the rank of junior lieutenant (*alférez*), but due to his being posted to the national militia of the Falange, as a result of his 47 years, he was again reduced to the rank of sergeant, the highest rank in these party units. The Winter War between the Soviet Union and Finland, which had just begun, evidently did not arouse any feelings in him, but on 11 December 1939 Shinkarenko, Amilakhvari, Tringam and Gogidzhanoshvili approached the Finnish consulate in Madrid in an unsuccessful attempt to hire themselves out to the Finns.[12]

In May 1940 Kovalevskii, who had just a few months before joined the Spanish Falange, was dispatched to national militia headquarters in the province of Guipúzcoa. Another two Russians also left for there. The first was an aristocrat, a colonel in the Russian service and a sergeant in the Spanish, Vladimir Abramovich Dvoichenko, who was born in 1884 in the

Crimea and who was, as noted above, Kovalevskii's uncle. The second was the previously-mentioned Bibikov, a native of Vladimir and veteran of the French Foreign Legion, who had fought in Spain in the ranks of the Spanish Legion.[13] The Georgian Gogidzhanoshvili was their fellow worker until the beginning of May.

This was a quiet place to serve. The Russians' task was the military training of youth under army control; taking into account the extensive experience of these people, this was not difficult. On the other side of the frontier, in French Biarritz, one could find Russians living there, if one had the desire. But the new war in the summer of 1941 and the immediate formation of the Blue Division interrupted the regular order of things. One may assume that Bibikov, Dvoichenko and Kovalevskii took part in a small anti-Soviet demonstration, which was conducted under the aegis of the Spanish Falange, on 25 June in San Sebastián.[14]

Only two of these three men were able to enrol in the Blue Division. Dvoichenko remained in San Sebastián, insofar as at the ripe old age of 57 he proved to be unfit for front-line service, and he could only wish luck to those who left for the 'East', even if he did not wish for a German victory. Dvoichenko died within a few years.[15] Kovalevskii's age was an obvious problem. During his first attempt to enrol as a volunteer, the candidacy aroused doubt among the Spanish high command: someone had written opposite his surname the word 'old' in the list of Russian personnel attached to the Division. This problem was somehow overcome and Kovalevskii was accepted.

It was planned to have him work as a translator. Actually, Kovalevskii alternated an entire series of roles: he was with the stables, in the rear areas, fought at the front, carried out tasks for the division's headquarters, and translated and searched for partisans. From 1 July through 29 November 1941 he was in the 262nd Infantry Regiment's 4th Machine Gun Company. In November he was transferred to general headquarters as a translator in the Second Section, dealing with counterintelligence tasks and propaganda. Also, according to his own notes, which were written three years later, he, together with *Feldgendarmerie* units, made up in the Blue Division by members of the Civil Guard (*Guardia Civil*), Kovalevskii was involved 'in operations to clear [the rear], was among the troops who seized the main headquarters of the snipers'. However, on 27 February 1942 he was evacuated to the military hospital in Grigorovo due to illness. He was moved the following day to the rear units, as a result of which Kovalevskii left the front-line zone for good and ended up in a military hospital near Cologne, where he remained until final demobilization.[16]

On 17 May 1942 Kovalevskii crossed the Spanish frontier and returned to his previous position at militia headquarters in San Sebastián. He resided there at least until February 1944, while trying to get recognition for meritorious service; this was evidently linked to the necessity of existing on something. He recovered from his illness and was fit for military service, although he no longer felt like going back: he preferred the position of accountant in the quartermaster service to duty on the front line.[17] We have not been able to determine whether or not Kovalevskii joined the Francoist Guard (*Guardia de Franco*) following the abolition of the national militia in July 1944, or whether they detailed him to some other kind of position.

Following 1944 his trail is practically lost. It is more than likely that he continued to live in Spain and from time to time at least socialized with Bibikov, Gurskii-Magometov and Iaremchuk.[18] In 1965 he published his brief memoirs in *Chasovoi*, which had been written as early as 1939.[19] In 1973 an article appeared in Spain about the Russian soldiers, the translation of which, three years later, was placed in the bulletin of the Gallipoli veterans in the USA. In the supplement, written by Iaremchuk, it was claimed that Kovalevskii was alive.[20] As you will read later on, it is likely that by the mid-1980s that Kovalevskii was dead. The details remain unknown. For now.

'A Tale of a Manuscript', or There and Back Again

Only now, with the third edition of this book, can we tell this story in its entirety. These memoirs were first unearthed in 2016, in the archives of the Hoover Institution at Stanford University (Palo Alto, California).[1] The anonymous typescript had been filed away in the archives of the old émigré publishing house Globus, which had been founded in San Francisco in the middle of the 1970s by Vladimir Nikolaevich Azarenko-Zarovskii, better known as Vladimir Azar.[2] The publishing house's archive was transferred to the Hoover Institution in 2011.

The unearthed typescript proved to be incomplete: the final pages were clearly missing. The tragic conclusion to these memoirs was found quite by accident at the other end of the earth in the form of a manuscript notebook – the original memoirs, which were stored in the documentary collection of the Central Museum of the Armed Forces of the Russian Federation (TsMVS RF) in Moscow.[3] These materials came to the collection of the former Soviet Army Museum, thanks to the American-Russian cultural-educational and philanthropic society 'Rodina'. These émigrés, who lived in the USA, believed in the new Russia and in 1994 made the decision to transfer for their permanent and unremunerated use of the exiles' cultural-historical valuables. This entire large repository of Russian fates and relics ended up in Moscow.

Nor did the manuscript notebook, consisting of 196 pages and written in a very poor hand, get by without losses, being cut off at the last page. Fortunately, in the Kovalevskii collection in Moscow there is a neighbouring source. Someone living in the municipality of Suances (Cantabria) in June and the beginning of July 1964 rewrote the last two chapters in a beautiful hand from Kovalevskii's memoirs, thus preserving them for history.[4] Back in 2019, we have rewritten the final pages from the original notebook and, by collating all the versions into one, have managed to recreate Kovalevskii's complete memoirs.

However, we continued to be bedevilled by the problem of how much the typewritten manuscript from the Hoover Institution differs from the manuscript in the TsMVS in Moscow. Is there anything left out? For this, it was necessary to get hold of a complete copy of the Moscow original, although this proved to be easier to wish for than to carry out. Unfortunately, not all the Russian archives are readily accessible and there exists a mass of bureaucratic obstacles, so for a number of years there was simply no opportunity to compare the two texts. Thus, the first edition of the memoirs (spring 2019, in Spanish, by Galaxia Gutenberg) became an inevitable compromise. The greater part of the text was taken from the American manuscript, while the ending was added according to the original and the small addition in Moscow. There then followed the Russian version of the book (winter of 2021, 'Nestor Istoriia' publishing house), in which the imperfections and shortcomings were corrected. And only in March 2021 were we able to get hold of the full-blooded copy of the original from the TsMVS RF. This was a fortunate coincidence, because we were preparing the English-language edition. We finally got the opportunity to collate both versions.

The manuscript from Moscow and the typescript from the USA contained a few different pages. Although for the most part the American and Moscow variants factually repeat each other, there are episodes in the notebook manuscript which were not included in the typewritten one. The opposite was also true: in the Hoover manuscript there is a small number of discourses and episodes which are absent in the Moscow manuscript. How is this difference to be explained? It is possible that there existed some kind of undifferentiated pages and notes which the author later sent to the USA, or which were transferred to Azar, and which subsequently were lost and did not make it to the archive in Moscow. For example, the notebook contains pages with later elaborations and separate notes with citations and preliminary outlines of future chapters – the author evidently recalled his life 'in layers', returning to some details. The fact that he so abruptly switches between the themes of the Second World War and the civil war in Spain is proof of this. Thus, it is quite possible that there was a part of the text which was subsequently lost. The fact that in 1964 someone read and rewrote certain chapters also confirms this hypothesis.

Some details enable us to claim that the text was initially written and then edited by the author during the period 1948–51 and that it was only a few years later that small corrections were made. There is no information as to the actual date of dispatch, receipt or typesetting by 'Globus' publishers. The following chain of events seems most logical. In 1982 Azar travelled to Madrid, where he met with Iaremchuk, who gave him his diaries and a notebook with the memoirs of the already deceased or still living Kovalevskii.[5] As early as 1983 'Globus' published a book about Russian volunteers in Spain and Kovalevskii's notebook was added to the publishing house's portfolio as a sort of 'continuation' of the Spanish theme.

Thus, having received the notebook, the American editor at 'Globus' carefully edited the author's language, correcting the numerous syntactical and stylistic mistakes that suffused the original. This was a logical decision, taking into account how much Kovalevskii's native language had suffered during his years of wandering. The sense of the author's words remained untouched, while the sound of the Russian text clearly improved.

However, the publishing house then decided on obvious, although not too may, deletions. For example, in the typescript version stored in the USA certain episodes are missing, in which Kovalevskii portrayed his émigré comrades-in-arms in an unflattering light. Simply put, an émigré publishing house decided to reduce negative comments about people from 'Russia abroad', although it did not erase them entirely. 'Globus' softened certain accounts of the abuses by Spanish officers, having evidently decided that the author laying the horrors on thick or simply inventing details. Some of the author's harsh comments were also softened. Finally, the publishing house completely got rid of the text's most unsightly part – Kovalevskii's long and prolix speeches, in which he castigates the Spanish people, their culture and Catholic Christianity. We will touch on this at greater length later.

Kovalevskii's text was not completely reprinted and redone by 'Globus', or either its ending was lost. Nevertheless, the book was not published, for which we can find a number of reasons. It is possible that it seemed to the émigrés not *comme il faut* to publish a text which so strongly differed from the myth of the glorious Russian volunteers and their smiling Spanish comrades-in-arms in grateful Spain. This difference is most sharply noticeable in comparison with Iaremchuk's earlier book on the Spanish Civil War: Kovalevskii's narrative lacks all patriotism and idealism, but only reflects disappointment, sorrow and anger. Kovalevskii also went against the hopes that had been cherished for many years among the émigrés. He did not attempt to buck up the reader's spirits; quite the opposite, he threw around phrases such as the White volunteers' role in the Second World War was not pretty, or that the émigrés would not have had a place in the future Russia. It is possible that all of this was the reason for the publisher's editing and even censoring. There was also a more significant reason: Azar died in the summer of 1984, after which the publishing house closed. Thus, the typewritten version remained unfinished and following the closing of 'Globus' someone passed on the original notebook for storage to the 'Rodina' society. As a result, one copy remained in the USA, while the notebook crossed the ocean and left for Russia, where it languished in obscurity from 1994.

'The Mirror of Trauma': The Russian View of Spanish Warfare

These memoirs are unique in their significance. Up until this day extremely few memoirs, and even more so diaries, were preserved from Russian émigrés who were on the vanquished side.[1] Kovalevskii's entries reproduce the émigrés' illusions and hopes in the summer of 1941 that forced them to make their fateful choice, but this does not signify the end of their value. Thanks to his own changing role and 'omnipresence', Kovalevskii was the bearer of a unique experience and an extremely rare view of the war. He undoubtedly saw things from the point of view of the aggressor, whose forces were invading the USSR. A peculiar feature of this is that it is a view from the ranks of the foreign part of the German army, but at the same time it is a Russian view, and not a foreign, Spanish or German, one. He has been freed of the clichés of foreigners who do not understand another country, which so set one's teeth on edge. In the context of the Second World War, by the word 'Russians' most of the people naturally mean Red Army soldiers or citizens of the USSR.[2] The loner Kovalevskii is made from something else altogether: he was a Russian, but anti-Soviet. He wrote like a man who had been out of the country for 20 years and now notices details which perhaps are already common and not so noticeable to the locals. Kovalevskii professionally evaluated the German-Spanish forces and combat operations 'from below', through the eyes of a junior officer and front-line soldier with a rich service record. At the same time, it was a view of matters in the rear area.

By 1941 Kovalevskii was more than a mature and educated man, both in the military sense and the general one, and a pilgrim who had for 20 years survived, studied and fought in foreign milieus and countries. He had mastered several languages – at least Spanish, German, Russian, Serbian and French – and thus was more perspicacious and distinguished Belorussians from Poles and Russians from Lithuanians, saw, heard and understood shades which, without a doubt, would have escaped the attention of his Spanish comrades, for whom everything was the same and foreign. This made him particularly useful in the role of a go-between who understood the stratagems of the occupiers, often when a man's life was at stake. Under hungry, dangerous and ruthless military conditions such skills ensured superiority and enabled him to control the flow of information and to achieve the necessary outcome.[3] At the same time, the role of a man torn into three parts – between belonging to the Wehrmacht, his fellow countrymen and his own émigré world, was obviously a heavy burden for him.

Despite his steely anti-communism, in his memoirs Kovalevskii renounced completely the saccharine story of his own life. He does not try to justify in retrospect his decision to enrol in the division in the summer of 1941 and does not try to make amends for his personal motivations in order to correspond with the apologetic narrative which dominated in the German and Italian accounts during the Cold War ('the struggle against communism for the sake of Christian European civilization').[4] Nothing prevented him from telling a tale of his own infallibility and great moral accomplishments, but he did not do that. On the contrary, Kovalevskii is an extremely critical and mournful chronicler. His text shows a bilious disdain for Spain, Germany and even for himself.

As early as his description of the fighting in 1939 we see elements of undisguised naturalism. The experience of the Second World War changed the author even more profoundly, forcing him to re-evaluate himself in war and the war in himself. It is possible that such a late crisis in the perception of a man's past, one who had gone through so many conflicts, coincided with some kind of stage of life. The author was already about 60 and he evidently had not fully adjusted to civilian life. Or, what is even worse, he remained an émigré and had not adjusted to life in another country. He clearly felt the necessity to write *something*, which is a characteristic trait of many veterans who have not found themselves in peacetime. Simultaneously, he wanted to pour out his soul and to rid himself of the disappointment of not just one war, but of a series of wars. It is possible that the practice of 'writing into the table' had a psychotherapeutic effect and helped him to cope with post-traumatic stress.[5] In this sense, it is noteworthy that Kovalevskii ends his narrative not in the spring of 1942 and his return to Spain, but significantly earlier, cutting it off suddenly, while describing in a distinctive crescendo the death of several surrounded Soviets during an anti-partisan operation at the end of 1941.

Without a doubt, these memoirs are not the 'truth', but only the insight of one, albeit very unusual, personage. As with any memoir source, they are not objective: taking into account the author's emotions and psyche, this lack of objectivity is very noticeable. The entries were created by a man filled with the gnawing of conscience, anger and disappointment. There is no doubt that Kovalevskii felt guilt for participating in the war, which he had entered for completely different reasons and which proved to be the opposite of the idea of 'liberating Russia from the Stalinist tyranny'. Yes, he remained a Russian nationalist, but it is possible that the he felt that he had become a participant in the torments of his fellow countrymen who had ended up 'under the Germans' (more accurately, 'under the Spaniards'). The text is rife with inaccurate dates and factual mistakes, including those relating to the people mentioned – at least the Spaniards – whom he often names incorrectly. Added to this is the usual Spanish confusion, when his comrades had two surnames, along paternal and maternal lines. There are more than enough harsh judgments and extreme evaluations.

In comparing the two versions of the text one notices a couple of additional facts. If in the typewritten version he emerges as a disappointed and bitter observer, then in the original there is also a peevish spitefulness. One may reliably call Kovalevskii an Ispanophobe: even having lived in Spain for so many years and fought for the country twice, he boils over with contempt for it. Naturally, the anti-Spanish tirades only increase his subjectivism and in no way do they paint a good picture of him. However, such was his view on life and his own fate, which was engraved in an historical source, so in this version we have restored all the unsightly episodes and his admission of antipathy for Spain, which were cut out by the original publisher. As historians, we believe that any source should be complete, no matter how contradictory it may be. We believe that it is precisely this spiteful subjectivism that shows just how strongly people are prisoners of their own personality and their own experiences. Exile, a multitude of wars and shattered multi-layered loyalties – all of this turned him into an extremely traumatized personality, and it is precisely his words, which became a mirror for his trauma and which have now been fully restored, reflect this in full. It is hard to imagine in just what psychological tortures he, a 'Russian without a fatherland', who had gotten tangled up in everything and who had become disappointed in ideals and no longer believed in anything, lived toward the end of his life.

It is just this complexity that makes Kovalevskii's testimony so valuable. This unique view is his personal one. This history of the war is the one which he saw, very harsh, full of contrasts and epic, full of cruelty, baseness, vulgarity, meanness and indecency. In this sense it corresponds to the criteria of the noted American author and Vietnam veteran Tim O'Brien as to what constitutes a true war story.[6]

What else do Kovalevskii's memoirs highlight? First of all, in describing in detail his tasks and fate, he does not mask his own prejudices. He is extremely biased against the Spaniards, both in the general sense and as regards their collective mentality; he despises Spanish culture, its religion and national character. He berates the military culture of Franco's army and this is despite living more than 10 years in Spain and his service in those very same ranks. The reason for this is the baggage of the past and the absolutely different mental wavelength of the author-wanderer and military polyglot, who constantly peppers his speech with words from other languages. As were many military men in old Russia, Kovalevskii was an 'aristocratic of the spirit': if life in the empire and military school created this feeling, then the subsequent misfortunes and conflicts in which he took part, only steeled it further. He perceives himself, first of all, through the image of a Russian officer and member of the military elite. In his patronizing and dismissive treatment of the Spanish military – their poor training, rarely-manifested sense of self-sacrifice and sloppy manners – he resembles many Russian officers who served in the ranks of foreign armies. Kovalevskii clearly exaggerates the numbers of deserters and with particular relish describes the comic-opera situations in which even the higher military command come across as complete ignoramuses. This is particularly noticeable in his description of those endless difficulties on the march to the front, when a column of Spaniards got lost and tried to get to its final destination on the front line, while a German unit waited to be relieved.

There are, of course, exceptions: the author retains respect for those whom he considers 'worthy', that is, disciplined and competent in military matters, and is particularly respectful of his red-bereted comrades-in-arms (*requetés*) from the *Tercio de Navarra*. As a junior officer, he was well disposed to sergeants and temporary junior lieutenants and NCOs, of whom there were many in the Blue Division. These were those same 'middle ranks' upon which the 'conscientious' Falangist volunteers looked on from on high and to whom they attributed coarseness, lack of culture, poor training and insufficient ideological zeal.

Kovalevskii saw it the other way around: for him it was precisely the Falangist 'seigneurs' and party members who were the locus of everything disgusting. He quite mistakenly thought that they were favoured in the officer corps. This may have been the result of a dislike for Falangists, who predominated in the subunits in which the author served, and on the part of those volunteers with a Carlist background. Nor were the Carlists looked upon with favour by the Falange, with which he cooperated. But in a number of cases, it seems that the author ascribes a certain political influence to the Falangists on how the war was fought. Such an influence was, in reality, absent, and in the sense of functions the Falangists were the mirror image of the institution of political commissars in the Red Army.

Like other Spanish authors, such as Dionisio Ridruejo, and other Falangists, Kovalevskii criticizes the Spanish army's military culture and the methods of supply, movement and conduct of military operations peculiar to it. He unmasks in a particularly caustic manner the corruption of the military quartermasters and other warehouse workers, and goes over the privilege of the officer element – the abundance of assistants, which lowers dignity, and the much greater ration from among the packages. Other soldiers, whom the cup of food and abundant equipment has passed by, experience shortages and 'compensate' for these shortcomings by robbing the civilian population. Of course, Kovalevskii is engaged in hyperbole here. At the same time, the author condemns the lack of initiative and pandering by the Spanish command to the 'errant' (*despistados*) troops, who abandoned their positions and headed for the division rear, a kind of deserters to their own rear. As a counterargument to such behaviour, he puts forward the supposedly ideal organization and discipline in the German units. With a certain feeling of *Schadenfreude*, he cites instances of a lack of understanding between the Blue Division's military personnel and their German instructors and allies. However, Kovalevskii all too soon begins to notice the far greater cruelty of the Germans toward prisoners of war, civilians and partisans. By the end of the memoirs his initial professional respect for the well-oiled German military machine has evaporated.

Kovalevskii quickly noticed that one should not await justice from those occupiers who were supposed to judge others for atrocities toward the Russian population. A system of collective responsibility reigned. In the Civil Guard, which in the division carried out the functions of the military police (like the Germans' *Feldgendarmerie*),[7] a number of officers firmly adhered their prejudices regarding the Russian population, which in their view was 'culturally backward'. Here we once again have Kovalevskii's peculiar position as a foreigner amongst foreigners. Even though he serves side by side with the Spaniards, they are foreigners to him, just as he is an outsider, and a participant and observer. Accordingly, his memoirs are free from corporate solidarity and they freely discuss those facets of day-to-day army life which are considered taboo in other war diaries and memoirs penned by Spanish soldiers, for example homosexuality. The loquacity with which the author describes the attempted rape by one sergeant by another one in the Grafenwöhr training camp is quite surprising. Beginning with a brief description of General Agustín Muñoz Grandes, all his sketches of cowardice in combination with military illiteracy, characteristic of a number of officers, ooze with spite. Kovalevskii does not pull any punches, writing about officers shacking up with Russian women. He is no less affronted by little phrases and degrading comments by his Spanish fellow soldiers about the Russian people.

Kovalevskii the translator intently examines the Blue Division, pointing the enormous magnifying glass of his criticism on the actions of the Spanish soldiers toward the civilian population. This is a very important distinction: in the Spanish corpus of memoirs and novels about the division, which arose following the war, the 'otherness' of the soldiers arrived from far-away Spain, who they say viewed the civilians with sympathy, was always stressed in particular. The sketches by the émigré Kovalevskii are in accordance with the observations of those German liaison officers, as well as the testimony of some civilians and collaborators. The Spaniards were chaotic occupiers who were often involved in pillaging. They directly or indirectly worsened the situation of the civilian population, whose lot was already bad enough and who lived in desperate poverty, but wrapped in the shroud of their own emotions, for them these sufferings go unnoticed. In some aspects, Kovalevskii does not paint a principally new picture: that same murder of the Novgorod *golova* (mayor appointed by the Germans), Fedor Ivanovich Morozov, was known earlier, as were certain details of the anti-partisan sweeps – his revelation of the details of these events is far more important.

Kovalevskii's memoirs confirm that during the period under investigation the Blue Division's occupation practices did not include collective repressions, which varies sharply from that which was characteristic of Army Group North's rear areas.[8] A flair for languages and his particular role as an 'engaged observer' enabled him to witness in a different light the human reactions which the 'average' Spaniards took for a manifestation of hospitality.

For example, the peasants received payment for requisitioned livestock and food in *Reichsmarks*, but this did not help them much in conditions of a collapsing military economy and shortages. Accordingly, it was clear to him that for the population there was not a great difference between forcible requisitions, paid requisitions and robbery – their resources in any event were absolutely irreplaceable and the consequences catastrophic. The author saw that families, who were forced to live under the same roof with quartered outsiders, were afraid both for themselves and their meagre possessions, and that this situation was not changed either by the compliments of uninvited guests in broken Russian, nor the accentuated politeness displayed toward the elderly, nor the sweets which the southerners shared with the children.

Kovalevskii stresses with bitter irony the Spaniards' emotional deafness. The peasant women complained sadly to the foreign soldiers about their hard lot, not because they wished to express the secret melancholy of the 'mysterious Russian soul', but simply because they were scared and hungry, and while they led a bleak life even before the war it had become a hundred times worse since then. Kovalevskii records instances of cruel treatment of the population and the conditions in which it had been placed. He reacts sharply if the situation forced women to engage in prostitution or to cohabit with the occupiers in exchange for a food ration and 'protection' for their families. Nor does he forget to mention the rare scenes of mutual understanding between occupiers and occupied people (the story of the peasant woman who treated a Spaniard like a son).

Kovalevskii launched an entire series of tirades against those of his Russian fellow servicemen – the division's translators – particularly those who took an active part in the requisitions, who grew fat on the sufferings of their fellow countrymen, and even more those who 'supplied' women for the Spanish officers' pleasure. He certainly exaggerates the crimes of Sergei Ponomarev, because he is reciting others' accounts, but does not condemn him for nothing, as Ponomarev's unpardonable acts are confirmed by documents. Quite the opposite, he depicts Ali Gurskii-Magometov as too good, while at the same time Spanish sources of his repulsive deeds have been preserved.

The author's perception of Imperial Russia is interesting, as well as what Soviet Russia proved to be at the moment when he set foot on its soil. The Tsarist 'overlay' puts a particular cast on his view: in travelling through Polish territory or the Baltic States, he feels himself 'in Russia', and for him these were little islands of the Motherland for which he strived and which he attempted to extract from under the rubble of a new war. He chatted with the local inhabitants, greedily grasping any details which would feed his nostalgia, the Russian hidden within himself, which he had seemingly acquired once again.

However, after a few weeks and having independently evaluated the results of Bolshevik rule, Kovalevskii adjusted part of his perceptions, hammered out over the decades. Judging by a mass of sources, many of those Whites who arrived in 1941 found confirmation of their worst fears. What most struck them was the other-worldly poverty of the peasantry. Tringam described his shock:

> The Russians here have changed greatly and the present war has so exhausted them all that they will agree to anything, if they could only be left alone and be given something to eat . . . . The overall level of education is very low. They know neither history, geography, nor literature . . . . Here even the teachers and professors speak as our cooks and yardmen used to. The level of our conversational language has fallen very low . . . There is no possibility of distinguishing, for example, a doctor from a peasant by his clothes. Everyone here is dressed gray, poorly and the same. It's funny and sad to see in the city mayor's waiting room a female translator in a scarf and bast shoes [peasant shoes or sandals made out of the soft wood lying immediately under the bark of a tree], while irreproachably speaking in German, French and English . . . . All one hears are questions and questions, chiefly about the émigrés and about life abroad. When you talk to them they don't believe you and think that you are telling them fables and fairy tales, but nevertheless each one asks that I tell them once again about 'such a happy life . . . ' Poor people, poor Russia.

Like many émigrés, Kovalevskii saw salvation in the Orthodox faith and the unshakeable spirit of the Russian people – which were for him the pledge of a bright future. In exile the ignorance of people's lives and the absence of information were compensated by apocalyptic visions of Russia, groaning under the Bolsheviks. Kovalevskii saw a much more layered picture. No, Russia in no way bloomed under the Bolsheviks, and he clearly sees that things were better under the Tsar. At the same time, progress is noticeable in certain areas, or the confluence of old and new principles. Kovalevskii attests in amazement to the fact that many traditions, including religious ones, which he believed to have been destroyed, had for better or worse adapted to the new conditions. He came to realize that the moving force of Soviet resistance was not fanatical devotion to Comrade Stalin or an unquenchable faith in the party system, but 'instinctive' Russian patriotism, which, it would seem, had learned to live with the Soviets.

This immediately raised the question: who, then, were the White émigré translators? After all, they saw themselves as the bearers of the Russian idea. How did it come about that what appeared to be the anti-national Soviet system was forging a path to the recesses of the Russian soul more successfully than they? That soul which the exiles believed only they had carried within themselves since 1920? In this case, Kovalevskii concluded with sadness, they are turning into everyday collaborators.

At the same time, Kovalevskii describes his situation in different ways. He was honest in his observations and paid attention to the aspects which did not fit into the picture of mass rejection of the occupiers, which also existed, and which predominated in the Soviet Union until the 1990s and beyond. He describes how some peasants cooperated with the Spaniards and Germans, moreover with enthusiasm; how glad they were to see him, a fellow countryman, from abroad, who would help and defend them. He describes the fear with which the local farmers often viewed the partisans, dreading their requisitions and repressions.[9] Patriotism was evident, but in that same space the citizens settled their pre-war accounts, while various segments of the population behaved in their own particular way.[10] Here Kovalevskii appears in another role, that of a chronicler of village life, while depicting the peasantry's world, with village elders, denunciations and the unhealed hurt over collectivization, above which hovers the war with its own code of cruel rules.

He describes in general terms those who cooperated with the new authorities, who include former Tsarist officers and peasants desiring to once again receive an allotment of land. Local prominent Bolshevik party members, who had not succeeded in retreating before the Germans' arrival, and, in general, people loyal to the Soviet system (teachers, for example), became the victims of denunciations. Kovalevskii makes an insightful comment: there did not always exist a direct connection between the peasants' social condition before the war and their attitude towards the occupiers. For all of these reasons he was always searching for the answer to the question: 'Why does the population react in precisely *this way*?'[11]

The theme of the banality of evil – life under occupation, suffused with violence and danger – is constantly present as a secondary theme of the narrative. In this strange and frightening space,[12] the dividing line between comedy and tragedy was a shaky one: if a man arrested for a dalliance with another man's wife should be caught during a sweep, he might be accused of collaborating with the partisans and executed. Kovalevskii's detailed description of combing the forests and villages for partisans is also full of suggestions in the same direction.

His sharp antipathy toward the Blue Division's officers reaches its peak when the narrative turns to the Civil Guard. For Kovalevskii its soldiers are like an assortment of people who did not know how to do anything, but with boundless ambition, greedy, cruel and prone to thievery. He precisely notes the absence in the Spanish division of the necessary means and training in anti-partisan warfare – a nearly anonymous struggle, far from the front line, in little-known villages, surrounded by impenetrable forests. The division really did occupy a large territory and lacked a coherent occupation policy, and also experienced a shortage of men and equipment to have effective control on the whole area of occupation. Kovalevskii does not spare epithets in describing Spanish logistics: chaos reigned during operations and the *divisionarios* were not even able to coordinate their actions with those of the Germans. At the same time, those responsible were 'pressured from above' by equally incompetent officers, who demanded immediate positive results from their subordinates, for which they could have yet another medal pinned on their chest. The circle was closed. If Kovalevskii's stories about his front-line comrades in the machine-gun company are contradictory, then in the case of the Spanish field *Gendarmerie*, the shadings disappear altogether. It is as though this part of the narrative is suffused with a grotesque spirit, while at the same time it is a tragedy and a picture of people's suffering.

Throughout the entire text there is one theme which Kovalevskii, despite his amazing frankness and very critical tone, 'trips over'. He did not avoid passing over things in silence and, without himself knowing it, ended up taking the same position as the majority of the Blue Division's veterans did who recalled the 900km march through East Prussia and Lithuania in September 1941. He barely mentions the Nazi practice of segregating the Jewish population, which the division's military personnel could observe directly, although they could not know its true scale and the later stages that led to the annihilation of the Jews.[13] Kovalevskii was an anti-Semite, which was a typical characteristic of the Russian officers of his generation. He almost never mentions Jews, although at the same time he uses the word *evrei* ('Jew'), and not the derogatory term *zhid* ('Kike'). Meanwhile, the Jewish population of the Grodno area was exterminated in January 1942, only a few months after the Blue Division marched through these places. Even ten years later, while writing his memoirs, Kovalevskii touches the theme of the 'final solution' with only a single phrase about the ovens. As for the rest, this does not interest him. The prisoner of his own concerns, the gnawing of conscience and the phantoms of the past, he did not hide that which was most important to him – his own relationship with Russia.

The spirit of war continued to live and torment not only Kovalevskii and it was not just the White émigrés that it forced to take up the pen. In the 1970s the member of the Hermitage Museum's scholarly council and a refined expert on the painting of the northern Renaissance, Professor Nikolai Nikolaevich Nikulin, began to write for himself. Thirty years before he had taken part as a private in the defence of Leningrad, was wounded and later made it to Germany. Nikulin's army gained the victory, but what he saw did not let go of him for decades. From the 1975 introduction:

> My notes were not meant for publication. This is only an attempt to free myself from the past: as people in western countries turn to a psychoanalyst, lay out their problems, concerns and secrets to him, in the hope of being cured and acquiring peace, I have turned to paper in order to rake out the recesses of my memory the loathsomeness, sediment and swinishness that have settled there, in order to free myself from reminiscences that have oppressed me. The attempt is likely unsuccessful, hopeless . . . [14]

The memoirs were published by the Hermitage in 2007. Published in a paltry edition, the book, under the clumsy name of *Memoirs of the War*, rang throughout the entire country, shaking readers with its frankness, depth of introspection and described scenes of violence. New editions followed and a wave of criticism fell upon Nikulin: logical and factual disparities, exaggerations and omissions (they are present, as in any text) were found in the text and the author's biography. Nonetheless, the success of his words was enormous. One can count on the fingers of one hand the memoirs of Red Army soldiers that have received *such* recognition in post-Soviet Russia.

Despite all of the mournful years of wounds, losses and tragedy, Mr Nikulin continued to live in his country after 1945, to speak his native language, made a successful academic career, started a family, raised his children, saw his grandchildren and lived to see the publication of his notes. Kovalevskii was unable to do any of this and died in a foreign land, having nearly forgotten his native language, without being able to relate to anyone, aside from his square notebook with the metal binder, about his regret and the ghosts which haunted his consciousness. It is almost impossible to compare these two different Russian people, who fought for opposite things, but if they had one thing in common it was the 'war within', in their own soul.

***

The text which we present for the readers' attention was the result of the joint work of two dissimilar historians from different generations and opposite sides of the planet. We have sought to be as careful as possible in compiling an academic apparatus, for which we brought in the holdings of almost thirty state and private archives and libraries in Australia, Andorra, Finland, France, Georgia, Germany, Latvia, Spain, the Russian Federation, the USA and Ukraine. We would first of all like to thank the custodians of the private collections and the workers in the state institutions for their professional and effective assistance. Carmen Jordá kindly agreed to review for us a number of materials from the Main Military Archive in Segovia, and our colleagues Miguel Alonso, Miguel Cabo, and José M. Faraldo, who seriously enriched the first version of the manuscript with their critical comments. Iñaki Fernández Vicente allowed us to become acquainted with his dissertation even before its publication. The original idea for such a book met with a friendly reception on the part of the Galaxia Gutenberg publishing house. Most of all, it was the indulgent professionalism of María Cifuentes that made the very publication of this witness, written by a Russian veteran-émigré at the end of his life, possible.

The Spanish-language version of the book was the result of a scrupulous translation and a stylistic and idiomatic proofing. Given the existing academic and general interest in the history of the Blue Division, this publication did not pass unnoticed and major newspapers and well-known authors wrote about it. Judith Keene, a professor at the University of Sydney, who has written the best book about foreigners in Franco's army, rated the book highly.[15] After only half a year the 'Nestor Istoriia' Russian publishing house became interested in the book. In preparing the Russian edition, we elaborated on a few details and added new information. The curator of Columbia University's Bakhmetev Archive, Tatiana Chebotarev, helped us unearth important accounts, and Olga Giralt i Esteve from the University of Barcelona and the employees of the University of North Carolina at Chapel Hill, at our request, digitalized the missing materials from their repositories. Mikhail Iur'evich Blinov, Nikolai Georgievich Dzhavakshishvili, Sergei Igorevich Drobiazko, Georges Mamoulia and Konstantin Konstantinovich Semenov put new sources at our disposal. Pavel Aleksandrovich Gavrilov and Viacheslav Al'bertovich Mosunov helped, with enthusiasm and patience, to unravel the numerous riddles surrounding the occupation of the Leningrad region. The book was extremely well received: major Russian academic journals, news outlets and private persons highly praised the memoirs themselves, as well as our work as editors.[16] The Hoover Institution wrote a favourable review of the Russian version of Kovalevskii's memoirs, saying 'it would be worthwhile to see an English translation'.[17]

The English-language version became possible thanks to the interest of Pen & Sword publishers and, personally, Rupert Harding. The main thing is that we managed to unearth the original version of the memoirs, which would have been completely impossible without the selfless assistance of the Very Reverend Dr Andrei Kordochkin and Vladimir Viktorovich Markovchin. The descendants of two Russian émigrés, Gurskii-Magometov and Staritskii, shared unique documents and photographs from their family archives. The kind attention of the American archivists Yves Franquien, Ivan Podvalov and Anatol Shmelev and their assistance with new sources, also improved this text.

This manuscript lay in a deep sleep in Spain for nearly half a century, in order to once again disappear among the papers of a Russian publishing house in the USA. One could say that the manuscript repeated the fate of the author, who was understood by no one and who until his death inhabited the vacuum of enraged solitude. The manuscript was not useful for the émigrés: Kovalevskii's text screamed that the schism between Soviet Russians and White Russians was irreversible and that the loss caused by the Revolution was irreparable; such thoughts were inconvenient and were thus pushed aside. The manuscript was of no use to many Spaniards before and after the end of Francoism: taking into account the enduring mythology of the Blue Division among conservative public opinion and readers of traditional military history, the Spanish publishers would not have gone for a publication so radically removed from the master narrative about 'our boys in Russia'. One could not even dream about publishing in the USSR: the war and occupation had become a social trauma of colossal proportions and thus any voice 'from the other side', all the more of a Russian man, was met with hostility.

But this does not mean that his voice must be silenced. Having left his extraordinarily partisan witness to the sadness of war and his personal fate, Kovalevskii, who lived in the emptiness of exile, clearly hoped that the day would come when his solitary words would at least be heard.

Will you listen to him?

THE 'BLUE DIVISION' AND THE CAMPAIGN IN RUSSIA

By Vladimir Ivanovich Kovalevskii

Take me away from the exultant, idle talkers,
Whose hands are crimsoned with blood,
To the camp of those who are dying
For the great cause of love.
   N.A. Nekrasov, 'Knight for an Hour'

In old age I live anew,
The past passes by in front of me—
Did it, full of events, rush on by,
Agitated, like the ocean sea?
Now it is silent and quiet,
Memory has preserved few faces for me,
A few words reach me,
While the rest has perished, lost forever . . .
   A. S. Pushkin, 'Boris Godunov'

Lo más divino que contiene el Corazón del hombre no sabe jamás de él.
(The most divine thing that a man's heart contains never knows about itself)
   Lamartine

Preface

In intending to write my memoirs on 'the campaign in Russia', I declare that I am taking up a work beyond my strength. Twenty years spent abroad, the absence of Russian society and Russian books during the last four years of my stay in Spain, mean that I have begun to forget my native tongue. In my 50 years I often find it exceedingly difficult to come up with the expressions and words adequate to the thought being put forward. The shades of the Russian language, the richest in the world in terms of its nuances, are now slipping from my memory. It is with bitterness that I have to admit that the best and the most valuable that I wanted to express, has frozen in dead and stiff phrases.

But, 'if there is no strength, then the desire alone is laudable'.[1] Therefore I think that the forewarned reader will read my memoirs with indulgence. I am writing both for those who are now on the other side of the front, as well as for my brothers in exile,[2] scattered all over the world.

I would like to explain our psychology, the people of the past, to a person living under the Soviet regime. That is, the psychology of people who did not want to reconcile with communist oppression and fruitless babble and who left the country but who have preserved, despite 20 years in exile, their passionate love for their abandoned motherland. And the émigrés, having read my notes, will understand how heavy was my cross in this struggle of the West against the USSR. How carefully I sought to separate the 'Soviet' from the 'Russian', and how it was often difficult to defend my brothers from the punishing hand of a ruthless enemy. Physically sick and morally broken, I returned to Spain without awaiting the denouement of this struggle.[3] Why? The reader will find the answer in my uninteresting account.

The future, the very distant future, will render its unbiased verdict. Will this verdict condemn those of us who struggled, insofar as it was possible, against the communists in Russia and beyond it, or will it stain as foolhardy the conduct of those states which aided the Bolsheviks' inhuman regime to bestially prevail in the USSR and which, in addition, turned half of Europe over to this regime?

PART ONE. THE PATH

June 1941. San Sebastián

As early as the middle of the month it was becoming clear that Germany was faced with a new war. A war with the USSR. The ideology of these two totalitarian states was so different and their interests often collided, as in the distant past (the war of 1914[1]) and more recently (the Balkans, the USSR's protest following the partition of Yugoslavia),[2] so that few believed in the durability of their 'friendship', the fruit of which was the partition of Poland.[3]

The 'allies'[4] were then concentrating their forces in this Poland. The press of both countries, as always, denied the possibility of a war breaking out, while recognizing only a few differences in their views. However, on the night of 23 June the German ambassador in Moscow presented a note containing a declaration of war,[5] while at the same time the Second Reich's[6] aircraft were already bombing Soviet airfields. Thus began this terrible war, in which armed forces of heretofore unknown size took part on both sides.

One may easily imagine the attitude of the Russian émigrés during the days preceding the denouement. Brunetti's words[7] fit the Russians very well: 'Like the Jews, with each clap of thunder and the approach of a storm, they peer out of their windows to see whether the hour of the Messiah's coming had arrived.'

Optimistic hopes inspired the émigrés. It seemed as though the hour of revenge had arrived and that the restoration of a National Russia was not far off. Projects were drawn up. The possibility of returning to the motherland with 'unfurled banners' was not doubted. Typically, Hitler, whom some had called the Antichrist two years ago, during the time of the German alliance with the USSR, was now raised to the status of a national hero.

To the majority the war itself seemed an easy and brief undertaking – something resembling a parade by the German armoured armies. The reigning opinion was that as early as Christmas the USSR would cease to exist as a state. It was not even safe to express doubts on this score, lest one be consigned to the camp of the Sovietophiles.[8]

We Russians, who had settled in Spain, were lucky: immediately upon the start of military operations in the East we already had begun to speak of a call-up of volunteers and the creation of an expeditionary corps. The newspapers, with typical Spanish bombast, began to proclaim the necessity for Spain to once again 'unsheathe the sword' for the defence of Christianity and the good of culture. Noisy meetings were held throughout the country, demanding that Spain take part in the campaign against Bolshevik Russia.[9] 'Let Russia die!' 'Communism is dead!' 'Lead us to Moscow!' – such were the posters at the forefront of popular anger. On 25 June the government, heeding the 'voice of the people', began to register volunteers.[10] Thus there arose the opportunity for us, the 'White Russians', to once again fight against the 'Reds', and once again on our native soil.

But IN PRACTICE, this matter proved not so easy to realize. Difficulties arose, one after the other. There was no point in even thinking about the recruitment of a separate Russian unit, which was the dream of our chief, N.N. Boltin.[11] He used to mysteriously say 'The enemy does not sleep?' The German embassy, in accordance with Hitler's order not to allow the participation of 'White Russians', forbade us to serve in the Spanish Expeditionary Corps at the rank acquired in the Russian army, although General Franco ordered: 'Send these gentlemen with those ranks which they had in the Russian army . . .'[12] But the Germans were in charge.[13]

We had to make the best of the little we had: for those Russians who, upon the conclusion of the Spanish Civil War, continued to remain in the army and Militia,[14] this problem was easily resolved and they were accepted with their officer's rank, while there was nothing for the remainder to do but to join as private soldiers. One must know the Spanish soldier's living conditions and his lack of discipline, but mainly the prejudice against any foreigner, in order to understand just how hard it was for us Russians to decide on the 'campaign against Russia' as a private soldier in the Spanish army. Thus the number of Russians who signed up was insignificant. In all, there were 11–12 men, of whom only four entered as officers.[15] My friend, A.V. Bibikov,[16] and I, who had served in the Militia in San Sebastián as sergeants, were 'lucky': we kept our rank as sergeants.[i]

The material conditions for enlisting were magnificent.[17] 1,000 pesetas for clothing, a monthly allowance equal to that in the Legion, which was increased by 30 per cent, but the main bait was that the position currently held by the enlistee would be held for him with pay, with his family receiving

---

i   Author's note. I later had occasion to become somewhat disappointed, for it transpired that during my years as a translator the private soldiers had a more quiet time of it.

the full amount while he was away, or he would receive it upon his return. The influx of volunteers was enormous.[18] There was a 20–28-year age limit for volunteers. Aside from this, one was supposed to be a Falange member.[19] I don't know why if this was because enrolment in the Falange was open to anyone or because the demands were not strictly observed (as is usually the case in Spain) during enrolment, but the fact remains that a 'red element' managed to infiltrate into the volunteers. Repeated cases of Spaniards going over[20] to the Bolshevik side at the very beginning of operations speak eloquently to this.

The enrolment itself, in its essence, was already pregnant with bad consequences, because the volunteers were not warned about the serious adversities which awaited them: about the harsh cold in Russia and the possible exhausting marches and, finally and mainly – about the bloody fighting. Instead of this, they spoke of parades in Berlin and Moscow and a triumphant march across Russia, but mainly they spoke of a quick return to their homeland.

They were so misinformed that many were scared lest they 'arrive late to the capture of Moscow' . . . [21] As testimony to this haste was the fact that they were already sending off the first echelon (1 July)[22] to the expeditionary corps's concentration area before the end of the enrolment period (2 July).

The send-offs were celebratory. They marched along the streets under the accompaniment of a wind orchestra. Bibikov and I were in front as standard bearers.[23] Behind us marched long ranks of volunteers. The imposing nature of this spectacle was only marred by the fact that everyone was dressed in a very motley fashion. In our registration bureau they only handed out a red beret (*boina roja*[ii]) and a blue shirt (*camisa azul*) to those departing. The spectators, of which there were a large number along our way, welcomed us coolly. Some of our relatives cried. This seemed almost funny to many of us: after all, we were leaving on a pleasant and short journey . . .

The authorities (*autoridades*[iii]) awaited us at the station in San Sebastián; a number of impassioned speeches were made obliging us to raise the mood of both those departing and those remaining. They then sang three national anthems (the royal march, the Falangist anthem and the Carlist anthem);

---

ii   Translator's note. In some cases the author makes orthographic mistakes (for example, '*Crusada*' instead of '*Cruzada*' or '*Espana una* . . . ' instead of '*España, una*'). Similar mistakes have been corrected in this edition without reservation. All foreign words have been highlighted in italic; all citations for these words belong to the translator.

iii   *Autoridades* (Sp.) – representatives of authority.

they shouted '¡*España una, grande y libre!*'[iv]; they shouted '¡*Franco! ¡Franco! ¡Franco!*'; and after distributing small icons and amulets, the train moved out. That was 1 July 1941. I did not leave on this day, but remained in order to lead another train.

On 2 July we left, one might say, 'without ceremony'. There was no one at the station aside from representatives from the Militia and the Falange. We, the two sergeants, were in charge of a train with a good 40–50 men. The San Sebastián Militia offered up only one officer as a volunteer. Others, as loyal Falangists, volunteered, but they did not consider it possible to take part in the Crusade (*Cruzada*) against the Bolsheviks due to health concerns.

I, having become the temporary 'leader' of this small detachment, and knowing the Spaniards' sloppiness, greatly feared complications and incidents along the way. But the boys, no matter how lightheartedly they viewed the future, grew quiet: they made a racket in the train car, but were not too bad, and at the stations through which we passed, due to the short stops we were not able to procure any wine and 'get loaded'.

It was only approximately halfway to Burgos, at Vitoria station, that we had a long layover. Here one mother, looking for her 17-year-old son, who had secretly run away from home, found him in my car. A soul-wrenching scene took place: she grabbed her son, who was trying to break free, with both hands and, fearing that they would take him from her again, sought to arouse the sympathy of the onlookers on the platform with shouts and wailing. 'They are taking my only son away, who's almost a child, in order to take him away to far-off and cold Russia. He'll die there from the cold, or those barbarians will kill him. I won't give him up, I won't, I won't!' But no one even thought of taking him away from her.

When they found out that I – the car sergeant – was a Russian, the hostile crowd literally besieged the car. Threatening shouts could be heard. We had to get out of there as quickly as possible.[24] I asked the conductor to cut short the stopover and we set off, leaving the son with his mother. Later on, in Russia, I recalled that mother, for whom the most attractive terms of service for her son could not dampen her heavy forebodings. In this way she saved her son.

Later on, during the second recruitment in the spring of 1942, I saw just the opposite: a debased father, who literally sold his son, against the latter's

---

[iv] *España una, grande y libre* (Sp.) – 'Great, united and free Spain' was a Falangist slogan, adopted by the Francoist regime.

wishes, in order to get drunk and play cards on the money he got for him. And when the Germans, due to the boy's young age (16 years), returned him to Spain, he nearly beat the child up in our presence in the Militia office: 'Why didn't you lie about your age? You probably didn't behave with sufficient bravery.'

Burgos

We arrived in Burgos, the capital of Nationalist Spain during the Civil War, after six o'clock in the evening. Here we encountered a large number of trains from other cities in north-western Spain. Files of the arrivals stretched through the entire town in the direction of the infantry barracks. There was an unusual amount of excitement on the large barracks square: soldiers, Falangists and simply people in civilian dress were darting here and there, or were conversing in groups. Here and there one could witness noisy meetings between friends, with typical Spanish embraces, expressed by the term 'slapping each other in the kidneys'.

Two or three officers officiously and pointlessly sought to conduct the classification of the newly-arrived soldiers. But the people, it appeared, did everything possible to interfere with this already difficult work: they walked away from their appointed spots, did not respond to the roll-call and, in general, contributed to the creation of an endless muddle. Thus it was possible to wait several hours here and not be assigned to any unit undergoing formation.

I viewed my situation quite hopelessly, but aid came from where I least expected it. There came up to me an unfamiliar man with a Russian face, who was completely unknown to anyone on the square, dressed as a civilian, and introduced himself: 'Pavel Ivanovich Rashevskii.'[1] That Rashevskii who 2–3 years earlier had aroused so much talk around his personage. A hero – one of the first Russian volunteers in Spain – and who as the result of circumstances which are still unexplained, was sent to prison, where he sat for about two years. He had now emerged from confinement by some kind of miracle and was preparing to once again travel to fight. Having learned of my 'unpleasant situation', he immediately set about putting things straight and within 10–15 minutes I had been assigned to one of the machine-gun units. I found out from him that there were only three of us Russians in Burgos and that he had been commandeered to one of the batteries, and Bibikov to an anti-tank unit.

I was amazed at Rashevskii's energy and lack of concern. After two years of confinement, with a broken family and his health undermined, he viewed the future with delight, in an almost childish manner. It did not embarrass him that he was only a Spanish *cabo* (corporal) in rank and that the threat of being thrown into jail hung over him. He repeated several times the phrase: 'I'll be at the front with my riding crop in my hand and in white gloves.' I don't know if he wanted to express in that way his complete indifference to ranks or contempt for the enemy . . . and for the Spaniards.

I soon presented myself to the commander of my machine-gun unit and then left for the city in search of a place to spend the night. It was already late and we sergeants were not authorized a cot. We also had to pay for our own meals. And because our stay in Burgos lasted 12 days, we had to spend 500–600 pesetas during this time. During the first days I rented a room in a private home and messed in cheap eating houses, but then I managed to find 'bed and board' for 13 pesetas per day.

My first impression of the company was not a bad one. The temporary commander was a half-blind captain from the Legion. His assistant was a lieutenant (*teniente*[i]), also a combat officer with four wounds from the Spanish Civil War.[2] He gave the impression that he 'had a screw loose', but overall he was an excellent and likeable man. Of the three *alféreces*[ii] only P. was a repulsive type: coarse and stupid, with a very high opinion of himself, a braggart. Later on he proved to be an outright coward and very soon slipped away from the front line to the rear. The entire quartermaster section and the headquarters rested on the shoulders of the *brigada*[iii] (*feldwebel*[iv]), a young man already weighed down by a family. He was not a bad person, but due to a lack of character he fell on the first day into the hands of 'dealers', artful and shameless people who cared more about their personal enrichment than about the company's interests.

There were a lot of bad rumours circulating about the new company commander, Captain Fernández[3] – that he was supposedly a petty tyrant and petty as regards small details. To be sure, to the Spaniards, as unused as they were to discipline, he at first seemed like a 'terror'. However, in my opinion, he was a brilliant officer, the best of all the Spanish officers I saw in Spain. Strict with himself, he always came to exercises before the other officers and often earlier than many sergeants. Punishments rained down

---

[i] *Teniente* (Sp.) was equivalent to a lieutenant in the Russian army.
[ii] *Alféreces* (Sp., plural) was the equivalent of a junior lieutenant.
[iii] *Brigada* (Sp.), the equivalent of a sub-ensign.
[iv] *Feldwebel* (Ger.), the equivalent of a sergeant.

on the spoiled and sloppy sergeants, but the captain finally achieved relative order (by Spanish standards!) in his company.

The day was apportioned as follows: we were supposed to be in the company by 0700. From 0800 to 1200 we had line exercises in the oak grove near the barracks. I must admit that for me, a man of 50 years, it was rather difficult to march for hours on end and do rifle exercises, but what can you do? – the position of translator in the team was not called for and I was the same sergeant as the others, with the difference only that they were from 22 to a maximum of 30 years old, and I was 50.

After lunch there was training from 1500 to 1700, usually theory. We were supposed to study the regulations, but the captain did not usually come during these hours, so people simply hung about the spacious courtyard of the barracks, waiting with impatience for the hour when they could go into town.

The days of our stay in Burgos stretched out woefully and monotonously. I spent my free time in the company of P.I. Rashevskii. He proved to be a very nice and most wondrous interlocutor. The necessity of accompanying him in his eternal visits to cafes and drinking houses was a chore for me, for I must mournfully admit that this very kind man was a zealous worshipper of Bacchus. I must say that he always behaved himself without reproach and it was only after one shot too many that he would become enlivened and recall the difficult years spent in prison and would make plans for the future, where he would cut a figure with his 'riding crop and white gloves . . . '.

But all things must come to an end. Everything was ready for our departure: the men were all decked out and the officers and sergeants fixed up their uniforms, while the regimental commander, Colonel Pimentel,[4] arrived to carry out an inspection. I don't know, but it's highly likely that in the past he was a good combat officer, but he now made the impression of an old and bloated woman. He treated us to a high-flown speech, which he hysterically shouted out, rolling his eyes in a terrible manner. A modern Mars in the image of Tartarin.[5]

On the morning of 13 July we set out on our journey. We passed through the streets of Burgos in a ceremonial march and at the station were once again favoured with a number of farewell speeches. The scene in San Sebastián was repeated, but only in a larger setting. In all, it was a lot of phrase mongering . . . I think that the Spanish Blue Division had to hear before its departure no fewer speeches as there were soldiers in the division . . .

I must once again mention that poor Rashevskii was unable to leave with our division. He was still on the rolls of the local Militia, which detained him. I found out much later that he nevertheless managed to get out of a Spain that was decidedly inhospitable to him and was commandeered by the Germans, I believe, to the Hungarian army. I don't think he miscalculated . . .

On the Road to Germany

The hopes of many that we would march past General Franco in Madrid were not justified. We were sent due north. We passed through San Sebastián, so dear to me, where I again had the opportunity to bid farewell to my fellow workers in the Militia. From here it was only an hour's ride to the border of German-occupied France.

In Hendaye we had our first meeting with the German authorities. The troops were given a light meal: the soldiers on the platform and the officers and sergeants in the first and second class waiting rooms. Here for the first time we saw the difference in the German and Spanish officers' attitudes toward their sergeants. At the same time that it seemed quite natural to the Spaniards that the sergeants ate in the same room as their officers, it was clear that this shocked the German officers, but they did not consider it possible to insist that we be put outside the hall. This German tendency to remove from the unhappy sergeant his inherent authority in the army later led to pernicious results.

A pleasant surprise for me was the receipt of an equipment parcel, which had been given to me by a teacher in Burgos, with whom I accidentally became acquainted on the street. The kindness of this almost unknown person touched me deeply. Not knowing my name, he wrote on the parcel 'For the Senior Russian Sergeant'. It's a shame that the Spanish military began their 'glorious' activity by considering it possible to open the parcel and removing what was most valuable, leaving to me a cheap box of bean preserves. Alas! It was already necessary to become accustomed to such a manner of distributing foodstuffs and everything else, up to and including decorations.

During the tedious hours of travel the Spaniards, true to their nature, lulled themselves with too sunny hopes – they already saw themselves marching around Paris and strolling along the thronged boulevards of the French capital and winning the hearts of frivolous French girls. But these dreams were not to be fulfilled: the train sped us through the backwoods provinces of France, and instead of willing French girls we saw the sullen faces of the inhabitants; clenched fists were raised and one could hear ironic cries and wishes that the Russians would cut our throats.¹ But this did not disturb the Spaniards much: they made noise, tried to pick up women at the stations, sang Falangist songs and, in general, behaved as though they were returning from an already victoriously-concluded war.

At night, on the second day, we crossed the French border with Germany. We were given dinner in the woods in the semi-darkness. German nurses handed out coffee, newspapers and a light snack.² The Spaniards, who after two days had already managed to miss women, set about courting, in their own way of course, the prim German women: '*guapa*',[i] '*niña*',[ii] '*rubia*',[iii] '*morena*',[iv] and other such epithets of Spanish gallantry enjoyed little success, but the rejected lotharios were not let down and were content, for lack of anything better, with greasy German sausages and sweet coffee.

We had a long layover the next morning in the first German city,³ for disinfecting clothing and getting shots. I should mention that many Spaniards managed to 'slip out' of getting shots, because at that time the Germans were insufficiently acquainted with the nature of the Spanish *picaro* (rogue). The result was that subsequently, while at the front, many Spaniards 'despite their shot', came down with typhus. It worked out that 'they had only themselves to blame'.

But now the journey presented another picture. The population greeted their allies who were coming to help. The absence of draft-age men was quite evident. You saw only old men, children and . . . women, each one of which was uglier than the other. These were fleshy and portly broads, lacking any kind of femininity . . .

At the station in the town of Karlsruhe (the former capital of the Duchy of Baden) a banquet was laid out for us: the station was all decked out with German and Spanish flags and tables were set up, while at a short distance, behind a file of rail gendarmes, the local population appeared, holding small flags. I must say that the snack was quite a modest one – evidently, given German fastidiousness, overspending on food was not considered possible . . .

But this did not detract from the warmth of the reception, and as soon as our lunch was over the population was allowed on to the platform, where they mingled with the guests. Acquaintances were struck up among the

---

[i] *Guapa* (Sp.) – beautiful woman.
[ii] *Niña* (Sp.) – here, meaning a girl.
[iii] *Rubia* (Sp.) – blond-haired woman.
[iv] *Morena* (Sp.) – brunette.

young people. It was striking that in such a short time (some 20 minutes), and what was most important, without knowing the language, our Spaniards had contrived to acquire friends, godmothers and, what was most important, *novias*.ᵛ What was even more striking was that many of these *novias*, entered fully into their role as fiancées and made plans for getting married to the black-browed Spaniards . . . I was sorry for these girls in the majority of cases, for one must know the Spaniards.[4] Shakespeare was right when he said that the Spaniards are perfidious.

We did not know where we were heading until the last moment. At first they spoke about our planned stay in Poland, where we would be outfitted and trained in the German way. But then they indicated other possible detraining sites. Thus it was a big surprise for us when on 17 July we arrived at our destination.

The train halted at a small station in a pine forest. All around were fog and a bog. Storm clouds were literally hanging over the tops of the pines. A light rain was falling. It was dank and cold.

ᵛ *Novias* (Sp.) – here, meaning girls or fiancées.

Camp Grafenwöhr (Bavaria)

We found out that we had arrived at the Grafenwöhr camp next to a small town of the same name. Even the happy Spaniards had become sad. As they say: 'Now we're in for it . . . ' We unloaded and headed on foot for the camp, which was two kilometres from the railway station. I, to tell the truth, did not expect anything good: I thought they would house us in dirty wooden barracks, just like the climate and the forest. And thus it was a pleasant surprise for me when, instead of hovels, they brought us to a barracks. This was not a camp, according to our Russian understanding of the word, but more of a military settlement. A good hundred two- and three-storey buildings were located along both sides of a broad road. Flower beds and lawns had been laid out in front of the buildings and nothing, it seemed, would betray the fact that here were barracks enough to house an entire corps.

Inside, the facilities were very basic, but with all the conveniences. The majority of rooms were laid out with iron bunk-bed cots. Some had beds with iron springs. Everywhere there were large iron stoves in expectation of the winter cold. The company captain was kind enough to set aside a separate room for me. It was hard to ask for more.

Overall, the first days of our stay in Germany were joyful for me beyond expectation. The machine-gun unit's NCO element had been well selected. With a small exception, the sergeants were sufficiently cultured and good comrades and treated me well.[1] To be sure, the daily marching on the parade ground was torturous, but the hours of rest allowed us to forget this morning torment. We went to the town in the evening, where we somehow managed to get something to eat without ration cards. I had a big appetite after expending so much energy, and they fed us wretchedly.[2] At this time I still believed the Spaniards that the Germans were at fault. It was only later that I learned the Spanish technique of distributing food supplies.

Before long things became worse for me: I was transferred to the battalion headquarters.[3] I had to give up my own room and move to a shared one, where four new fellow soldiers lived. The company was not very likeable. The new leadership also left a lot to be desired: there was the splenetic and eternally peevish battalion commander, Enrique;[4] his adjutant was Lieutenant Izquierdo,[5] who had the habit of issuing orders that only created confusion. Everything went very badly, but when the adjutant joined in then any hope of restoring order would disappear. Two junior lieutenants (*alférez*), devoid of personality, rounded out the headquarters.

And then the order came down to distribute duties among the sergeants. It turned out that there was a great shortage of the latter. At the same time, a month ago, in Burgos, twenty sergeants had been sent home because there was no need for them. I was appointed personal property (baggage) chief; to this day I still don't know what I was . . . One thing was clear, that I was to be with the secondary rear transport.[6] To my observation as to how I was supposed to carry out my duties as a translator for the headquarters if I'm going to be tens of kilometres from the front, they replied that, on the whole, there was no translator position in the establishment.

The future would show just how absurd was my appointment: all of the personal property was lost and stolen, while in Russia all of the battalion's transport came down to three or four nags with the kitchen and food vehicles (sledges, to be exact), while I, as the translator, was supposed to take care of everything, bearing an enormous responsibility. For if it was sufficient to point to one's open mouth with a finger and repeat '*Agua, agua*', in order to request water for the billeted troops, then in intelligence work and while questioning prisoners, the Spanish 'genius' was insufficient and a translator was needed.

Whatever the case, in Grafenwöhr they commandeered me to the battalion's stable, where there were at the time about thirty-five horses. This is how they got at me: each day I had to get up at 0400 or 0430 (depending on how the unbalanced adjutant felt) and wake the drivers. This was the most difficult part, as no one wanted to get up: you can threaten, cajole and beg, but almost always without success. Of the 20–25 men obligated to be present at the morning feeding, there were usually no more than 6–7 men, and always the same ones, the more conscientious ones. The remainder was, as the Spanish say, *despistados* (those who have lost their way), and who only appeared at the stable from time to tie in order to find out 'if there are any orders . . . '

Two of my fellow sergeants, who were also assigned to the transport detail, would appear at about 0800–0900, having first breakfasted well, and sometimes they did not appear for duty at all. It was completely useless to complain to anyone about this state of affairs, for one of the features of Spanish military service is the leadership's fear of 'complicating the situation' by resorting to punishments. Here the goodness of the higher-ups played no role, but rather their fear of ruining their mood by getting into a conflict with those who were punished, and particularly their protectors. And the latter will always be found among the Spaniards . . .

According to the testimony of the Spanish themselves, nowhere in any country (with the exception of the Latin American countries) are misdemeanours committed without punishment as in Spain. Often the criminal, no matter how serious the crime he has committed, does not even lose the position he occupies in society, if he only has influential relatives or friends. He who protests, or even points this out, is threatened with serious consequences. Of course, a change in regime entails a reshuffling of cards, and thus it is not surprising that today's influential friends and pals will tomorrow prove to be simply ordinary (I'm not speaking here of political ones) criminals . . .

But let's return to camp life. The more time passed the fewer soldiers reported for service and the more unruly became their conduct. Here, for the first time in my life, I lost my self-control to such an extent that I beat one of the drivers. And, I must admit . . . with success, for that yielded brilliant results: after this that driver became my dependable assistant and . . . a good friend.

In this regard, the higher-ups held to an original position: those few souls who, 'through their good will', came, or those whom I managed to drag to the stable, were detailed to other work by order of one of the *alférez*,[i] or by that same adjutant. I often remained alone at the stable. The unwashed, hungry and unfed horses, standing up to their ankles in manure, presented such a pitiful sight that I, taking off my sergeant's coat, took up my brush and shovel and began to work. General Muñoz Grandes,[7] the division commander, once found me in such solitude in the morning. I don't know if my solitude surprised the General, and it seems as if it did not! He was only surprised that I was a Russian.

They finally began to dress us in German uniforms and equip us. Along the way there arose the question of our ranks. This question, having been decided unsatisfactorily, resulted in unpleasant consequences. The difficulty

---

[i] *Alférez* (Sp.) – an Ensign or Junior Lieutenant.

was that in the German army the transition from a *gefreiter* (corporal) to the first officer's rank comes about through a highly-developed hierarchy, while the Spanish have only a *sargento* and *brigada* (sergeant and *feldwebel*, or sub-ensign), while the latter is more often not a rank, but a position. And it was here, in renaming the Spanish Sergeants that one had to be extremely careful.

The gulf between officers and men in the Spanish army is enormous. The Spanish officers, with their institution of 'honorary officers' (*honorifico*), represent a sort of anachronism in Europe. I have never met such an enormous number of officers completely lacking military training as here. In the regiment a good third of the officers did not know how to command. This was an **aristocratic estate**. They were not interested in the life of the soldiers and the entire burden of maintaining discipline fell on the NCO personnel. Order in the company depends upon the sergeant's authority. He must be a friend to his subordinates, but not to associate with them in either their work or recreation.[8]

In the beginning we sergeants were given rank insignias for German sergeants – epaulets, trimmed with silver lace (as with the Russian cadets) and with a small star, but within two or three days, following protests by German Sergeants and due to considerations of economy, we were ordered to remove the small star. And so we became junior sergeants, but, it would appear, that didn't satisfy the Germans either, so steps were taken to reduce us to the status of plain sergeants. And because in the German army the latter live, work and eat with the soldiers, this meant that we had to mix with the soldiers. The fact that some sergeants, in the face of repeated orders, continued to wear the small star on their epaulets, likely did not improve the situation, but rather worsened it, because everyone knew that they were *embusteros* (rogues, cheats). And every Spaniard is an *embustero* by nature. And now the unfortunate sergeants hung around in lines for meals, to receive uniforms, and simply in order to get into the movie theatre. And anyone who tried to break the line, as in the past, was pursued by cries of '¡*A la cola!*' ('Get back in line!'). And because in reality a line was never strictly observed, and the more shameless and artful would break forward, then the sergeant, while maintaining his dignity and not wishing to resort to illegal tricks, always remained at the tail end of the line. All of this led to a situation in which the poorly disciplined Spanish soldiers, lacking any kind of restraint and reins, turned into bandits.

My new sergeant comrades from the battalion headquarters were not very likeable. Sergeant Tomillo,[9] the 'signals chief', was repulsive. He combined a boundlessly high opinion of himself with a really low-life personality. His endless wish to play some kind of role, to intrude with his observations and to run everything, combined at the same time with his personal lack of control, knew no bounds. I was once woken by the sound of cries. What had happened? Sergeant Tomillo had attacked his friend, Sergeant Cortez,[10] and tried to . . . rape him. The latter only managed to save himself by running to the light switch and illuminating the room. The two sergeants standing in their underwear painted a pretty picture, of which one was defending his honour in such an original pose . . . I informed Tomillo in the morning that henceforward I would not tolerate any complaints, either relating to his duties or his personal life, and that I would prefer not to be a witness to such scenes. Sergeant Cortez only reacted by not showing up for two days out of a feeling of shame. But he did not consider it necessary to complain to the authorities.[11]

The days passed – for some spent working, while others lounged about with nothing to do. The people under the command of German instructors were supposed to acquaint themselves with the weapons issued to them. Modern war demands the employment – even in the infantry – of such various types of weaponry that the two-week period we were given was insufficient for instruction, even given a maximum effort.[12] Given Spanish laziness, it worked out that people went to the front without any kind of preparation. Inherent Spanish valour and their nature as carefree adventurers saved the situation. Perhaps the saying that 'God looks out for drunks and little children' applies to them.

Spanish sloppiness and lack of discipline made the German instructors, who had been assigned to us, indignant. At first they attempted to 'shake up' the Spaniards: they shouted and complained to the Spanish commanders, but then, seeing that had no effect, fell into a sort of apathy and lack of concern, as if to say 'Do as you please'.

The Spaniards, for their part, criticized everything German, calling the Germans 'human machines', bragging about their Spanish 'healthy discipline', and got out of all manner of exercises as much as possible.[13] I feel that in one sense the Spanish were right: the German standard (both light and heavy) machine gun[14] was not worth much. Later, at the front, it would freeze up when it was particularly cold. During this time we sought assistance in the light Russian Degtiarev machine gun,[15] captured from the enemy.

Our departure for the front was drawing closer. The battalion would march out for a training march or firing practice almost every day. They pulled me out of the stables at this time and, to the amazement of many, I did not disgrace myself – my service in the French Foreign Legion stood me in good stead – and marched without getting tired. At the same time, many Spaniards, even the young ones, quickly fell out from exhaustion. I believe that this can be explained by the fact that they had not yet accustomed themselves to the heavy German boots, and they were not allowed to go to their exercises in their favourite *alpargatas* (canvas shoes with corded soles).

Not long before our departure my commander suddenly remembered that I, as supply sergeant in charge of personal belongings, was authorized to ride a horse. I thus became the 'supply cavalry'. This happened in the following way: in the beginning there was a great demand for all of the 10–12 supply horses. Each man wanted to get on a horse, prance around the town's streets and to wear high boots with spurs, but then it transpired that this pleasant exercise was associated with a lot of discomfort, especially for poor cavalrymen. Some horses proved skittish in unskilled hands. The horses also demanded upkeep and the harness and saddle cleaning, while the riders themselves had to go to riding exercises. In the majority of cases, the Spanish are poor cavalrymen and care for their horses is completely foreign to them; for this they lack both constancy and love for the animal.[16]

I was questioned by the adjutant for a long time whether or not I could ride and whether I would fall off my horse, before they gave me one. Later on, due to the capriciousness of the horse issued to me, I understood why they asked me these questions. What could I reply? In the past I had to ride a lot, but I never learned to ride properly; I did not have time to do it in military school due to the beginning of the October Revolution, and while serving with the British in a remount squadron, I, as the chief of the officers' stable, rarely had to take charge of the squadron's daily ride. But I believe I sit well on a horse. My evil-wishers expected my fall and finally my refusal of the refractory horse. The horse issued to me was nervous during the first days; it was skittish, it kicked, reared up on its hind legs, and even bit, but then we got used to each other a little: I came to love it and it became attached to me. It followed me around like a little dog and at night, if we slept out under the open sky, it would stand over me without being tied up, or if resting, would lie down beside me. During the long campaign nearly all of the battalion's riding horses disappeared for this or that reason. They began to tell me that it was not right for a sergeant to ride when the battalion commander, captains and the doctor went on foot. They repeatedly took my horse from me, but not for long. They would return it with curses, such as this is '*animal de diablo*' (the devil's horse), adding among themselves that '*Dela misma estirpe que sargento ruso*' (the same breed as the Russian sergeant). And even when they hitched it to a wagon, it, upon seeing me, without paying attention to the driver, would pull the wagon toward me. It was a good horse. It had only one defect: it did not allow any other riding horse to move ahead of it. More than once the commander, raising his hands to the sky in despair, would shout 'Sergeant Kovalevskii, do you command the battalion, or I?' Evidently in the past – the Germans took it from the Poles – it had been the property of some unit commander.

It was just as difficult to win boots and spurs for myself as it had been easy to acquire a horse. It was only in Russia that I was able to equip myself fully. The vain Spaniards, although they were dismounted, loved to jingle their spurs . . .

Before leaving for the front, we still had to swear allegiance to the *Führer*. This act was organized with great solemnity and took place on a large parade-ground 12–15 kilometres from the camp. At first, you might say, they organized a general rehearsal for us. It took place in very unfortunate conditions, because we were caught in a downpour. We looked just like 'wet chickens' and our march past the reviewing stand resembled more the stampede of a frightened herd. It was already better the next day for the oath-taking. We passed by the reviewing stand in ranks of eighteen men, maintaining an almost irreproachable line. A Spanish colonel and German major marched in front of the regiment.[17] It was interesting that during the religious ceremony the German band played, among the other marches, the Russian 'How Great is our God in Zion'.[18] If this was purely a coincidence, then what irony!

On the Road to Russia

Finally, on 20 August our 'Pimentel Regiment'[1] began to load up in order to leave for the East. In view of the large supply columns, each battalion required two trains. The train, in which the battalion headquarters and the first and second companies were to leave, departed at six o'clock in the evening. I, who had wisely foreseen cold nights, preferred to ride in the wagon with the horses. I chose wisely, for while at the same time the people in the passenger coaches suffered at night from the cold and were exhausted from the close quarters, I was in heaven, resting on a saddle among eight horses and in the company of three very likeable orderlies.

To be sure, sometimes, especially when the train jerked hard, the commotion and the stamping of the horses would wake us, interrupting our sweet dreams. But a light shout was sufficient for the upset horses to quiet down and to the accompaniment of the horses' snorting and the rumble of the wheels, we would once more fall asleep. During the day the greetings of the population were even more cordial, evidently because they overestimated the role assigned us. It seemed to the civilians that there were thousands and thousands of us travelling. Actually, the 'Blue Division' numbered 16,000–17,000 men, of which about 10,000 were combat troops,[2] while the remainder belonged to the headquarters, the quartermaster service, transport, hospitals and veterinarian stations.

All of these non-line units made up the division's 'cream'. They, having connections in the party and finding support among the command, interfered in everything, demanded a lot and – this was the main thing – ate up two or three times more than they were authorized. This was the real 'internal enemy'. They, being disorganized, headed for the rear during the winter months, terrorized the population and filled up the hospitals. Here one could see these mama's boys who had never come under fire, but they were already decked out in Spanish and German decorations. With the onset of spring they flooded back to Spain and, boasting, related their 'feats'.[3]

The people who served in the line of fire were divided in the following manner: three infantry regiments (Pimentel, Vierna and Esparza), each consisting of three battalions, a reserve infantry battalion and numerous artillery – battalion, regimental, heavy anti-aircraft and anti-tank. The division had no cavalry. There were also Spanish planes, but outside the 'Blue Division' and they worked with German units.[4]

We were finally ordered to unload in Suwałki. Unimaginable confusion followed. People forgot a lot of things in the train cars and a lot that was unloaded was lost as well. Bales of hay, bags of barley, canvas buckets, and individual bits of harnesses lay strewn along the rail bed. I attempted to gather up some things which would be so necessary for us on our long journey, but it was already late and we had to hurry and line up. The soldiers were strung out in a long column and, without stopping in the town, which was once Russian, moved on. We had a 30–35 *verst*[5] march ahead of us to get to Seiny[6] (I don't know how it was called earlier in Russian).

By the end of the march twenty or thirty of the battalion's soldiers had gotten blisters on their feet[7] due to unfamiliarity with marching, and had to be loaded onto wagons and *camions*.[8] By evening we had reached the outskirts of the town, and were settled in a large four-storey building. We remained here for two days. I was too busy in the stable to go into town often, but it was here for the first time, after 20 years, that I was able to speak to people from the USSR, and who had borne to the end the communist yoke.

Refugees from the so-called second emigration,[9] such as Solonevich,[10] Besedovskii[11] and Dmitrievskii,[12] laid on too much drama with their eyewitness accounts, while often sinning against the truth in their all too subjective evaluation of unrecognized leaders. A Russian-Polish family with which I became acquainted struck me, first of all, by its solidarity and, what was most amazing, its optimism. A Russian man, who had weathered a serious disease and, having freed himself from Soviet tutelage, amazed me with his sunny world view and limitless energy. Though there be poverty all around and hungry days await him, he is drunk on freedom and the opportunity to soon be working for himself and not for the ruthless communist machine. The Soloneviches did not tell us about this.

What also struck me was that the town's Polish population, which had lost its independence, was less antagonistic toward the Germans than the Bolsheviks. The 12-month rule of the people from Moscow was sufficient to instil a distaste for the communist 'paradise'. The overall opinion was 'better the Germans than the Bolsheviks'.[13] Unfortunately, in their subsequent behaviour the Germans (through their coarseness, greed and psychopathic behaviour, in which they were hardly better than the Soviets) managed to turn both the Polish and Russian population against them. The deification of the *Führer* in Germany and Lenin in the USSR was revolting to people. But I did not notice any hostility toward me as a Russian. Quite the opposite! Everywhere, whether on the street or in the shops, the population readily spoke Russian, while the older generation still mournfully recalled the Tsarist days, when everyone lived so free of care. They tried to be of service to me as best as they could and through their joint efforts managed to knock together some straps, which were so necessary for my spurs.

But the Spaniards rarely had the pleasure of spending the night with a roof over their heads during the march across Poland. It's difficult to say what the reason was for this: the Germans' tendency to keep the Spaniards as far away from the Poles, their co-religionists, as possible, or our commanders' desire to 'play at being soldiers', by carrying out a march according to all the rules . . . But the goal was not attained in either case. Upon arriving at a halting place, the men would abandon the camp in search of the closest village and it was already impossible to keep any kind of watch over those who had left.[14] And if the night halt was near a village or in the village itself, then no one spent the night in tents – most of all, of course, the commanders.

I found the going difficult. The muddle-headed adjutant did not let up until he had forced me to strictly spend my nights in a tent, near the carts and horses. During the cold September nights our tents were already covered with hoar-frost and I often lay curled up in a rotten blanket and shaking from the cold. But I had little time for sleep. It was a rare night when the hungry horses did not break free from their tethers and run off into the fields. Searches were organized and then goodbye nighttime sleep! And at 0400 or 0500 one had to be on one's feet in order to feed and water the horses. We would warm ourselves by the dying embers of a fire, and then hit the road. Frozen people, without greatcoats – the wise commanders, in order to toughen up the soldiers, could find nothing better than to take them away – tried to get warm, hopping from one foot to another or marching rapidly.

Everything around interested me. After all, this was the old Russia! I would forget that I was in Poland and that its inhabitants were Catholics and that the young people could often not speak Russian. For me, this was RUSSIA.[15] I sometimes encountered a resident who, if not a Russian, at least spoke and thought like a Russian. We would then recall 'the good old days' and then it seemed as if that had not been so long ago. The Spaniards constantly interrupted our conversations and, due to their inherent feeling of envy and outward posing, sought to attract attention to themselves. There was only one cure for this: to point out that they were Catholics, and not schismatics, like myself . . . Then they would pull out their crucifixes and small icons and zealously kissing them, would show their loyalty to the Roman Catholic Church. Alas! They were mistaken, as this moved the Poles little.

But before long the Spaniards encountered open hostility toward them on the part of the population, when thievery and looting began in the villages through which we passed.[16] How then ungrateful was my role! It was useless to relay the population's complaints to the battalion commander. His only reply was: 'These are not our people.' They usually stole animals: sheep and chickens. In one landlord's house they did not limit themselves to even this: they broke down the door during the night and took away a suitcase, a suit, a watch and money. I was sorry for the old Polish gentleman, all the more so because the Spaniards had christened him a 'Bolshevik' for his 'slander of the Spanish army'.[17]

However, they met us in a decidedly unfriendly manner in Lithuania. The Lithuanians treated me, a Russian, with a great lack of trust and none of them wanted to speak Russian. We crossed the boundary of this country twice and I can't understand where Lithuania begins and ends . . . One of the most painful sights I've ever seen is linked to this country.

During an exhausting march in the woods our battalion column suddenly halted: an endless column of Russian prisoners of war was moving toward us, but in what condition! Lined up in rows of five men, they had to hold with their hands barbed wire, which was strung from the first ranks to the last. The people inside the column had to strongly hold on with their hands. No one was supposed to fall behind. It was terrible to watch how these living skeletons, with indescribable fear in their eyes, and tripping, relentlessly moved forward. The rear rows practically had to run. A terrible rubber stick, held by the soldier (the majority of these were Latvians or Lithuanians, which the latter deny) escorting them, hung over those who fell behind. And if this did not help, then a shot from a rifle would save the unfortunate from further torments. People could not halt in order to recover as the inhumane 'bearers of culture' drove them like cattle. No one was spared. Along our route we encountered the bodies of three who had fallen behind, all with smashed heads.[18]

I don't know how many kilometres this nightmarish column stretched. In any event, there were thousands of people. Thousands of candidates for sure death. The impression was so awful that many of the Spaniards later sighed for a long time and could not understand why was this so.

One thing was clear to me: how cruel can one be and, the main thing, how can one be so short-sighted, bordering on idiocy, to believe that one could quickly and victoriously end the war, given such treatment of prisoners? It was hard to do a greater service to Stalin, for there, among the ranks of the 'Red' soldiers; they already knew what awaited them in captivity.

Our path lay toward Grodno,[19] but we went through the city without stopping there. Only the centre of the city had been destroyed. The streets were narrow and dirty and full of Jews,[20] who were particularly noticeable now by the yellow, five-point stars on their right breast. In general, the condition of people of this race in those places occupied by the Germans was quite bad. From morning until evening all the Jews, without exception, had to work to repair the road. It was pitiful to see, without forgetting even the crimes of their fellow tribesmen, the young girls, yesterday's young ladies, puttering about in the dust and serving as a laughing stock for any passer-by.[21] They were only allowed to live in defined quarters of the city – the 'ghetto', and where there were few of them – in concentration camps.[22] They were forbidden to associate with Christians. Neither their rights nor their lives were protected by the law, and if they got in someone's way, or as a means of repression, they could 'taken out'.[23]

The division did not move by the shortest route during its march, but for reasons unknown to us chose out of the way and long routes. From Grodno, instead of heading directly for Vil'no, we moved on Lida and Zhidom'ia,[24] and we set up camp 15–17 kilometres from Grodno, on the outskirts of the village of Obukhovichi. I mention this village because we stayed there for three days and the time spent there was one of the most pleasant recollections of the march.

I became acquainted here with the likeable Polish family of Osip Obukhovich. The mother, in her youth, had lived for a long time in Moscow and was completely Russian. The father and three grown sons also spoke Russian freely. I spent all my free time from duty with this family. They sent me off like one of their own and supplied me with all sorts of eatables for the long journey. I asked myself, where is the old Russian-Polish hostility, about which the foreign press spoke so much? The policy of this state issued, it seemed, from an indisputable truth, and we now see the result of this short-sightedness. Only in sorrow did the Poles understand that an anti-Russian policy would be a policy of suicide for them.

Our stay in this village was marked by a phenomenon rare for the Spanish army: a marauding soldier was publicly flogged. As our *teniente*, Nikolai Krivosheia,[25] who served in the regimental headquarters, told me later, this took place at his insistence. Whether this is true or not, it made a powerful impression on the soldiers. For a time after this nothing was heard of robberies, but later, while already in Russia, they were renewed, and at the front, under the protection of the commanders, they took on a shameful character.

Up until this time, since I was riding a horse, I did not often get tired, but it became obvious that I did not have long to take advantage of this privilege. First one and then another draught horse fell out on the road as the result of poor food and heavy burdens. The German four-wheel wagon was not itself heavy, but then they would load it up with all sorts of junk, and then a pair of horses could only pull it along a level road. Once the road went uphill or we turned onto a dirt road, then the horses' sufferings would begin: neither pushing nor whipping helped, and the poor horses would raise up on their hind legs and break their traces, but the cart would not budge. The only way out in this case was to hitch up another pair of horses to help, but this took up a lot of time and delayed movement. The majority of the saddle horses were rendered useless due to poor care and careless saddling. Almost all of them had swayed backs and, the unskilled riders, afraid of being thrown, did not risk getting on their horses.

I preserved my horse longer than anyone, but I finally had to part with it and turned it over to be a work horse. This took place near Vil'no. We did not enter the capital of Lithuania, but our staff workers later told us that the city did not suffer any damage and that life there was going very well; that is, they found a place to entertain themselves.[26] One of the last Lithuanian towns we passed through was Molodechno.[27] Here we left a large part of our train and the sick horses to be loaded onto rail cars. We then continued our journey on foot. I still recall Molodechno because it was there that I met a 'Ukrainian', a captured Russian soldier who had been released for free work thanks to his coming from the Poltava *oblast'*.[28] There was little of the Ukrainian in him: he mocked the Germans' plan for carving up Russia, and that very 'independence'[29] among the population that had so bloomed under Petliura[30] and the *hetman*,[31] could, in his words, no longer be.

PART TWO. RUSSIA

First Impressions

Ich habe so viel Elend gesehen, dass es nicht zu sagen ist
(I have seen so much sorrow that I have difficulty speaking about it)

Finally, on 17 September 1941, at one o'clock in the afternoon, we crossed the border of the USSR.[1] A small bridge divided the kingdom of the Soviets from Lithuania. On the other side, along the slope of a small hill, a number of pitiful hovels huddled together, on the walls of which there already hung German posters with Hitler's portrait. Two or three hours still separated us from the nearest village of Maslovichi (Minsk *oblast'*), and we stopped for the night near there. Outwardly, the Belorussian villages were not very different from the same villages in Poland or Lithuania. Only the presence of collective farm buildings reminded us that we were in the 'Soviet paradise'. These structures – barns, threshing barns (drying barns[2]) and the collective farm club – are located, for the most part, on the outskirts of the village and often occupy a large area. Throughout the day the entire life of the village revolves around them, while at the same time one can only find old men and children in the huts. Everything that is capable of work is working off the 'Soviet corvée'.

We still found this system in operation, for the Germans did not touch the collective farm system upon their arrival, so forced labour still remained, although under freer conditions, which did not arouse sympathy for the newcomers.[3] They left the resolution of the land question until after the war, replacing only the collective farm chairman and promising a better salary for work days in dividing up the profits and an increase in the size of personal plots for the more vigorous workers.[4] Of the livestock, only horses were distributed amongst the families, while the remaining livestock was either requisitioned for the army's needs or strictly inventoried, and these animals were issued livestock 'passports'. All of the collective farm's bread, potatoes and hay were also catalogued.

The villages, with the exception of the collective farm buildings, were a pitiful sight and there was poverty everywhere. Inside the cabins it was clean and there was an abundance of icons.⁵ It's hard to be sure whether the latter, upon the approach of the Germans, did not take the place of the 'Lenin corner'. According to the inhabitants, the religious persecutions had ceased during recent years and religion was freely practised.⁶

You didn't encounter any men of draft age. They'd all been driven off to the war. Despite the fact that each family had one or two of its members in the ranks of the Red Army, no one, in my opinion, desired the Soviets' victory. The sincere joy of liberation from the Bolshevik yoke was visible on everyone's face: 'If only this war would end as quickly as possible, so that we could work, work for ourselves.' This is the slogan of almost everyone.

In order to understand all the charms of the Soviet regime, you only have to listen to the inhabitants. Each head of a household was allotted 50–60 hundredths of a *desyatina*.ⁱ For this he had to pay a tax of 500–800 rubles per year. Before, the peasants could rent a *desyatina* for 20–25 rubles per year.⁷ But the very use of this land was restricted: you could plant vegetables, but you couldn't plant wheat. In the event of a violation, the peasant was obliged to pay a heavy fine. One could keep only a single cow, while paying the state the cost of 35 kilograms of meat for it. Whoever kept chickens (one or several) paid the state 180–200 eggs per year. Aside from this, there also existed an entire series of small requisitions.

What did the peasant get from the state farm? He almost never got hay for his cow. Sometimes, very rarely, the collective would furnish a horse, so as to travel somewhere, or for work. They gave the peasant bread to feed his family, but not in a sufficient amount. And the peasant nearly always had to buy bread in the town. But here he also ran into restrictions – a kilogram per person. And if he wanted to buy bread for all the members of his family, he had to take all of them into town.

A work day in the collective farm was rated in different ways, depending on the work being performed, the number of hours worked and the season. The day was rated at 15 kopecks and more. Sometimes, in a bad harvest year, when the production norms still had to be fulfilled, the collective farmer received nothing.

Our battalion was not the first to move along the road near which the village of Maslovichi was located: everything that had existed had already been requisitioned, bought or simply stolen; there were no sheep, pigs or

---

ⁱ   A *desyatina* is an old Russian form of measurement equal to 2.7 acres of land.

chickens to be seen anywhere. In defiance of the most severe order by the German authorities on the inadmissibility of the forcible purchase of livestock from the inhabitants, the Spaniards entering Russia 'to eat white bread' considered it their inalienable right to requisition everything edible, while in the majority of cases not paying anything.[8] But despite all of this, the inhabitants of the 'Soviet paradise' joyfully greeted the strangers coming to free them from their own government.

As to their attitude toward me, a Russian, I won't say anything. I, who in Spain thought that they would shoot at me, as a traitor, from around every corner, was completely amazed by the tenderness and joyfulness with which I was engulfed in Russian villages. If there was something to be procured, I was the only one who could do it. This finally placed me in a torturous position, for the Spaniards began to employ me widely to shake down the population of its last article. What could I do? If I was unable to refuse the commanders' demands, I at least was able to force them to generously pay for what was bought. But what does money mean to a hungry population when there is nothing to buy? . . .

The first impression I took away from people under Soviet rule was as follows: the degraded morals of the population, which I expected to encounter, did not jump out at me. The absence or non-requirement of a church marriage did not break down the family. Pre-revolutionary Russia's old family way of life had not suffered. The authority of the father and mother was still strong. I did not notice any impudent behaviour or even simple disobedience by children toward their parents. The mutual relations between the youth of both sexes were simple, but not undisciplined.[9]

But there was something new as well. In the majority of cases, adult children, with a high school education, continued to work to help the family. It was so awful for me to see a female student,[10] dressed like the other girls in the village and working barefoot in the fields. Here there was not even a hint of posing in the spirit of Lev Tolstoi . . . [11] It was clear that to work was not a burden for her and among the youth in the village there were no lords and no serfs.

Following a meeting with the youth, I always took away a feeling of tenderness and faith in Russia's future. They were physically healthy and morally uncorrupted, with a great hunger for knowledge and a great desire for work. I took away the impression that we, the Russian émigrés, should radically change our opinion of the Soviet man in Russia.[12] Maybe the Soviet regime was horrible, as was usually thought, but a Russian, and particularly the Russian woman, having gone through suffering, had maintained this purity of soul. After a couple of months I became acquainted with a no-longer young Spaniard in the division headquarters. He, being a sincerely religious person, had gone to Russia as in a crusade against barbarians and atheists, and had been particularly struck by the Christian simplicity and beauty of the Russian soul. He said that in his opinion the Russian people stood closer than all other peoples to the ideal of Christian life.[13]

After having stayed for a day and a half near the first Russian village, our battalion moved on. On our first march I was seized by such pains in my stomach that I had to halt from time to time and lie down. Finally, on the edge of a small grove, I was no longer in any condition to hope to continue the march. Company after company passed by without paying any attention to me, and it seemed to me that I was in danger of being left behind, had not one kind-hearted *aléfrez* expressed his concern: 'Hey, people, it seems as if someone is dying here!'

They picked me up, just as it was starting to drizzle, and placed me on one of the carts, where I slipped into a state of semi-consciousness. I don't remember how long I lay there half asleep, and when I came to the sun was shining as if in springtime and people were cheerfully walking along a road that was as straight and smooth as a parquet floor. This was the famous 'Stalin road' (highway) from Moscow to Minsk, which had been completed not long before the beginning of the war.[14] One must admit that the road was a lovely sight. I later saw many highways in Germany, but I never saw anything like this one. The Germans used it as much as possible: dozens of cars, tanks and motorized guns passed by every minute, in this or that direction, but even then traffic never to a standstill. There was room for everyone ... even for us, a living anachronism, strung out in a long line, with heavy and clumsy carts, hauled by horses that could barely put one foot in front of another ...[15]

My senior command remembered me during our first stop for the night. They found me and ordered me to go out and search for food. I was to buy up everything that was edible. (Seeing that the money was not worth anything.) I can't say that such assignments gave me any joy. Knowing the poverty of the surrounding population, I was quite ashamed to buy, actually by force, the last of what remained in the villages.

The price, no matter how laughable it was, always seemed high to the Spaniards. I paid ten marks for a calf (five marks by German calculations), three marks for 100 kilograms of potatoes (one mark and 75 pfennigs by German calculations), but the Spaniards were not satisfied with this. Every day 25 pfennigs were taken from each soldier's pay for improving his food. Thus, in a company of 160–200 men, 40–50 marks per day were earmarked for purchases. In reality, not even half of the sum taken from each soldier was spent in our battalion. The 'remainder' was taken by whoever was responsible for feeding the battalion.

But if I could not get out of delivering food for the battalion, I absolutely refused to take on the purchase of chickens, sheep and piglets for the lordly officers. I saw so much sorrow and tears in each peasant family when they had their last bit of livestock, the family's last resource and joy of their children, taken away.[16]

It was exhausting, following a long march, while the others were resting, to set out on foot to search for food, often for tens of *versts*. I once had to drive cattle that I had bought across the Dvina River and came under fire from an enemy plane. Another time I had to interfere in an argument that threatened to turn into an open fight between the Spanish 'purchasers' and the German field police.[17]

But all of this was made up for by the pleasant minutes spent in this or that Russian family. It was autumn and it was not so long ago that the guns roared here and soldiers mercilessly killed each other, but good people, despite their misfortune and poverty, joyfully looked to the future, just like in springtime. 'Once the war is over, we will work.' There's some kind of cult of work here: how far the new Russia is from those countries where they view work as some kind of punishment from God!

Nobody knew which front we were going to. As early as Spain, and later in Germany, we were making plans. Everybody wanted to go to Ukraine. And although the Spaniards did not know much about Russia, they knew one thing, and that was that in Ukraine the climate was easier and, what was the main thing, there they could 'eat white bread' (*pan blanco*), which so attracted them following the hunger in Spain.[18] However, the route we took after detraining in Suwałki promised no good.

But not all hope had been lost until we turned off the Moscow highway to the north, in the direction of Vitebsk. We entered onto a narrow forest road. Nights in the woods were very cold and devilishly cold and damp in the tents when the sun went down. We rarely came across villages and there was no place to get warm. We were visited at night by Red aviation, so we were ordered to extinguish our campfires when it began to get dark.

In the morning, well before dawn, we would strike our camp, for the short autumn days were not enough to cover 30–35 kilometres. The companies got smaller and were down to less than 100 men, and those were limping and tripping over every little thing. The heavy German boots were sheer torture for people who were used to walking in *alpargatas* (canvas sandals with hemp soles). The medical automobiles gather up the sick and lame every day. And yet we move on and on . . .

Finally, we are at Vitebsk. We make camp 8–10 kilometres from the city and wait for our train, in order to continue our march by rail. I was able to acquaint myself with the city's life in the three-four days of our layover. The centre of Vitebsk had been destroyed, but the outskirts were intact and full of life. Everyone from the camp was trying to make his way there in order to have some fun. I was there two times or so. The place was of especial interest to me. After all, it was the first Russian city I had seen following a 20-year absence.

But the first impressions are not very good: the streets are full of poorly clothed, I would say 'wan', people hurrying in search of something. There is poverty and hunger. There are long lines of people by the numerous stores with empty display windows, bakery shops with broken windows, and cheap eating places. There's a 'market' near the bridge, on the city's main square. Suspicious types move in and out of one scrum of people to another, while asking what is being bought and what is being sold. One can buy anything: beginning from women's stockings, which are by no means new, and ending with an exhausted and painted up woman-child of 14–15 years . . .

But the best-selling item is vodka. Its main suppliers are the German soldiers. But this is the highest quality vodka and expensive. The population makes do with some kind of surrogate, involving a mixture of moonshine and gasoline. Unbelievably repulsive! But it all gets sold, because the drunks, of which there are evidently a sufficient number, need something to get drunk on. I got into a conversation with two or three such types of an already advanced age. There was the unnatural tone, the artificial manners and the desire to appear noble, along with a drunken belch. There was the semi-fascist gesture: 'I greet the warrior for the liberation of Russia! As a former officer under the Tsar, I am with you, heart and soul.' There follow unexpected tears from an upwelling of feeling and, finally, the request: 'Friend, can you spare anything for half a bottle?'

Not wishing to dine in a public canteen, I agreed to the suggestion of one inhabitant to dine with him. In order to somehow recompense my host, who flatly refused to take money, I bought something to drink for lunch. To tell the truth, I was later sorry for the money (20 marks) and the time spent. The lunch itself was not so bad, but the entire setting and the subsequent outpourings of emotions were disgusting. There was a widow there of about 40 years of age, not unpleasant, who was, as they say, the 'highlight of the lunch'. And when she, following good drink and heavy snacks, instead of the promised charming singing, began to howl, I didn't know where to turn. As they used to say in the old days, 'Get out while you can'. After the widow's drunken tears and vile revelations, I couldn't take it any longer and considered it best to withdraw, leaving my host the last drops of the expensive alcohol and the widow to call with her caterwauling either her deceased husband or one of her numerous lovers. The Spanish '*maestro herredor*' (the regimental blacksmith), who was with me, preferred to remain and later told me, while smacking his lips, that this broad was 'to his taste'. I won't even risk trying to express, even in Spanish, his literal evaluation.

Vitebsk was gloomy with the onset of night: lonely chimneys from the destroyed buildings stick out along both sides of the empty streets. Not a soul or an inviting light is to be seen. Even the barking of dogs did not disturb the deep silence, for these animals had been killed by the Germans due to precaution and fear of spies. From time to time the air is shaken from the far-off explosions of aerial bombs, and then the sky is lit up by a red glow – Soviet aviation is bombing the 'Blue Division' along its way.

But it is not only enemy bombs that lie in wait for the Spanish volunteers. They have covered their path through Russia with corpses: and it was here, near Vitebsk, that death found one of our battalion's more likeable sergeants. He accidently pressed the trigger while checking his sub-machine gun. A number of shots followed and the Spaniard fell. There was nothing anyone could do. The unfortunate's stomach was peppered with bullets. But this was not the first death in our regiment. The Spaniards are quite careless in the rear and nervous at the front. Either an abandoned grenade, one of the ones that litter the path of the Reds' retreat, will explode, or a friendly patrol will send a fellow countryman to the next world, which will increase the list of those 'who gloriously fell for the glory of Spain', but not killed by the enemy. I believe that this list is already quite long, filled with those who perished for the most various reasons ... [19]

Finally, boarding began. They brought up a freight train without a single passenger coach. This time, the temporary battalion commander, that very kind old man, De Rivera,[20] ordered me to bunk with him in the same compartment. Our journey was mitigated by the sounds of the radio. Concerts were sometimes interrupted by Soviet propaganda, where the communists, who suddenly fell into a fit of patriotism, reminded the Russians of the distant past (during the time of Tsarina Elizaveta Petrovna), the occupation of Berlin by the Russians and nearly all of Frederick the Great's East Prussia, while praising the valour of the Russian General Saltykov.[21] The Spanish would be interested: 'What is it, what are they saying?' But my explanations could hardly satisfy their curiosity.

I would play chess with the doctor at the halts, or argue with the battalion adjutant. A Catholic priest in a German officer's uniform (I believe this was the first such case in the German army) rounded out the staff.[22] To tell the truth, I was much better off in the car with the horses. Here I had to be always on my toes with the commanders and had no time to myself. There I was in charge of the car, rested on fragrant hay and, what was most important, did not suffer from the cold. But what can you do? – *noblesse oblige* . . . [ii]

We proceeded very slowly and would spend hours standing at the halts, while letting other trains by. Any kind of movement along the railways would cease at night, because the partisans had already begun to make themselves known. At Dno station they loaded us onto train for the narrow-gauge railway, which had already been built by the Germans. The cars were more convenient and our movement faster. They now no longer hid from us the fact that we were going to Chudovo station (the Nikolaevskaia railway), in the neighbourhood of which we would occupy our front.

We are unloading. We move 15 kilometres along the road in the direction of Novgorod. We halt for an hour or two in a small railside village, in order to rest and have a bite to eat, but end up spending two days here. Our regiment's second battalion is already taking up position on the opposite side of the river. But a new order arrived to pull up stakes and load onto a *camion* and head for Novgorod, 40–45 kilometres away. I must admit that this was fortunate, as later on this sector of the front was overrrun by the Reds and very few of the defenders of Chudovo and its environs managed to get out alive.[23]

[ii] *Noblesse oblige* (Fr.) – the situation requires it.

With the red berets from the *Tercio de Navarra* on the Northern Front. On the far left is Elizbar Vachnadze, behind him is Petr K. Odishariia, wearing the light coat is Aleksandr V. Amilakhvari, and the first left sitting is Konstantin A. Gogidzhanoshvili. Escoriaza, spring 1937. From the album of Petr K. Odishariia. (*Private archive of military antique photography https://www.photo-war.com/*)

Georgian émigrés from the *Tercio de Navarra*. Petr K. Odishariia in the middle, Konstantin A. Gogidzhanoshvili on the right. From the Nino Vachnadze-Koval'ski archive. (*National Parliamentary Library of Georgia*)

Nikolai V. Shinkarenko convalescing after a head wound. Vitoria, 14 June 1937. Previously unpublished. (*Private archive, Russian Federation*)

From Russian Major General to Spanish Lieutenant – Nikolai V. Shinkarenko. Note the small Russian tricolor on Spanish uniform. Salamanca, 26 October 1937. (*Private archive, Russian Federation*)

Russian officers in Spain. On the left is Aleksei P. Ergin, Aleksandr Esaulov (in an overseas cap), smiling is Nikolai V. Shinkarenko, and standing behind is Nikolai N. Boltin. (*Private archive, Russian Federation*)

After the victory. Head down below: D.K. Golban. Sitting: N.P. Zotov, N.E. Krivosheia, N.N. Boltin, standing next are V.A. Klimenko and S.P. Brilliantov. Second row, standing: N.E. Bark, N.I. Selivanov, L.N. Pylaev, N.S. Artiukhov, M.A. Sal'nikov (in the shadow), G.M. Zelim-Bek, P.A. Zotov, M.N. Iureninskii, B.V. Il'in. Behind: N.K. Sladkov, A.A. Tringam, V.V. Boiarunas, V.E. Krivosheia, A.P. Iaremchuk II. End of May 1939 (*Stanford University, Hoover Institution Archives*)

'The dean' of Russian émigrés: Spanish Colonel Nikolai N. Boltin. After 1939. Previously unpublished. (*Private archive, Russian Federation*)

Officers of the 3rd *tercio* of the Spanish Foreign Legion. On the far right is Konstantin A. Goncharenko. Larash, Morocco, 6 June 1941. (*Stanford University, Hoover Institution Archives*)

Konstantin A. Goncharenko. Previously unpublished. (*Gurskii family archive*)

Vladimir I. Kovalevskii's Blue Division enrolment card, 30 June 1941. (*Archivo General Militar de Ávila*)

Back on native soil. Ali (Sergei Konstantinovich) Gurskii-Magometov. Miasnoi Bor, 12 October 1941. Previously unpublished. (*Gurskii family archive*)

First Soviet POWs. On the left with papers in his hands is Igor Perchin, in the centre is Captain Pedro Martínez de Tudela García. October 1941. (*Gurskii family archive*)

Panikhida. Orthodox memorial service at Konstantin A. Goncharenko's funeral and the funeral itself. The officer standing on the right behind the priest is Nikolai E. Krivosheia. Grigorovo, 22 March 1942. Previously unpublished. (*Gurskii family archive*)

Zoning in on the enemy. Ali Gurskii-Magometov, Captain Martínez and Captain Ackerman. March 1942. Previously unpublished. (*Gurskii family archive*)

Ali Gurskii-Magometov and Igor Perchin. Grigorovo, winter 1942. Previously unpublished. (*Gurskii family archive*)

Russian reunion in Spain. Vladimir I. Kovalevskii and Aleksandr V. Bibikov walking down the Calle República Argentina in San Sebastián. The picture was taken by Ali Gurskii-Magometov. Early August 1942. Previously unpublished. (*Gurskii family archive*)

Despite losing both legs during his service with the Blue Division and having prosthetic limbs, Vadim A. Klimenko remained a staunch rider. Madrid, 28 March 1954. Previously unpublished. (*Private archive, Russian Federation*)

The golden years. Georgii A. Staritskii. Palma de Mallorca, early 1960s. (*Staritskii family archive*)

Lost tales from the Russian past. Vladimir I. Kovalevskii's original manuscript. Late 1940s–early 1950s. (*Central Museum of the Armed Forces of the Russian Federation*)

64

В ШТАБЕ ДИВИЗИИ.

В последних числах ноября 1941-го года прибыл я в Штаб Дивизии. Не могу сказать, что бы было легко вырваться из батальона. Командир наотрез отказался отпустить меня, несмотря на официальное извещение. Не знаю, вчел ли он мой уход из батальона за личное оскорбление, или же действительно считал, что я ему так необходим, но понадобились длительные переговоры со штабом полка и Дивизии, пока удалось заставить командира батальона выполнить распоряжение. Лично я ему напомнил его слова "убирайтесь с моей дороги", сказанные мне в первую ночь нашего пребывания на позиции, а на его жалобы, что он остается беспомощным без переводчика, я ему сказал, что при штабе батальона есть один испанец, которые понимает то, что ему говорят по-русски и даже довольно прилично изъясняется на этом языке. Это испанец всегда следовал за мной как тень, не знаю с какой целью - совершенствоваться ли в русском языке, или вернее для наблюдения за мной, так как испанцы весьма недоверчивы и ко всем питают подозрительность. Во всяком случае, разставание с командиром батальона было очень холодное, и старик на прощание даже не подал мне руки. Что-же делать ? Всем не угодишь ...

По прибытии в Штаб Дивизии, меня поместили в одном из бараков, в комнате, набитой жильцами. Убобств было мало : полати в четыре этажа, жара от печки горящей день и ночь, сама комната была проходная, так как через нее проходили в уборную. Но несмотря на все это, после моей дыры в окопах, барак мне казался весьма комфортабельным.

Одно только смущало меня : начальство, по его словам, "временно" отвело мне койку моего соотечественника Игоря П. О нем говорили, что он сын генерала, говорит прекрасно по "испански и весьма предан Национальному движению. Я навел справки. Русских в испанской дивизии было человек двенадцать, но никто не выставлял свою преданность режиму, никто не говорил в совершенстве по-испански и никто не выставлял себя сыном генерала ... С нетерпением я ждал возможности с Игорем П.познакомиться, так как хотел узнать у него сведения о других русских переводчиках и об их обязанностях при Штабе Дивизии, чем они живут и

Made in America. Vladimir I. Kovalevskii's typescript from the Globus Publishers, San Francisco. Early 1980s. (*Stanford University, Hoover Institution Archives*)

Novgorod and Its Environs

I cannot believe the history of the past, having seen how the history of the present is written . . .

We arrived quite quickly in Novgorod, or, to be exact, to that place where Novgorod used to be . . . Instead of a city, we saw only ruins. In Vitebsk there still remained some untouched environs, but here – there was nothing, or nearly nothing. The numerous cathedrals in the Byzantine style rose mournfully among the ruins. The majority of them had cupolas leaning to one side, but two or three of them were entirely intact. Even the fortress walls remained and, in an irony of fate, the monument to the thousand years of Russian civilization on the main square . . . And nevertheless, people still lived in this city that had disappeared from the face of the earth, as I later had occasion to testify.

But this time we did not stay in the city, as we had to hurry. We halted somewhere in the rushes far from the city. After we unloaded, they called me to the commandant (a major). He and Captain Fernandez and two men from the 'liaison office' were getting deep into some thickets. After a lengthy examination and discussions of the map, the major ordered me to take them to two neighbouring villages – Bol'shoe Lobanovo and Maloe Lobanovo. After lengthy fumbling we find the first of these villages. As opposed to its name, the village was very small: there were few huts and the village elder proposed putting at our disposal the large collective farm barns to house the soldiers for the night.

Maloe Lobanovo was a half-*verst* away, but the Germans were already there. There was no way we could squeeze our troops into there. Our companies were beginning to arrive. I roamed through the village in order to somehow set up our officers and the supply unit. Then there began the eternal fuss over potatoes, a product without which the Spanish cannot imagine their stay in a village. Alas! Now that the dreams of 'white bread in Russia' have evaporated, this somehow has to be made up with potatoes.

And I should admit that they gobbled up potatoes in such quantity that a thousand kilograms per day was barely enough for the battalion. And this was only the official norm. Besides this, each soldier, either through theft, purchase or begging, boiled some separately for himself.

Thus when potatoes (*patata*) for the soldiers and milk for the officers and the 'privileged' were secured, I was summoned to the major, where a surprise awaited me – we're in the wrong place . . . We have to move to two other villages, Bol'shie Khlevishcha and Malye Khlevishcha, 15 *versts* distant. This sad misunderstanding happened because the battalion commander could not read the maps in Russian. Now that everything was mixed up, they turned to me. They placed the map at my disposal: 'Take us out of here!'

Night was coming on and it began to rain. The mud was impassable. People were tired. The transport had not yet arrived. We had to look for a guide. Following Kipling's[1] advice, I prefer to trust a young boy, almost a child.[i] I asked this boy beforehand if he knew the road like the fingers on his hand and whether he could find his way at night. For greater assurance, I cleared up various details of the way and we set out. We took with us only one peasant cart for ammunition.

A difficult night lay ahead for our people, especially the machine gunners who carried parts of the unassembled machine guns on their shoulders. It was pitch black, especially for me, who sees so poorly at night. We slipped and slid, tripped and fell along the ruined road. The road seemed to be endlessly long. More than once the adjutant ran up to me to ask whether I'm sure that we're heading the right way. I sensed a certain lack of trust in me.

Finally, we crossed the line of the railway, which, according to our guide, was halfway to our goal and we ran up against a barbed wire barrier. What to do? It's too late to go back. And, while fully trusting our guide, we took the barrier apart and filled up a ditch with logs and ended up in the centre of a German position, to the great amazement of the Germans. During this time the major, and particularly the adjutant, believed I was either crazy or a traitor. They later admitted this to me.

They showed us the road to the highway and everyone perked up upon reaching it. But we still wandered around for a long time until we reached Khlevishcha. But it turned out that we were not supposed to be quartered here. Only the regimental headquarters was to be located here. We still had

---

[i] Author's note. There is a passage in Kipling's *Kim* that reads: 'If you want to entrust a secret, entrust it to a child'.

another 7–8 kilometres to go. We changed guides and set out. We reached the village of Bol'shie[2] on the shore of Lake Il'men, in the dead of night. We roamed the village for a long time, looking for the village elder's hut. We knocked at the door. A frightened female voice informed us that the owner had left for Novgorod. We demanded to see the 'foreman', or his assistant (the village policeman, in the old days). A great amount of insistence was required to force her to obey.

But we had to wait a long time for her to return and the major and the adjutant began to grumble, accusing me of a lack of efficiency. When the foreman, a very pretty girl, finally appeared, we began to go through the village in search of quarters for the battalion's people. This was not easy, particularly at night: it was especially so with the lordly officers and the 'privileged' ones. There were a lot of the latter and they were always dissatisfied. All of these clerks, quartermaster sergeants, weapons experts or simply people close to the commander of the battalion or company, are an unmitigated misfortune. I recall the saying: The Tsar reprieves, but not the huntsman. I don't know how it is in other armies, but in the Spanish army one is forced to depend on the 'huntsmen'.[3] To Captain Fernández's credit, I must say that he asked me to show him his room only when all of his people had been quartered.

We had nearly finished quartering the battalion, when on one of the streets some sort of character joined us and insistently accompanied us in our searches. I called our pretty foreman's attention to this: 'Who's this and what does he want from us?' 'Why, that's the village elder!' was the reply. It turned out that the village elder had not gone anywhere and it was only when we knocked at his door that he, upon hearing Russian being spoken, thought we were partisans operating in this area and thought it better to hide. This was certainly understandable.

Hard is the fate of the shoreside Lake Il'men villages: when German units were stationed here they suffered from levies and endless requisitions; in their absence, the partisans visited and even detachments of regular Soviet troops from the other side of the lake.[4] This village elder, a very prudent man, later showed himself to be very businesslike. We stayed in the village for about a week and, as far as was possible, he and I did a fine job of organizing the supply of our units with both food and fuel. The latter was a critical problem, for the winter cold suddenly set in. And as I now remember, on 7 October there fell the first snow, which did not disappear until the end of winter.

By edible foods one must understand, first of all, potatoes – the sole resource of this impoverished country. We bought them for three marks per 100 kilograms – a price established by the Germans for free trade. Alas, you could buy almost nothing for a mark, this was outright robbery. In order to meet the needs of their troops, the Germans requisitioned potatoes at the price of 1.75 marks per 100 kilograms. And, besides this, they demanded potatoes for feeding the Soviet prisoners of war for free. This latter delivery was carried out quite readily by the population and with amazing rapidity. In a half hour to an hour the old women would bring dozens of sacks and load them onto wagons heading for the prisoner of war camps. 'Our boys should not have to starve', the old women would whisper to each other, and there were few of them who did not wipe away a tear, remembering their own son or husband 'there': 'Let him be a prisoner, but at least let him live . . .'[5]

But our Spaniards never had enough. Despite the fact that each company boiled in its kitchen every day more than 100 kilograms of potatoes, which I purchased, each group of volunteers quartered among the huts always wanted to cook potatoes separately for itself. If they were unable to cheat or beg potatoes, then they simply stole them. And it was in just this village that they broke in a cellar door and stole six sacks of potatoes that had been procured for planting. The village elder howled and protested and threatened to complain to the German authorities. I calmed him down as best as I could, promising to track down the perpetrators and to pay for what they stole.

It was not hard to find the guilty parties, for I knew them, but I was powerless to punish them. Everything was done with the knowledge and on the initiative of the supply personnel (*suministros*). These 'gentlemen', for the most part party members,[6] made a profitable venture out of the 'campaign in Russia': they got rich, made a service career (and what a career!) and in order to satisfy their purely Spanish vanity, which does not eschew any means, embellished their chests with various signs of distinction, beginning from the Iron Cross to the endless Spanish awards created especially for the occasion.

For some reason our command counted on a lengthy stay in this village. I, along with the village elder, undertook to repair quarters for people, and for the horses they rebuilt the stable almost from scratch. Unfortunately, this effort was expended for no reason. We did not remain here.

I have impressions of the images of Soviet girls from this village. The hut in which I lived belonged to two female orphans. It would be hard to imagine two more modest and hard-working people. They were on their feet from morning until evening. There was no labour too hard for them, for women were used to doing everything on the collective farms, even ploughing and mowing. They sought to do me a good turn in every way they could, sharing their last scrap of food with me. And, to my shame, I must admit that I did not refuse the latter, for because of our idiotic rules, I was assigned to and lived with the staff, but in order to eat I had to hike to another village three kilometres away. Thus, when it would rain I preferred not to walk 'a long way for nothing'.

In contrast to my girls was a girl who carried out the *brigada*'s duties on the collective farm, an interesting brunette, 18–19 years old, who had completed high school and who had previously lived in the city, and who very quickly mastered Spanish, and our *chicos* (boys) were positively crazy about her. And no matter how lazy they were, she was never short of volunteer workers where she was in charge.[7]

Finally, when we least expected it, we received orders to move out. There had been confusion in the battalion lately, because newly arrived Major (*Comandante*) Enrico[8] had fallen ill and it was hard to understand which of the two majors present commanded the battalion . . . Thus everything went from bad to worse. The order to get ready was issued at night, but they did not bother to warn me. I guessed only because at dawn I found out that the battalion was already drawn up on the outskirts of the village. The heavy German carts, hitched to puny horses, moved with difficulty over streets covered with snow.

It was clear to me that we would not get very far with them. I therefore mobilized four sledges with their gear (the Spaniards christened them 'troikas') in the village, with one sledge per company. But it took time to do this and I, sitting like a lord on a sledge, caught up with my battalion only after several kilometres. We would have had a very difficult time of it without those sledges, because the German carts were completely wrong for the Russian roads, especially in winter. Our poor horses slipped, fell and exhausted themselves in order to pull the heavy carts. The march was not a long one, but we lost almost an entire day. We finally loaded the most necessary things – machine guns, rifle rounds and food – onto the sledges and left the carts behind.

On the way, in one of the villages, we were witnesses to the sad picture of a village fire. The fire was caused by the troops' carelessness. This carelessness, light-heartedness and the Spaniards' complete contempt for the villagers' interests made of our 'conquerors' a sort of ulcer for the population. The villagers feared the Spanish lodgers like fire.[9] And if fires broke out in other villages in the deep rear, then the peasants would say, with a humility characteristic only of someone living under the Soviet regime: 'The Spaniards set fire to this . . . '[10]

This was the case here as well: a hut, where two families had taken shelter, was already burning out. The charred corpses of the horses spread the smell of fried meat and the mother, gone crazy from sorrow, was rushing around, searching for her three young children. Two or three lackadaisical Spaniards, and with them some foppish officer, were holding forth with jokes and facetious little phrases about the 'strange coincidence': how could a fireplace, located inside the entrance hall, set fire to a hay thatched roof? . . . And the fact that it was precisely they were who guilty of the sorrow inflicted by them on these poor Russian people, who had already lost everything, did not even occur to them. But they managed to find a lot of comic aspects in this 'adventure'.

I blew up. Forgetting about any kind of subordination, I 'straightened out' the officer, pointing out to him how out of place jokes were and how this was inappropriate for him, who, was evidently responsible for the fire. Having shamed him and pointing out the poverty of those who had suffered, I advised him to do at least something to help. This was, so to speak, not nobility, but an obligation.

The officer was at first taken aback, and then he turned red and suggested organizing a collection among the numerous Spanish gawkers. Within a quarter of an hour the sum gathered had reached 615 marks. In order to distribute the sum amongst those who had suffered, the officer, who was probably a very good man, called me and the village elder, asking our opinion. He personally insisted on giving the owner of the burned hut 500 marks, with 115 for the lodger with the three children. The elder and I suggested dividing the sum in half. But the Spaniard insisted on his opinion, but promised to increase the amount gathered. I don't know how this affair ended, because our battalion moved out. I think that the money was nevertheless turned over to those who suffered in the fire. However, it's possible that this was not the case. It was a lot of money and the temptation was too great!

In the Trenches

We pass through the city of Novgorod. There is nothing but ruins on both sides of the streets. Somewhere in the distance Soviet heavy artillery is roaring, the shells of which explode quite close by. We cross over to the other side of the Volkhov River over a pontoon bridge on to the old commercial quarter: half-destroyed buildings and parks, and the main thing – monasteries and monasteries . . . Curious heads stick out of small huts with glassless windows and roofs without shingles.

On the corner of the former streets stands a girl in sky-blue sport clothes. Golden braids frame her kind and childlike face. Her blue eyes smile gently. The war is forgotten – for such welcoming faces can only be among Russian women. Such were our mothers and our sisters. The tired Spaniards perk up. Cheap compliments rain down: *'guapa, guapa'* (good looking), *'rubia'* (blondie) . . . But we have to hurry: twilight is coming on and we still have far to go.

And here we are, already on the edge of town. There is the city park.[1] Half of the ancient trees have been destroyed by shells and aerial bombs, but here and there colourful kiosks remain, and coloured paper wreathes hang here and there like dirty rags over the abandoned avenues. A cold piercing wind blows from the river. One thinks about the approaching night with horror. It's creepy. Even the tireless babblers have quieted down.

We go out into a field, and here, on a knoll, whipped by the wind from all sides, take a break. It's cold and there is no place for people to sit down. We have a snack while standing. I eat up my appointed portion of meat products, but feel an ever greater hunger than before. And this is hardly surprising: you should divide a small can of tinned goods into seven parts, and a larger can for ten people.

The 'aristocracy' assigned to the kitchen or to a specialized worker eats its fill even more, without shame, in front of everyone: there are tins of fish (from Spain), butter and preserves. And why not – millions were collected in Spain for the 'valorous' soldiers of the 'crusade' (*Cruzada*). All of this is generously washed down with vodka or cognac. The majority of the company's soldiers make believe that they don't notice the feasting by their privileged comrades, but the weaker spirits and the more brazen ones hang around those feasting in the hope of getting something edible from some satiated *señor* and, what is most important, a swallow of the alcohol that so pleasantly warms one.

I already began to fear that we would have to spend the whole night here. In order not to become stiff from cold, people stamp their feet in place, wave their arms and wrestle, but it's all in vain, as the frozen clamminess penetrates the entire body and the soul is seized by a kind of condition of helplessness . . .

But my fears proved groundless. The signal was given to set out and everything began to move. Those who had managed to lie down jumped up, shivering from the cold. The feasting 'privileged' ones begin to stuff various foodstuffs into their sacks. Everyone is glad. What for? . . . To go there, into the dark distance, there, closer to the enemy. There, from where many will never return, or will return crippled and frostbitten, with stumps instead of limbs. But such is the fate of man – to take joy in that which will prove his doom and to fool himself with cheerful hopes, even then, when only suffering and death await him. In this is his weakness, but in this is his happiness. Thanks to this quality, the beginnings of religions were possible, and together with this so-called 'culture'.

It is pitch dark all around and one's feet get stuck in the mud. We pass through some sort of small village, the streets of which are occupied by wagons, field kitchens and guns. One has to be particularly attentive in order not to get lost in the darkness and confusion and to not fall behind one's unit. There is a glimmer of hope that perhaps we'll stop and spend the night in some kind of hovel. But alas! We move on in the darkness. It feels as though we are approaching the front line. We are ordered to maintain silence and not to smoke. Ahead of us rockets ceaselessly rise up and sometimes, somewhere in the distance, a gun bellows.

An orderly runs by, bypassing the companies, asking something in a semi-whisper. I, in my frozen and half-asleep state, am little interested in what goes on around me. Finally, someone quite rudely pushes me in the back: 'Why don't you say something? After all, they're looking for you . . .' It turns out that they want me to report to the major, the battalion commander. I don't know why, but the 'old *commandante*' is a little bit tipsy. He greets me as his saviour. 'They finally found you! Corporal V., the German interpreter, has gone missing and I can't come to any agreement with the Germans we're supposed to relieve. Come here quickly!'

We come out onto a crossroads. The sky seems to have grown lighter: I don't know why, perhaps because of the rockets launched by the enemy, or because the sky has shaken off the overhanging clouds. To the left one can clearly make out the white trunks of a birch grove, and to the right of the road one can see some kinds of piles of dirt, which prove to be the dugouts of the battalion headquarters. A narrow road winds between the shell holes.

A German *feldwebel*, shivering from the cold, is clearly burning with impatience to get away as quickly as possible and to go back to rest with his battalion. But it's not so easy to come to an agreement with the Spaniards: the companies that have gathered toward the crossroads were impatiently marking time in one place at the same time that the commander, the one who was 'a bit tipsy', was painfully coming to the realization of the facts, so primitive and clear to the Germans being relieved – that to the right was one company, with two machine guns. There were two *seccion* (platoons) and three machine guns with the headquarters. Everything seemed clear, only not to the commander [Rivera]. He fussed over every word. He got fouled up in his thinking and couldn't see the difference between sub-machine guns, which the infantry platoons were supplied with, and heavy machine guns. He finally realized that he had left the machine-gun company in the little village we were passing through. He sent to fetch the 'forgotten' company, while the soldiers settled in the roadside ditches in order to smoke a forbidden cigarette. It was very clear that the German was extremely upset: '*Donnerwetter!*'[i] and other more pungent curses escaped his lips.

Finally, after a good half hour, the panting machine gunners came up, but at this point a complication arose: two machine guns had already 'infiltrated' ahead to their position on their own. We tried to find out – where, where to? After a good half hour the entire battalion had dispersed and there remained only we three – the battalion commander, the German and myself. Having worked up a sweat over his completed mission, the commander, with a realization of his own dignity (like the Saviour resting from his labours), turned to me: 'Now tell him (the German) that he should set up my quarters!' The German took us to the headquarters dugouts. The major's dugout turned out to be under the largest pile of earth. The German and I expected that the

---

[i] *Donnerwetter* (Ger.) – the devil take you.

major would then give orders to find a place for me, but he only said: 'Why are you hanging around here underfoot?'

The German finally took the initiative. Politely, with respect for my gray hairs, he asked me: 'You are apparently the battalion priest. Where do you plan to establish yourself for your rites?' I did not try to disabuse him that I was not a priest. Because I was evidently no longer of any use to the major and, remembering the kind attitude of Captain Fernández, the commander of the machine-gun company, toward me, I asked the German to take me to this company's position. 'But this is in the trenches in the centre of the position, under enemy rifle and machine gun fire!' the German declared in amazement, but led me somewhere in the darkness. He had evidently come to deeply respect Spanish priests who performed their rites in the front-line trenches . . .

Captain Fernandez was quite vexed to see me: it's one thing to invite someone, which is quite characteristic of the Spanish, but another to put someone up, all the more so a Russian with undefined responsibilities. But he did not pass up the chance to employ me: 'You go with the German along our trench line and let him point out to you where it's planned to place our guard posts, and while you're doing that I'll take measures to find you a nice place.' Despite my being tired, I had to crawl out of the captain's comfortable dugout and go out into the night. We went along the entire trench line. The Germans had nearly all left for the rear and only a few sergeants remained to explain everything necessary for us. Thus my arrival at the machine-gun company proved to be quite opportune.

We finally finished the rounds of the position and I could return to the captain's dugout. There I found a German ensign with the face of a child. It turned out that before our arrival he had been the chief of the position now occupied by the 4th Company. I once again assisted in the conversation between these two officers of different nations and felt satisfaction that during this day I had earned my bread, and then some.

I was fearfully tired and could barely stay on my feet. I looked forward to going to sleep as pure bliss. But my labours were not yet at an end. After the German left, the captain kept me for another half-hour with conversation: 'Is your home far away? When will you go home? You were probably a Colonel in your country?' I finally got up the nerve to interrupt this interesting, for the commander, conversation and asked the question: 'Captain, sir, where will you be putting me up for the night? Excuse me, but I'm awfully tired'.

'Oh, yes, I quite forgot about that . . . Orderly! (*Enlase!*[ii]). Take Sergeant Kovalevskii to the *brigada* (*Feldwebel*) and tell him that the Sergeant will be living with him . . . Until tomorrow, Sergeant; come to me in the morning and we'll inspect the positions together.'

I crawled out of the captain's cosy dugout and, shuffling along in the darkness, followed behind the 'orderly'. We fell into some kind of holes twice along the way, in one of which we came down on some kind of body got incredibly dirty, but we finally made it to the sergeants' dugout. Without a doubt, it was far inferior in comfort to the captain's quarters, but was nevertheless quite cosy. Here there were no glass mirrors on the walls and the roof was not upholstered with plywood, but it nonetheless had its creature comforts: a tiled stove and a water filter. I, who had come in from the cold and was chilled to the marrow from the damp, was immediately entranced by the pleasant warmth of well-heated quarters. It was obvious that the people who had just arrived had set themselves up with all the comforts of home. The smell of strong coffee pleasantly tickled the senses and there were all sorts of food on a large table: tins of fish, butter and preserves.

My appearance, accompanied by the 'runner', evidently made an unpleasant impression on the inhabitants. Although the sub-ensign and his inseparable clerk were usually friendly towards me during work hours, 'slapping me on the kidneys' (something akin to a friendly embrace), but here, at the front, in such a privileged position, they did not consider it necessary to treat me very considerately. They considered the commander's order to put me up with them to be a direct insult to them. Where did their Spanish politeness go!

The sub-ensign raced off to the commander like a bullet, while Echeverria,[2] the clerk, as my old 'friend' (we had served together in the *Navarra tercio*[3] during the Spanish war and whom I gave my nearly new winter coat upon leaving Burgos) set about explaining to me the impossibility of cohabitating with him. I did not consider it necessary to dispute the conviction of his arguments, for during my short stay in Spain I knew that no matter what I did for these gentlemen they would never give a foreigner (particularly a Russian, with no homeland) the opportunity to share their comforts and privileged situation. And truly, the sub-ensign did not make me wait long. Upon returning, he had dragged along some sort of small and dirty corporal: 'I present to you, Kovalevskii, your future dugout cohabitant.

---

ii   *Enlace* (Sp.) – liaison. Here the word can also be translated as 'orderly'.

The Captain agrees with me that it will be very uncomfortable for you to live with us. A lot of people come here and you would be bothered. You will live with the Corporal-weapons man and mess with us. See you soon!'

While I lingered, crawling out again from the dugout into the cold, the nimble corporal-weapons man managed to swipe something edible from the 'lords'' table. While choking on some tasty piece of food, he would mutter something to himself and belch with relish. I understood from his incoherent mumbling that it was very tight in his dugout and that it was filled with water, but that if you wrapped yourself up in a blanket and covered yourself from above with a waterproof canvas, then one could sleep . . .

We arrived at some kind of hole. 'Do you have an electric lamp?' 'No'. 'Then light a match, or you'll fall into the water . . . Here you have to jump onto the planks.' I lit a match. The wind blew it out. After having ruined ten matches, I had adjusted sufficiently to the situation to jump on the boards that were to serve as my bed. The corporal occupied the second bunk, jumping first and then clambering up. It was dank in the dugout and melting snow rolled down the walls, while the water at the bottom reached up to the sleeping benches. Taking the corporal's advice, I wrapped myself up to my head and shivered from the cold and could not close my eyes for a long time. The corporal fidgeted above me on his bed, sprinkling me with small bits of straw, which fell down from cracks in the boards. He belched the entire night while chewing something: evidently his supply of provisions was quite large, or he had the ability of ruminant animals of endlessly chewing his cud . . .

I examined our home in the morning. It really was a water-filled hole that was not meant for living in. It was not quite a machine-gun nest nor a hole for a mortar: it was a metre and a half deep and was covered from above by a sheet of iron. The walls were not upholstered with boards, as was the case in German dugouts, while the entrance hole did not have a door. The water nearly reached the lower bunk and its level continued to rise. The first thing that I had to do after waking up was to bail out the water with a tin can. That I was put here did not much surprise me – I didn't live in Spain for three years for nothing, but why did the corporal-weapons man also suffer the sad fate of sharing this hole with me? This was unclear to me.

I was able to orient myself in daylight. Our 3rd Company, along with its Captain Leiva,[4] who was famous for his cruelty, was located to the right, in the direction of Novgorod and the main branch of the Volkhov River. Of all the battalion's companies, it was the one closest to the enemy, from which it was divided by a narrow stream, an arm of the Volkhov. The trenches here were deep and were guarded by a thin line of barbed-wire obstacles. Our 4th (Machine-Gun) Company was in the centre of the position, some 250–300 metres back from the stream and a small lake. The enemy trenches were located about the same distance from the water. Our trenches were shallow, but small bushes and some bunches of dry weeds enabled us to move along them by crouching down and not being seen by the enemy.

To the left, the 2nd Company occupied a large section of front, while in the thickets of reeds on the other side of the stream was a small *tête-de-pont*[iii] near the enemy which sometimes enabled the Spaniards to practice their favourite means of war – fighting with hand grenades: when there's a lot of noise and fuss and it's so easy to show off one's bravery.[5] In war the Spanish prefer to close with the enemy, although they know nothing of fighting with a bayonet! They get bored (*aburren*) while sitting in the trenches under enemy artillery fire and get depressed, and even panic under an intensive bombardment.

And here I am, far away, along a quiet position. The first company, the captain of which is a very likeable and intelligent man, interested in the Russian language.[6] The company maintained contact with the 213th Regiment.[7] The battalion headquarters was located about 500 metres behind our company. The dugouts here formed entire streets and were furnished with greater conveniences than along the front line. Headquarters personnel changed often and its strength varied. Although located not far from the enemy, it was nevertheless a little safer than where we were. But when it occurred to the Red command to bombard the close-by rear areas, all these headquarters personnel scattered among the trenches of the closest companies, looking for shelter from the shells. Mass was held on Sundays in one of the headquarters dugouts, but there were few visitors because of the dugout's small size.

Captain Fernandez, my company commander, soon moved into the headquarters, in order to actually command the battalion, because Rivera,[8] although a very kind man, as a result of his limited intellect and excessive love of drinking, proved to be incapable of command. Two *alférez* (junior lieutenants) remained in our company. One of them, Bobadilla,[9] is one whom I still recall with sadness and deep respect: he was the embodiment of the best Spanish valour, which is almost no longer encountered. As opposed

---

[iii] *Tête-de-pont* (Fr.) – a bridgehead.

to the majority of his fellow countrymen, he was quiet, brave, modest and simple in his relations to his subordinates. I became close to him as early as the march, because both of us often had to prance ahead of the transport or hurry up those carts that had fallen behind. At the front we went out together a couple of times on reconnaissance, accompanied by two soldiers. We went out together, holding hands, not out of tenderness, but because of my deafness: after all, you can't shout when you're near the enemy, but you need to exchange remarks in whispers. Unfortunately, he did not remain with us for long. In the middle of November he left our company in order to move to the 267nd Infantry Regiment of Colonel Esparza,[10] about whom I will speak in greater detail later. This regiment suffered heavy casualties and mainly needed machine-gunners from the division's other regiments. *Alférez* Bobadilla was sent to reinforce the machine-gun crews. Within three days after his arrival at the new front, he perished in a night attack, suffering a serious head wound.

Our company's other *alférez* was the exact opposite. They would have called him a crook (*proshchelyga*) in Russian, while in Spanish a *pícaro* or a *listo*.[iv] One might say that he was the son of our age: a repulsive man and a braggart who was distinguished by sadistic cruelty. He occupied Captain Fernandez's dugout after he left for the battalion, which prevented me from taking advantage of the free space. A desperate coward, he was unable to withstand more than three or four days at the front and migrated to the rear to the village of Derevianitsy, where our transport and kitchen were located. There, of course, it's safer and you get more to eat.

At one time the 'leakage' from the front reached such an extent that the defence of our position for a good half-kilometre lay on me and another sergeant. Only 55–60 soldiers remained at our disposal, ten of whom did not have any weapons because they belonged to two mortar platoons. They were not authorized rifles, according to German regulations, but only revolvers. But the Spaniards did not distribute these to their soldiers. Officially, their motives were quite understandable: either the soldiers would lose them, or they would begin to employ them in their internal feuds, and I'm not even mentioning the fact here that they might 'go over' to the other side with such a light weapon. However, officially, I saw these weapons in the hands of rear-area quartermaster sergeants, repairmen, orderlies and other 'privileged'

[iv] *Listo* (Sp.) – smart boy.

persons. It would have made a great story if the enemy had known how weakly our front was held! This was particularly the case at night, when the mortars could not have been of much use.

The days passed mournfully and monotonously. At night we slept 6–7 men in a dugout, without undressing or taking off our boots. It did not become more roomy with the departure of people, because the empty dugouts were broken up for fuel – doors, floors and windows. Of the 25–30 dugouts built by the Germans, the Spanish only occupied 10–12, while the rest had been abandoned and were filled with water.

Upon waking, we would heat the stove. Before the arrival of the hard frosts, we would go out to the field and along the road to the battalion headquarters, looking for potatoes. We dug them up with great difficulty, using pickaxes and shovels. This was dangerous, as the enemy took people looking for potatoes for those digging trenches and would begin to ruthlessly bang away at them with artillery. We had to send people out for potatoes in rotation and then we had to halt these expeditions altogether, as the cold would go down to 30–35 degrees centigrade and the ground became as hard as a rock. But even if you managed to dig up a potato, it would crumble in your hands like powder.

This was a disaster for the Spaniards, because they so skilfully distributed their rations that with each day it became more pitiful, differing greatly from the German soldier's rations, which were satisfactory and, with a small difference, were authorized to us. While the rations made their way to the soldier, it went through six Spanish stations: the quartermaster service, the regiment, battalion, company, platoon and section. Each time the 'distributors' would take something for themselves, especially the most edible things: butter, which was issued twice a week, did not make it to the trenches. Sugar, which in the beginning was distributed, at least in microscopic amounts, remained for 'the insiders'. It was impossible to determine the 'leakage' of meat, because little pieces of fat sometimes floated in the hot meals that were issued once a day, but you really couldn't speak of portions.

Of course, I would have believed the Spaniards' stories that 'The Germans have us by the short and curlies',[11] if I had not had the opportunity to repeatedly see our 'aristocracy' – the quartermaster sergeants living in the nearby rear by the company kitchen: bread, bountifully buttered, the large amount of sugar, beefsteak the size of a large plate, jam, preserves, and coffee. As the Germans told me, and which I later had occasion to believe, the Spanish ration was supposed to be significantly better than the German one, because they got a lot of things from Spain, where collections were made from among the population and, besides, a certain part of the soldiers' pay was withheld for improving their diet.[12] Individual packages were prepared for everyone for the approaching Christmas holidays. They did not reach the front-line soldiers, but at the headquarters I saw people with one or two such presents.

Once, following the food distribution, I, with a box of spoiled cheese, went to see the commander in order to show him what I had received. He was upset: 'Kovalevskii, take this butter, this box of preserves, and, in general, don't be shy about coming to me if you're short of something!' I just laughed: 'I speak Russian, I can work it out with the Germans, and so I won't die of starvation. But your men in the trenches are exhausted beyond belief. Do something for their feeding!' 'But what can I do. It doesn't depend on me. This is *suministro* Pablo's affair.' 'Private Pablo! Send him to me for two days in the trenches. I'll place him in the "listening post" not far from the enemy'. 'What do you mean, what do you mean? After all, Pablo has a high position in the Falange. He's the *jefe local* [district chief], and . . . ' I did not bother to listen to the old man's further explanations and returned with nothing.

I'll make a small digression, while getting a little ahead: I met Pablo a year later in Madrid – embraces, that is to say 'slapping me on the kidneys', and we were both in military uniform. For some reason he was very glad to introduce me to his *novia* as a combat comrade 'from the Russian steppes'. Seeing the *Cruz de Hierro* (Iron Cross) on his chest, I asked him where he got it. 'What do you mean, Kovalevskii? Do you really not remember how I came to the front one night with the field kitchen?' What could I say? I only thought how cheaply the Germans now hand out their medals, which once enjoyed great prestige.

I now return to the front in my memoirs. Real hunger reigned in the trenches as early as the end of November 1941: anyone who was able left for the rear, closer to the sources of food, while the remaining unfortunates roamed like shadows, rising from their beds with difficulty, covered with lice and dirt.[13] It was practically impossible to sleep at night, because there were a lot of details due to the shortage of men and the situation was very troubling. The enemy set off signal rockets of different colours all night, all the more so that the Spaniards, not being able to decode these signals, made the most panicky assumptions.

On my advice, the listening posts were moved up about 300 metres in front of the trenches, as earlier they had been located in the immediate proximity and were useless in the event of an enemy attack. But my efforts were in vain in getting the guards to observe the 'password': they could neither pronounce nor remember the German words, and could not bring themselves to come up with their own. This circumstance served as the reason for two unfortunate incidents. One of them took place not long after our arrival at the front. The Germans, before being relieved, reported that an agent-informant was supposed to return 'from the other side' within the next few days. He was to reply to the password with '*Rittmeister von . . .* ' We communicated this to the companies, but before long we found out that one deserter had been killed. He proved to be the German informant: the Spaniards got a little too nervous.

In another incident, the Spanish themselves suffered because of their carelessness. At night, while making the rounds of the listening posts, we did not find them. They had been removed by the Reds, who had moved up with impunity and in reply to the question 'Who goes there', usually replied with the common word, taken from the Spanish: *España* (Spain). The enemy captured them together with their rifles. It's not surprising that the Soviet soldiers knew this password well, as there was no small number of deserters 'to that side' on the part of the Spaniards. I particularly recall an incident, when three Spaniards from the 3rd Company ran away. Our troops fired on them and killed one. Of the two who made it to the Reds, one spoke a little Russian and, as we later learned, had been sent by plane to Moscow.[14]

We learned of these details a few days later from a pair of Russian deserters who had come over to us, led by their sergeant. They had been sent out on reconnaissance on a boat, docked on our bank and surrendered to our listening post. They summoned me to battalion headquarters to interrogate them. The major, inspired by such mass desertion and the information gathered, proposed that I return with the deserters to the other side and throw bombs at the enemy's guard posts. The major, not seeing any great enthusiasm on my face, got so excited that he expressed the desire to take a personal part in this raid. We had to expend a lot of effort in order to extinguish his ardour and to get him to forego this escapade.

Within a few days an entire section (five men) came over to our side, with a sergeant and even with a light machine gun. This was along our 2nd Company's sector. The sergeant made an excellent impression on me – a cultured man from Turkestan, with training as an artist. At his own behest, he drew a picture of his captain, which caused a lot of gaiety. According to established tradition, I had to escort them to the rear, to division headquarters. So as not to take any more extra soldiers for escort duty, I made the prisoners carry their own weapons, removing the bolt beforehand. The appearance of Soviet soldiers in the rear, and with a machine gun to boot, caused a panic. I had to explain that this was a special honour for those Soviet soldiers who went over to us voluntarily with their weapons.

This time, having covered the 15 kilometres into the rear, I decided to visit my fellow countrymen three kilometres away, in the village of Grigorovo, as well as those who were residing with the headquarters in a forest settlement. In Grigorovo Captain Tringam[15] (a sergeant in the Spanish army), had been seconded to the veterinary company. He lived with a Russian family with all the comforts of home. He came to the office at set hours and sometimes in a car – by himself or with his captain – in search of forage. He was among the privileged as regards food and lived very well. He was very thrifty and he was evidently not particularly shocked by the Spanish view of Russia and the Russians. The Spaniards even liked that.

I arrived in Spain with him from Yugoslavia and thought that I knew him well. But his Scottish ancestry told strongly in him and it came to the fore here. I found him surrounded by hay cart drivers at the very height of a 'commercial deal': holding a bottle of German vodka high over his head, he proclaimed its qualities, while convincing them to take it as payment for the hay and transport, this pure, clear and strong, 'just like the old days', vodka. The Russians were hesitant, but I left my fellow countryman without waiting the conclusion of the deal. Later, while serving as a translator with the *Feldgendarmerie*, I could understand why the drivers had hesitated: the women of many of the distant villages implored me to set things up so that they paid their husbands with money for hay, and not vodka. This was the only thing that they could sell and German marks, although they were not worth much, at least gave them the opportunity to buy something or to save up something for the future. Captain Tringam managed to accumulate a sizeable fortune during his long sojourn in the 'Blue Division' and, upon his return to Spain, acquired an estate near Madrid. This was the only example of such among the Russian émigrés in this country.

I never cared much for another Russian, Totskii:[16] a coarse man, a cynic, and a materialist to the marrow of his bones, he was always under the influence of wine fumes. He was always sullen and sought out quarrels, which distinguished him from Rashevskii. Totskii served as a driver with the hospital and was evidently satisfied. Politics, patriotism and the motherland were of little interest to him: the main thing was to have a full belly and live well.

Our second-echelon transport was located in this same Grigorovo, along with a uniform depot and our soldiers' packs. The armaments chief and the battalion blacksmith headed this colony of people firmly ensconced in the rear. They lived, you could say, like lords. The armaments chief was a man my age (around 50) and unusually religious, in the Spanish way, of course, and his religiosity came down to the daily reading of required prayers. His assistant had to repeat after him, in accordance with Catholic ritual. This was done publicly, with a lit candle on a candle holder in the shape of a small skull. This mumbling was interrupted by the armaments chief's observations that had nothing to do with the Lord God. I myself witnessed how the old man slapped the face of his assistant, when he messed up his refrains . . .

I recall this armament chief because he was the first one to predict the Germans' inevitable defeat in Russia. Our march to the front near Novgorod coincided with the first frosts and icy conditions. Upon seeing our soldiers in the most pitiful condition, the armaments chief became desperate, while cursing the hour when he volunteered for the Blue Division. Since then he would categorically tell anyone who would listen that in these conditions the war was lost.

The blacksmith was a man of another type: he wasn't interested in either politics or predictions. All of his activity during his free time was devoted to conquering the hearts of the local females. Lacking both enviable looks and youth, he spent all of his not inconsiderable pay and privileged rations on winning the affections of the fair sex. Whether it was in Poland, Russia or Germany, the only thing he talked about was how he had won the heart of some broad or skirt . . . He finally ended up in Germany in a hospital for venereal diseases. We were great friends and even the sorrowful incident with his lackey did not ruin our relations. This incident is worthy of telling, as it characterizes the Blue Division's mores.

I once had to go on business to the rear, Pablo's kingdom, where the smithy and officer were located. While going back to the front, I could not find my mess-tin. I was told in secret that the blacksmith's orderly had unhooked it from my field pack and taken it away. This meant that it was

13–15 kilometres from the place where we were. Not losing a minute, I set out and within about two hours I was already in Grigorovo. The blacksmith was pleasantly surprised at my arrival right at lunchtime, while looking forward to a confidential talk about the news of the day, mostly about women. But I asked him to grant me time to take care of one matter. My mess-tin, the 'material evidence', lay on the table and the orderly was quietly drinking coffee from it. Despite my many years of service in the armies of various countries, I had never gotten into a fight before my enrolment in the Spanish army. But alas, here it was often the sole means to force people to respect you. Despite the severe prohibition on beating subordinates, I gave the thief two smart whacks and he crashed down on the bed. 'You can complain to the commander if you like', and with these words I left the hospitable blacksmith, not forgetting to take my mess-tin. I don't know how all of this became known, but within two days everyone in the battalion knew that 'Kovalevskii is into boxing' . . .

The Blue Division's ulcer was all kinds of thievery. I often blessed that hour when I left my suitcase in a German private home, and not with the quartermaster. They stole everything of value out of my field pack that was at the depot. There even disappeared that very same 'emergency ration',[17] the loss for which they threatened the most severe punishments. My reports about thievery, both at the depot and in the battalion headquarters, had no effect. They only smiled condescendingly, as if to say 'And how could it be otherwise!' I was lucky that they didn't accuse me of slandering and insulting the noble Spanish *caballeros*.[18]

Certain recollections are linked to my constant travels from the front line to the division headquarters. One of these is my find of a large library in one of the semi-destroyed buildings in the suburbs of Novgorod. How glad I was upon finding, after many years without having Russian books, entire volumes with the works of Aksakov, Gogol' and Saltykov-Shchedrin, as well as many works on history. My eyes popped out upon seeing this bounty. But the question arose: how to use this wealth? I could bring a book or two to the trenches, but how could I read them there without light? It was impossible to store them, as they would rot from the damp, plus the Spaniards might toss them somewhere out of carelessness. I only managed to read two or three books out of the entire library.

I knew that libraries survived in many of Novgorod's buildings: there was a public library of great value in the palace, where the regimental headquarters was located. It would have been a pity if all of these treasures had been plundered, trampled into the dirt, or tossed to the winds. How hard it was to see mountains of corpses scattered around the fields of our motherland, and the same feeling manifested itself when viewing the destruction of works of the Russian genius – books and historical monuments. I had the idea of saving at least a part of what might be lost tomorrow, before it was too late.

Our lieutenant (*teniente*), N.E. Krivosheia, a good man, was with the regimental headquarters serving as an interpreter. I shared my thoughts with him, requesting his assistance in procuring permission to visit the palace in Novogord and other surviving libraries, in order to remove the most valuable things from there. Upon finding some kind of suitable location, it might be possible to preserve the books until better times. But, alas, nothing came of this. Because of typical Russian slackness and an unwillingness to burden oneself with any kind of worries, the *teniente* did not heed my requests, excusing himself on the grounds that 'the game is not worth the candle', and that there was nothing of value in the libraries.

I often had the opportunity of meeting with another Russian, also a Spanish officer, Second Lieutenant (*Teniente*)[19] Goncharenko,[20] who had been seconded to the headquarters of our 263rd Regiment.[21] He was the only person in our rear area with whom one could share one's impressions. Once I was given the task of taking a group of old Russian women, accused of espionage and caught at our battery, back to headquarters. They were digging potatoes in their field and this struck the Spanish as suspicious. I brought them to headquarters and Second Lieutenant Goncharenko quickly put an end to the affair, ordering them to be set free, to the great dissatisfaction of the Spaniards.

A strange metamorphosis took place with my fellow countryman. In Spain he had been one of the few Russians who quickly assimilated with the local population: he drank with them, played cards and courted interesting women, among whom he evidently enjoyed success, and his career was secured, which his officer's rank guaranteed. But hardly had he stepped foot on Russian soil than all of his '*Hispaniolism*' disappeared. He often caused arguments with his Spanish fellow tipplers (to tell the truth, he often rendered homage to Bacchus), rejecting the power of Spanish culture (worst of all!) and the inerrancy of Catholicism; he openly made fun of the showy valour of the Spanish *caballeros*, contrasting it with the quiet fearlessness of the Russians.

I once had occasion to witness this 'lack of understanding', when I arrived with a Soviet newspaper in German, which had been dropped from an aircraft. This included Stalin's speech, given on the anniversary of the revolution and which played on the patriotic heart-strings of the Russian people.[22] As a result, a violent verbal fight broke out between Goncharenko and the Spanish officers. Upon leaving, I warned Konstantin Andreevich in private about the danger of frank shows of feelings before the Spaniards: suspecting both their own and us, who served under them, of disloyalty, they were capable of 'taking us out' without trial and under any handy excuse. Unfortunately, I became a prophet, although I did not wish this.

In February 1942[23] he perished under unaccountable circumstances on the ice of Lake Il'men, during a nighttime raid on the Reds.[24] The division headquarter even established a special commission for investigating this and our Russian lieutenant from the Legion, Ali Gurskii,[25] who would not hesitate to tell the entire truth to the command, took part in it.

Goncharenko was slightly wounded in the leg and was abandoned by the Spaniards, as a result of which he froze to death in the -30-degree centigrade cold.[26] Only one circumstance defies explanation: on that same night and at that same hour died his beloved bride, Nina Zhemchuzhina,[27] who served as a nurse in one of the hospitals in the suburbs of Novgorod. This is one of the secrets that defy explanation . . .[28]

Main Headquarters

'One may judge the master by the actions of his servant'.

The tedious sitting in the trenches, the mud, lice, the semi-starved existence and conversations with the nearly always half-drunk battalion commander drove me to look for something better. I was particularly indignant at the 'scattering' of the front. The trenches were empty, because anyone who could, legally or illegally, 'evaporated'. I often found my major poring over his battalion's list in search of his people. But his efforts were in vain: the old man threw thunder and lightning and cursed in the most vulgar language, but he proved to be incapable of keeping his people in the trenches.

He who enjoyed any kind of protection from the command or in the party got transferred 'for the good of the service'. The officers did not lag behind their men and despite the fact that the battalion had suffered no combat losses, there were no people. It would have simply been stupid for me to remain. At dawn on each day, while crawling out of my dugout, I witnessed how, while still in the morning fog, individual emaciated soldiers would hurry to the rear. At first I could not understand what was going on, but I subsequently understood that the soldiers figured that the enemy always carried out his attacks at dawn and, taking into account their small numbers, abandoned their trenches for a while. They would later return. An original precautionary measure and a peculiar means of waging war![1]

While visiting the division headquarters, I found out through the *alférez*, the Russian Gurskii, that there was a great demand for Russian interpreters.[2] It was only now that the Spaniards understood that they could not take a step without the Russian language. That which was impossible to get from the population, either with money or threats, was now easily acquired with the assistance of interpreters, and to the mutual satisfaction of both parties. These were needed more in the rear than in the trenches, where their responsibilities came down to questioning prisoners and deserters, who became fewer and fewer with each day.

I was presented with two proposals: to transfer to the *Guardia Civil* (the Field *Gendarmerie*), or to the 'transport' – the division supply service, where it was quieter and you lived better. I sought to get into the division supply service. But after the leadership, following a short examination, became convinced that I freely spoke German, they transferred me to the Second Section (counterintelligence), without taking into account whether I wanted this or not.³

Service did not smile on me there. Ali Gurskii warned me: to close my eyes to a lot of things that I, as a Russian, would not like, and be on the lookout, because the *Guardia Civil* – that's the personification of the higher command's will and its actions may be neither disputed nor judged. Having landed in this institution, I did not clearly understand what this 'guard's' activities amounted to and which role I would play in it. I understood after a month of service.

Before describing my service, I want to offer a brief sketch of the Blue Division's headquarters and its life. In order to understand this division's role in Russia, one must hang around its headquarters a bit and see just what kind of people this 'cerebellum' of the army consisted of, what it lived by and to what such a command could lead to. In a word, to see the confirmation of the Russia saying: a fish stinks from the head down . . .

The settlement of wooden barracks was located 3–4 kilometres from the nearby village of Grigorovo. I don't think that it arose during the war, for it is already noted on a Soviet one-*verst* map from 1937. Some of the barracks were certainly of new provenance. They were probably built by the Germans, for I never saw that the Spanish built anything in Russia. They only destroyed . . .

There were a good ten of these barracks. They were strewn among the woods and, in this manner, were hidden from the 'eyes' of the enemy air force, and although anti-aircraft guns were visible everywhere the settlement never once suffered from the Reds' air force during my time there. The camp was separated from a nearby road by barbed wire and three or four huts served as apartments for the division's officers on the other side of the road. It was precisely at Christmas 1941 that the Spanish command undertook to move the civilian inhabitants of these huts out. I don't know if this was carried out. I only know that this created a great deal of panic among the Russians.

Among the barracks occupied by the Spaniards, the 'stain', so to speak, was the barracks occupied by the Germans. Although outwardly the Spanish supposedly acted independently, in actuality they were completely dependent on their hosts. The Germans commanded them, even in small matters, despising them simultaneously for their lack of discipline, and in particular for their lack of seriousness in war.[4] In my position, and given my knowledge of both languages, I had to more than once (of which I will speak later) smooth over disputes between them.

But for the great majority of Spaniards, thanks to their great vanity, this remained a secret. The division commander, General Muñoz Grandes, the 'genius' Falangist general, was for the party-minded Spaniard the personification of wisdom and military valour. He was surrounded by a bunch of assistants or, to be more precise, spongers, for nowhere except in the Spanish army, and particularly in the Blue Division, could there be such a number of parasites.

Here, as opposed to the regular army, the main officer cadre was the so-called *oficiales honorificos* (honorary officers) and party people. Although party members did not have ranks, they proved to be powerful and invulnerable to any kind of discipline. The party 'aristocracy' – *camarada* Guitarte[5] and many other *camaradas*, including women – were more terrible for the division commander than General Franco himself . . . Within the division's ranks these party *camaradas* were surrounded by a group of enforcers who issued their own laws and who were themselves beyond reach of Spanish laws. And woe betide the officer, no matter how high his rank, if they did not like him. General Varela,[6] who at that time was the military minister and the holder of two Orders of San Fernando (the highest Spanish order for bravery[7]), had a lot of unpleasantness due to the divergence of his views with the party's policy.

Aside from his services to the party, General Muñoz Grandes did not possess the necessary qualities of a military leader: bravery and efficiency and, what was most important – military training. I never saw him visit the front line. The complete collapse and indescribable robbery of both state property and the local population is proof of his inefficiency Alas, as never before I recall the wisdom of the words: 'It's easy to make a thief out of a soldier, but you'll never get a good soldier out of a thief . . . '

A certain justification for General Muñoz Grandes may be the circumstance that during the discovery and conquest of America by the Spaniards in the '*gloriosos tercios españoles*',[i] there became engrained a certain conception

---

[i] *Gloriosos tercios españoles* (Sp.) – glorious Spanish *tercios*. Kovalevskii refers to the sixteenth-century infantry regiments of the Spanish imperial army.

about the rights of the conquerors to the property of the population of the conquered countries: thus the rights of the Russians for them were hardly more worthy of respect than the rights of the Indians of Peru and Mexico. The principle that 'the ends justify the means' justified all the excesses of the *Cruzada* in Russia.

Another justification – but for the soldiers – was the commanders' view on the soldiers' feeding and supply: the authorized money was spent at the whim of the commander. Thus in the Blue Division the feeding of the soldiers fell into the hands of the party members, while the starving soldiers could do nothing but steal.

General Muñoz Grandes barely showed his military training. They said that his chief of staff, Colonel[8] [the name is not indicated], carried the entire weight of operations on his shoulders. Muñoz Grandes, a party general, was a tyro in military affairs. The Spanish tactic of the Civil War of sitting 'on one's navel' (fortified posts in the mountains, not connected with each other), was criticized in one weighty German work on Spain (*Kampf um Spanien*, by Werner Beumelburg).[9] It would seem that this tactic could not be employed on the Russian plains. But this doctrine had embedded itself too deeply within the Spanish command, while pride and a sense of independence prevented them from renouncing it.

For example, Colonel Esparza, who had a deserved reputation as a monster both among the soldiers and the population, was unable to forego an attempt to undertake an operation along the far bank of the Volkhov, in the area of the villages of Sholokhovo, Posad and Sitno. This attempt to establish a strongpoint in a dense forest, which was separated from the Spanish positions by 15–20 *versts*, ended disastrously. Almost the entire 267th Regiment[10] perished in this operation and a number of guns were lost, and the machine-gun platoons from other regiments, which had been dispatched as reinforcements, suffered enormous losses in men and materiel.[11] But because Spanish vanity was unable to recognize its defeat, this ill-starred operation was inflated both in the Blue Division, but particularly in Spain, to a battle of enormous scale, ending in the Spaniards' brilliant victory. It was spoken of the heroes of Posad and Sholokhovo as of the heroes of Thermopylae and Lepanto. All of this very much reminded one of Tartarin from Tarascon . . .

I must go back in time in order to relate an amusing incident from the civil war, when the Russians serving in Spain became heroes, which they least expected. The detachment, formed from Russian volunteers, occupied a quiet area of the front, either by the wish of Boltin, our representative, or by the Spanish, who were always afraid that suddenly these Russians might prove to be too brave, which might damage the Spaniards' prestige. It was Russian Christmas and I arrived from my unit (the *Navarra tercio*) to visit my fellow countrymen. There was no shortage of strong drink and the guys, due to the holiday, had a little too much to drink. Those who had drunk too much began to fire their rifles and machine guns somewhere in the distance, in the direction of the imagined enemy. There was a squadron of Spanish cavalry at one of the nearby 'navels'. Upon hearing the intense firing, they rushed to aid us. Upon arriving, the 'misunderstanding' was cleared up . . . but what Spaniard could refuse to have a drink, particularly with appetizers and in good company. The hosts and their guest drank until late in the night, with the commensurate firing. But this was not the amazing thing, which of itself was almost commonplace. But in the following days the *Parte Oficial* (communiqué from the army headquarters) described the engagement, the enemy's attack on the Nationalist post, and the victorious repulse of the enemy. There was even a definite mention of prisoners. The location of the engagement – our post – was pointed out. Some of the 'heroic participants' were confused, while others were flattered, but of course no one tried to refute this, all the more so as a share of the 'glory' belonged to the cavalry squadron.[12]

General Muñoz Grandes did not so much spend time at his headquarters near Novgorod so much as he toured the headquarters of his German allies. He was often in Berlin. In singing the division's praises, he also praised himself, not forgetting his Falangists in the lists of citations. An Iron Cross of the First, then Second Class, and [the Knight's Cross] on his neck was a more than generous award for a general who, while commanding the division for an entire year, did not advance a single step . . .[13] The division's officers earned hundreds of Iron Crosses. It seems as there was not a single officer who remained without this high decoration, while the 'remainder' of the undistributed medals adorned the puffed-out chests of the cooks, orderlies, medical workers, drivers and simply those Falangists whom the commanders liked. I'm not even speaking of the fact that all of the party bosses, who swarmed the headquarters and were in Berlin, were decorated.

But in the majority of cases the real feats and acts of bravery were not awarded with medals. While in the hospital in Germany (Bad Neuenahr), I met a Spanish youth of about 17–18 years, who had had all the fingers of both hands amputated. They had become frostbitten at the front, while he was escaping from Soviet captivity on all fours. The German doctor who sawed off the ten fingers nearly lost consciousness and the nurses present were very surprised and asked me was it really true that such a young hero had not been awarded the Iron Cross. What could I say in reply? For those of us who served in the Blue Division this was just one of several such incidents. Spain does not need such heroes: this boy, an inhabitant of a remote village, should not have an Iron Cross, for whom is he going to show it, and for what? It is somehow inappropriate to even write about it in the newspapers. For the tawdry glory of the country, and mainly for glorifying the party, they should adorn the chests of the Madrid *chulos* (clotheshorses)[ii] and young degenerates with this Cross. It's not important that they did not accomplish feats of any kind. An unbridled fantasy can even create such feats there, where there was only shame: there was the case of one captain, who returned from Russian captivity, where his conduct brought him (by the Falangist press) the aura of a hero.[14] For this he was awarded the Order of Saint Fernando and raised in rank, first to colonel and then general? Contrast this with Soviet Russia, where all prisoners, upon returning home, were temporarily sent to Siberia.[15]

The accumulation of an enormous number of idle and unnecessary people placed a special stamp on a Spanish headquarters. Because the Spanish hate boredom more than anything else, the newcomer was struck by the free-wheeling lifestyle of this 'military establishment'. A barracks occupied by the Germans was the complete opposite of a Spanish headquarters.

Instead of a gloomy, glowering and dry *hauptmann* and *major*,[iii] there flitted scented and constantly smiling captains and majors, who now and then would stop in order to flirt with the pretty girls who moved in and out among the soldiers. One was struck by the plenitude of these Katias, Natashas and Olechkas, who with a red beret on their golden hair had seemingly completely come to terms with their roles, either as servants or concubines (*odaliski*).[16] And because in Spain, as nowhere else, 'all ages submit to love', so all of the regimental commanders and the general as well, had their concubines.[17] Officially, all of these girls were considered headquarters kitchen and dining hall personnel. Regardless of the time of day, one could often hear the sounds

---

ii Kovalevskii uses the word '*shchegol*" in Russian, which has both positive and negative connotations depending on the context. However, the Spanish *chulo* might also mean 'scumbag' or 'pimp'.

iii *Hauptman, major* (Ger.) – captain and major.

of music coming from the headquarters mess – this was one of the Ninas or Katiushas delighting the ear of the 'tired' and bored officers. All of this female world created a mass of intrigues, comical scenes, and sometimes tragedies.

On the first day following my arrival at headquarters, I was witness to an unpleasant scene, when one of the insulted women came in person to General Muñoz Grandes with a complaint against Lieutenant Ali G.[urskii], who supposedly had taken her record player. Ali G.[urskii], who had not slept following the previous evening's carousing, offered some incoherent explanation.[18] This problem was smoothed over Spanish style: the guilty woman was escorted to the door and soon removed from the headquarters area.

The Spanish were always true to the principle: 'Why complicate life and cause tragedy, when life is so gay and pleasant?' I don't know where and how they dug up these 'beauties', but all the girls were pretty, as if they had been chosen for this. It happened that girls would come from the neighbouring starving villages to offer their services for working and doing laundry. 'Doing laundry' would end up with the girl finding herself a protector. I witnessed how a handsome German captain kicked out a pair of such beauties, pointing out to the women the Spanish barracks: 'You're mistaken. Go there and they'll take you and satisfy you . . . '

Clerks, orderlies, cooks and an innumerable swarm of various small parasites were not behind the command in the art of 'living the good life at someone else's expense'. To each according to his abilities and, what was most important, according to his means. In this case, German marks did not rate very high. Only bread, which was completely absent, was valued by the starving population. Much of what had remained to the Russians was requisitioned by the Spaniards and then returned to the population as payment for the purchased caresses of impoverished women. I knew of a case, when several cart drivers gave a girl a cow which had been taken from her village. With my assistance, the 'gift' was returned to its owner, for generous cavaliers proved to be small pawns.

There were amorous escapades which became public knowledge, because important people got mixed up in them and the intrigues ended with a tragic denouement. In one such case the 'hero' proved to be none other than Colonel Esparza, who had acquired a poor reputation as a result of his cruelty. Like any Spaniard, he had two weaknesses – he liked to eat well and enjoy himself with the weaker sex. He satisfied the first weakness easily, having a French chef and carrying an entire poultry-yard in his train. (The cook constantly told his Russian translator, '*Mon cher ami*,^{iv} you have to get me a turkey at any cost, because this is the colonel's dream'.)

As for the second weakness, he had a girl on board, almost a child, and a deaf and dumb one at that. It's not known where he dug her up, but her physical shortcoming made for a lot of comforts . . . Everything went well until . . . the unfortunate became pregnant. One could not call this a scandal, for what does Russia and its unhappy residents mean for a Spaniard? . . . But this provided fodder for ridicule and jokes behind the terrible colonel's back.

Colonel Exparza eliminated this problem in a purely Spanish way, as befits a *hijodalgo* (gentleman).^v He decided to publicly condemn this 'debauched girl's' 'cardinal sin'. A court was convened and its chairman and accuser was no other than Colonel Esparza himself. It would be morally difficult to imagine a greater mockery of a person. The picture was worthy of the pen of Dostoevskii or Shakespeare: the poor deaf and dumb girl and the ruthless judge who was the main guilty party in this 'cardinal sin'. A modern Inquisition of the twentieth century . . .

Justice, and most of all, immorality, must be punished. The guilty girl could alleviate her guilt, but not before an earthly court, but before God by a frank admission of her sin and by naming her co-respondent. And this admission had to be torn from her with the assistance of a Russian interpreter. This heavy task fell upon the shoulders of Sergeant Aleksandr Bibikov. In this case the subject of mockery was not only the woman, but the interpreter. This meant to know that this was a lie and a repulsive comedy and to humbly expose oneself to the monster. You can't please a petty tyrant: for this the two preceding interpreters (the Georgian Konstantin Gogoshvili[19] and Igor' Perchin[20]) were the embodiment of toadies and lackeys and they managed to save themselves by running away from their terrible commander, knowing that he could take revenge on them, accusing them of espionage and relations with the enemy, while they would be forced, as was the reigning practice here, to dig their own graves. But this digging of graves, so as to be buried in the ground, was a privilege reserved for the Spanish. Local Russians and killed partisans were to be undressed after death and stacked up like cordwood. This collection of corpses was the pride of the colonel, who carried out a periodic inspection in order to insure that the body of any one of those executed not be 'traitorously' taken away by relatives. The

---

^{iv} *Mon cher ami* (Fr.) – my dear friend.
^v *Hijodalgo* (Sp.) – archaic word for *hidalgo*, member of the petty Castilian gentry.

Revista de cadavers (inspection of corpses) was the pride of Russia's 'liberators'. One must assume that Muñoz Grandes knew about this.[21] No way did Bibikov, the timid sergeant-translator, want to be killed to add to the collection of corpses.

They could not manage to get any kind of admission out of the deaf and dumb girl. The poor unfortunate only wailed, covering her pretty little face with an apron. But the judge did not need this admission: taking advantage of his intuition and logic, he declared his own orderly to be the guilty party. His protests did him no good and he was sent away to one of the companies. Being sent away to a company would be a sufficient punishment for the sinner and his meditations on his sin and zealous prayers would complete his spiritual cleansing and return to the bosom of the church. As for her, an inveterate heretic who debauched a Spanish soldier, there was neither justification nor indulgence. For the sake of her sex and, observing the onlookers' sense of shame, she would not be added to the collection of corpses. But she was to be driven from the village into the -30-degree centigrade cold. A Spanish patrol was to see that none of the inhabitants sheltered the exile. Let those living here know that 'justice' reigned with the arrival of the Spanish. Following this 'wise' sentence, the court adjourned, praising the colonel's resourcefulness and the 'immorality' of the Russian population, which had moved so far from God . . . [22] All of these facts are horrible and nightmarish and seem hardly possible, even in our time, with its horrors of exterminating humanity by whatever means available. But these 'feats' of Colonel Esparza seem, particularly for the Spanish, with their *tortuoso* (tortuous) manner of thinking, based on casuistry, no more than a joke.

The fate of this 'hero' is an interesting one. Having completed his mission in the Blue Division, he, along with two other colonels (Pimentel and Vierna) was promoted to general. But the Second World War had hardly ended when we read about his death in the newspapers. His death was officially ascribed to a road accident. It's possible that 'Vengeance is mine, sayeth the Lord' from the Gospels and the simple Russian people's 'and so the ground still tolerates them' could not find a better employment. It's just strange that the driver and the general's adjutant were unhurt.[23] And it was at this time that the hunt for *criminales de Guerra* (war criminals) was in full swing and that Spanish pride would not allow them to openly hand him over to the

Allies as a war criminal, so he might have shared the fate of the German General Rommel.[24]

In another case, only the timely intervention of the interpreter, Lieutenant Ali Gurskii, prevented a tragic end. This was how things stood. One of the Captains of the star-crossed 267th Regiment,[25] having settled into an apartment with a Russian family, cast a favourable eye on the owner's daughter. Sure in his vanity that this was a great honour for her, he insistently set about to 'storm the fortress'. The girl flat out refused to give in to his demands. The failure infuriated the captain and he went over to threats, promising to accuse her of espionage if she continued to be stubborn.

In the end, this is what happened and the death sentence had already been signed. The division commander stubbornly refused to believe Lieutenant Gurskii that this matter had nothing to do with espionage. It ended when the informer himself got caught, cynically bragging over the telephone about his 'feat' and it was suggested to Muñoz Grandes himself to listen to this confession. It was now awkward to execute the accused and it was suggested that they abandon their native village. And the captain only received a mild rebuke for his 'crude joke'. Of course, the Spaniards really rose in the Russians' opinion from such jokes!

At Division Headquarters

I arrived at division headquarters during the last days of November 1941. I can't say that it was easy to leave the battalion. The commander flat out refused to let me go, despite my official notification. I don't know if he considered my leaving the battalion a personal insult or really did consider that I was so necessary to him that lengthy negotiations between the regimental headquarters and the division were needed until they managed to force the commander to carry out the order.

I personally reminded him of his words, 'get out of my way', which he spoke to me on the first night of our stay at the front, and as to his complaints that he would be helpless without an interpreter, I told him that there was a Spaniard with the battalion headquarters who understands Russian and even expresses himself quite well in the language. That Spaniard always followed me around like a shadow, although I don't know for what purpose – perhaps to improve his Russian or, what is more likely, to watch me, as Spaniards are very untrusting and are suspicious of everyone. In any event, my parting with the battalion commander was a very cold one and the old man did not even shake my hand to say goodbye. What could I do? Besides, 'the battalion was not authorized an interpreter', as I have mentioned before; officially, I was either some kind of a chief *de bagaje* or *equipaje*.[i] The Germans were often surprised and indignant about the situation with interpreters (particularly with me, an interpreter in two languages – Russian and German) in the Blue Division. The Russian interpreters held officer rank in the German army, and if they were listed as civilian employees their situation was much better than that of an average army officer. Thus the Russian population of the occupied areas viewed me as such.

Upon arriving at the division headquarters, they put me in one of the barracks, in a room filled with other lodgers. There were few comforts: four layers of bunks, heat from a stove, which burned night and day, although the room itself was cold, as the passage to the toilet went through it. But,

---

[i] *Jefe de bagaje, jefe de equipaje* (Sp.) – baggage or equipment manager.

despite all of this, the barracks struck me as quite comfortable after my hole in the trenches.

Only one thing made me uncomfortable: the commander, in his own words, had 'temporarily' allocated my fellow-countryman's bunk to me. 'Oh, of course you know Igor' Perchin, the son of a Russian general', which was the first thing my housemates told me. 'This is a man! (¡*Este es hombre!*). He speaks Spanish as well as we do and is very loyal to Nationalist Spain'. Alas, I could not reply in the affirmative and satisfy their curiosity. I did not know any such general's son and such a rabid partisan of the Spanish regime. As far as I knew, up until this time there were 10–12 Russian interpreters in the Blue Division, of whom anyone of them spoke Spanish perfectly, and none of them called himself the son of a general. I awaited his arrival with impatience.

The Russian Interpreters

I think that it is now appropriate to say a few words about the Russian interpreters; about the position they occupied, how they lived, why they joined the division and, what is most important, how they ended up in their motherland, how they behaved themselves and how they dealt with the population. The majority of interpreters, with the exception of two – Bibikov, with whom I served earlier in San Sebastián, and Igor' Perchin – belonged to the older generation that had left Russia 20 years ago and more. The majority of them, while roaming around various European countries, 'had not set down roots', living in the past and making plans for returning to their motherland, to a Russia liberated from the communists. I don't think that any kind of feeling of revenge played a role here. I also think that, in allowing for a German victory, it was clear to everybody, with a few exceptions, that it was unlikely that there would be a place for us in a future Russia. But there was the desire to see the motherland, maybe even to die on its soil and to breathe that unforgettable Russian air. This desire was overpowering. And what price would each of us have paid to embrace and press to one's breast relatives and simply acquaintances. There was no price too great!

There was so little of value left for those who were already old. How many dreams did we émigrés have about Russia? For many these dreams were life itself, while the rest was only a terrible nightmare, which would end only with our life. Those who lived in France, North America and Yugoslavia, thanks to their large numbers, were able to create there something akin to a 'little Russia': they had their own churches, theatres, restaurants and libraries. Many Russians did not even enter into any kind of relations with the local inhabitants and did not even know the language, despite the fact that they had lived in the country for many years. If the Russians lacked a motherland, then they lived a Russian cultural life, while consorting with their fellow countrymen. And they did not need anything else. I remember one old woman in Belgrade (Yugoslavia), who exclaimed with indignation: 'These Serbs are so incompetent: we've been living here for 15 years and they still haven't learned to speak Russian!'

The Russians in Spain were in a completely different situation. A small group of Russians, numbering no more than fifty, the majority of whom were veterans of the Civil War, were scattered throughout the entire country, among a people of different culture and, I will say more, hostile due to their faith and their race. And one could not even speak of Russian cultural institutions. A Russian, lost in a Spanish city, was for years deprived of the opportunity to speak his native language. So as not to forget it, he would exchange rare letters with other fellow countrymen. There existed not a single Russian library in Spain. Worn-out Russian books were preserved as holy relics and were passed from hand to hand throughout the entire country.[1]

One could meet in Spain fellow countrymen who had forgotten Russian and who preferred to speak Spanish. Those who married Spanish women did not teach their children Russian, while the Catholic Church, which was so insistent and openly aggressive, tried to destroy those remnants of faith and Russian frankness among these Hispanicized Russians. Worries about earning their daily bread swallowed up their attention, but aside from that one still had to live for something. The nightmarish lie that reigned in the country penetrated everywhere: into the state, religion, the family and even into relations between individuals with each other. And it was this that unbearably pressed on us, the émigrés, who still possessed something holy and Russian. For me, each embrace, which the Spaniard so often has the habit of expressing his liking for us, reeked of betrayal. And I would ask myself the question, will I really over the years, if I am fated to live here into old age, turn into such a repulsive and two-faced scoundrel to the marrow, for whom there will be nothing sacred and who will lie in wait his neighbour and 'friend', waiting for that moment when he can stick a treasonous knife in his back? No matter what the price, I must break out of this stifling atmosphere. And if someone enlisted in the Blue Division so as to make a service career, or for the sake of monetary gain, then upon crossing the border of Russian Poland he immediately felt compassion for the poor inhabitants. And nearly every interpreter did what he possibly could to help his fellow countrymen in their relations with the Spaniards and Germans. But I must confess that there's a 'rotten apple in every barrel'.

The sole and most notable example of the unconscionable and bestial treatment of the Russian population was the adventurist Sergei Ponomarev,[2] who styled himself the 'The Most High Prince of Imereti'. He was finally turned over to the division court, accused of brigandage, robbery and violence against women. The division's first decision was (in accordance with German laws) the death penalty. But because Spanish officers were involved in this matter, Ponomarev was sent to Spain and sentenced to 10 years in prison. Upon arriving in Spain he was released and within half a year he was serving in the censorship bureau in Madrid, with a decent salary. Ponomarev was the only one of the Russians who had the Old Guard Medal [founder of the Falange].[3]

Aside from Ponomarev, there were another two Russian interpreters, who for the sake of their careers or simply to praise the commanders were ready to act against their conscience. Stifling the voice of their conscience, they were 'bigger monarchists than the king', as regards their treatment of the population . . . The Georgian Konstantin G.[ogidzhanoshvili] whom I knew well, because we had served together in Spain in the same *tercio* (a battalion of Carlists, or *Requetés*), was thought by the Spanish to be a model of valour and in accordance with this was decorated with medals and promoted to *teniente* (lieutenant). But I very much disliked his hysterical bravery, as it was too much for show. When the day came when the *tercio* was threatened by great danger of being completely destroyed (or be taken prisoner), near Monterubio in 1939, he and the *tercio* commander and several other officers shamefully abandoned their men. The enemy attack was beaten off and the brave *requites*, without officers, fought with hand grenades and rocks, captured four Russian tanks and damaged five others. On the following day this 'brave' *teniente* came to judge and threaten with a military court those who on the previous evening had in desperation strongly criticized the unworthy commanders.[i] I have never witnessed a more revolting scene.

Here, in the Blue Division, in order to get an Iron Cross, he was not content with running after every colonel and general, but created out of thin air plots and acts of espionage, contriving denunciations against the innocent and even those who had died long ago.[4] The Germans would laughingly tell me stories about these denunciations.[5]

The second was the youth, Igor' Perchin. He officially worked in the newspaper, which was published in the division headquarters,[6] but unofficially was an employee in the Second Section, who spied on not only the local population, but also us, the Russian interpreters. He served with

---

[i] Author's note. The Russians Fok and Captain Polukhin shot themselves in similar circumstances. Better death than the shame of surrender.

the *Gendarmerie* and as a reward for his service he received some crosses. He was my 'shadow' in particular, because the commanders' faith in me was limited.

But, I repeat, these were exceptions. Ali Gurskii, the chief interpreter at the division headquarters, through whose hands a lot of prisoners passed, was more than just and saved the lives of many Russian people. After all, a lot depended on his words, and if he was unable to save a lot of people, then that was not his fault. They began to trust him less toward the end of his service and 'blew away' many innocent people behind his back.

I had occasion to be present at the interrogation of people stopped without documents. Despite the fact that the Spanish clerk wrote down the questions and answers in Spanish, there was always an 'unofficial conversation' in Russian, where we spoke heart to heart. Ali Gurskii usually warned them: 'You can trust me as a former old Russian officer; so you should stop all your lying and tell me right out that you ran away or were liberated; I'm not going to betray you, and I only want to defend you . . . '[7] And the prisoners would eventually tell the truth. For the most part, they belonged to the Soviet 88th Division,[8] which was encircled in the forests, and the interpreter did everything he could to supply them with documents and send them to the rear and not to a camp, which meant certain death for the prisoners of war. Only in one instance did someone under interrogation prove to be a spy, whom I later had occasion to encounter in the front-line area and who later managed to evaporate in the forests.

The Second Section and the *'Guardia Civil'*

'When a country is seized by war, everything is shaken up and the dregs rise to the top'.

Confucius

With the passage of time I became acquainted with the new commanders and with my new duties. But I never saw the chief of the Second Section[1] and I could not find out his name. According to Gurskii, he was a complete non-entity and a pawn in the hands of his immediate assistant, Captain Martínez.[2] The more I recall this captain the more clearly and in greater relief do I see him. This was a typical representative of the Spanish people and its culture. Not very tall, rather fat, red-cheeked, good-natured, and with a gentle look . . . But it was only necessary to serve under his command for about a month in order to be see how Captain Martínez, with his good-natured smile, would issue orders to shoot completely innocent people and, what was most important, that he was able to do this so that no one knew nor guessed what was going on.

His refined politeness in no way interfered with him covering up the most brazen robbery of the population. When he would sing arias with his melodic voice, he was probably at the same time contemplating intrigues of the lowest sort. One should not be surprised. After all, during the *corridas* (bullfights) splendid women of angelic beauty fall into raptures when the enraged bull disembowels the *picador*'s pitiful nag, or when the same bull sinks his horns in to the velvet-adorned and gold and silver-inlayed stomach of the *torero* (bullfighter) . . .

Of course, Martínez considered himself the true son of that church that kills faith in people with the aid of the horrible medieval Inquisition and its 'indulgences' (remittance of sins) and inflames hostility between rich and poor. Of course, for him Russians were heretics and to 'blow them away' was even pleasing to God, since it was impossible to return them to the bosom of the true Catholic church . . . An attempt to put one heretic on the right path, which was undertaken with the assistance of interpreter Perchin, was unsuccessful: the sinner, a lame communist teacher from the village of Dolgovo, was nevertheless executed, without having repented . . .

When I became acquainted with Captain Martínez, the *gendarme* captain, my first impression of him was quite a pleasant one. His closest assistant and accomplice was a German lieutenant, who served as liaison for the Second Section with the Germans. Without him, Captain Martínez, despite his experience in investigative work, would not have achieved anything. This German had earlier served in the Spanish Legion, spoke Spanish with a slight German accent, and lived for a long time in Spain and had Spanish citizenship. Despite this, he retained his German traits: restraint, an ardour for service and the absence of religious fanaticism. It was he who insisted on my transfer to the *Gendarmerie* (*Guardia Civil*) as an interpreter.

But this *gendarme* detachment was commanded by a semi-literate Spanish lieutenant, who had come up from the ranks and whose entire duty consisted of collecting 'trophies from the grateful population'. One of the sources of his income was the soldiers' rations, because when the *gendarmes* set out on an 'expedition', all of their food (with the exception of bread, sugar and tobacco) came from the population. As to the remaining questions – headquarters security, intelligence and interrogations – he didn't understand anything. In this case the captain's main adviser was Zeiss,[3] the *brigada* (sub-ensign). I usually had to deal with him, as I was directly subordinated to him.

As opposed to the captain, he did not represent the type who radiated the joy, self-satisfaction and politeness that charm one. Nonetheless, he did not cease being the personification of 'Hispanism', if one may use the term in its 'opposite sense'. You don't have to eat a pound of salt to understand a Spaniard: if you're rich, if he has need of you, if you're the representative of a powerful state, or even simply a foreigner who might leave the country tomorrow and might talk overseas about his impressions of Spain, then you see them all, beginning with the numerous marquises all the way to a simple *barrendero* (street sweeper), then they lie down and put themselves out for you with their *obsequio* (gifts, expressions of love), *homenaje* (honours) and *agasajo* (hospitality). You will see before you only joyful, hospitable and incredibly polite people. Your slightest wish is not only fulfilled, but is foreseen. Thus there is no better country for rich tourists than Spain. But woe betide you if you are poor or if you are unemployed, and especially if you are careless and see or find out what you are not supposed to know and, on this basis, come to a different opinion that is not so flattering about the inhabitants of the country. Then you will see the other side of these people's character. Remove from them this veneer of politeness, this notorious (in words) Christian mercy and before you stands such a Spaniard as he is in reality: incredibly cruel, extremely envious, not believing in any good and noble, a greedy egoist who is at the same time possessed by pride and a sense of self-importance, despising the entire world. Culture, to his way of thinking, exists only in Spain and it was created by Spain. Thus Europe must be Hispanicized . . . This slogan was openly propounded in the Spanish newspapers at a time when people here were drunk with the Germans' success (?!). And this Spaniard, without his mask, is a coarse clod. And this coarseness is not the same as that of a Serb, for example, as a result of his lack of culture, or a German, as a result of his being withdrawn and with a distaste for any kind of sentimental outpourings and sugary phrases. In these cases you don't become so insulted like here, where it's as if they hit you with a whip across the face with their contempt.[4]

It was *Brigada* Zeiss who represented this secondary nature of the Spaniard. And here I will state frankly that, having worked with him for a month, I preferred him to Captain Martínez. I squabbled with him often; he would play me any such dirty tricks that he could and I even think that had I not left in time (maybe the day before the death that was hanging over me[i]), he would have put a bullet in the back of my head somewhere in a remote forest. But I could at least foresee this, and so we played this game, one might say, 'openly'.

I did not live long in the division's central barracks. Perchin, whose place I occupied, returned, and then the *brigada* insisted that I move to his place, because he always wanted me close at hand. So I moved into a barracks with the *brigada*. This was an enormous building in semi-darkness, without partitions, full of smoke and fumes from two large stoves, which burned day and night. The door was always opening and someone would come in or go out, letting in the cold air. Taking off your greatcoat was out of the question, because the warm place near the stove was reserved only for the privileged, among which were included the *brigada* and a bunch of his friends, but not me . . .

---

[i] Author's note. I've seen too much that I'm not supposed to see.

Among these was a *gendarme*. Corporal (*cabo*) of venerable age, Galeote.[5] Later on, after leaving the Blue Division, I had occasion to become acquainted with him more closely and to even become friends. He had a gentle nature and appeared to be inoffensive, but, alas, he was possessed by a thirst for enrichment. He was accompanied in his wanderings of many months around Germany by an enormous sack with tinned goods, which were not shared with his fellow soldiers. He was a quartermaster sergeant and, by Spanish standards, not a bad one . . .

If Galeote was the oldest out of this privileged group, then the youngest was a 16–17-year-old Falangist, just a child, who was very nice and obliging. I asked him what he was doing among the *gendarmes* and what his official position was. I was quite surprised when he gaily replied: 'I'm under arrest for murder.' 'How is this? What could such a child do?' And he, without changing his tone, replied: 'I killed the *alcalde* (mayor) of Novgorod.'

And he, without waiting for my questions, began to relate in detail all the particulars of this crime. He arrived with his friend to rob and the latter wanted to take a ring from the mayor's hand; the latter put up a fight: 'And so I raised my rifle and fired. I could not allow a Russian to insult my friend . . .'[6] Straight and to the point. One of the *gendarmes* interjected: 'I don't think that he was severely punished for that. First of all, he acted according to legal self-defence and, secondly, one Russian more or less is no big deal . . . '

They gave me a place on the second storey of the sleeping benches, warning me that I would have a lot of work to do tomorrow. During the night I could not sleep under two blankets and my greatcoat because of the cold, and my bunk companion was evidently teeming with lice. In the semi-darkness of the barracks it was impossible to hunt for the lice even during the day, because it was so cold in the barracks that it was impossible to undress, while outside there it was -30 degrees centigrade.

In the morning my 'first steps' in the *Gendarmerie* began: the *brigada* warned me that in Novgorod I was to detain a female spy, who spoke Spanish quite fluently.[7] 'You have to find out where she learned to speak Spanish fluently and for what purpose', the *brigada* said to me. 'I suspect that she was among those Russian beauties that were sent to Spain under the Reds.'

I knew the Spaniards' 'spy mania', but it appeared that in this regard the *brigada* broke all records. Because the motor in the captain's car had frozen, I had to go into Novgorod in a truck. It was bitterly cold and I was frozen through. The commission, which had been convened for the interrogation, consisted of three men: the *brigada* and two *gendarmes*. One of them, López,[8] was more cultured than the others, but also more repulsive than the rest: in all instances he sought to place all the blame on the local inhabitants and to hide the Spaniards' misdemeanours. We became enemies upon our first acquaintance and he tried to play dirty tricks on me wherever he could.

In Novgorod, despite the seeming complete destruction, there still remained buildings fit for habitation, and one of these was the former museum, where the interrogation was to take place. At that time one of the Spanish *Gendarmerie* posts was housed there. I don't know if it was under them or even earlier that the museum was plundered completely. One thing was clear, that it was the Spaniards' doing, for as one guard told me, the Germans did not touch any of the relics stored there.[9] Some of what was stolen was later sold in Spain and, I must admit, at a high price. For example, the icon that was presented to Tsar Aleksandr III following the train wreck in Borki (near Khar'kov),[10] was quoted at 25,000 pesetas!

And so, while we were warming ourselves by the museum's hospitable stove, the adroit López set off to find the guilty woman. But he did not make us wait long. He came back, accompanied by two girls. What was striking about them was that they were dressed a little more fashionably that those whom we usually encountered around us. Of course, this coquetry was more than relative, for given the overall destruction and poverty which reigned about us, any kind of new kerchief on one's head and undarned stockings almost reminded one of luxury.

I don't remember, but it seems they were named Katia and Natasha, and the first one was the assumed spy. It was already clear from the first glance that the *brigada* had overdone it with the accusations. This girl knew about thirty or forty Spanish words like *beso* (kiss), *dinero* (money), *guapo* (good looking), and *pan* (bread), etc. In the majority of cases, these were the most common words, or were similar to French words. As a result of the accused woman's intelligence and her frequent contacts with young Spaniards, this knowledge was understandable and necessary for her. I did not insist on knowing the reasons for her being acquainted with the soldiers, one could see from her behaviour that they were more than evident. Nor did she hide the fact that she had a lot of 'friends' among the Germans as well. In any event, there was very little here to accuse her of.

The *brigada* saw this: it was clear that 'nothing would come of this matter'. López and his comrades tripped over themselves in coming up with cheap compliments for those who only an hour before they were ready to shoot. It was decided to postpone the matter until new evidence could be acquired, and then the *brigada* and I set out for headquarters, while our two comrades left to accompany the girls in order to set a day and hour for the next session of the court. But I was not invited to that hearing, because they evidently had no need of an interpreter.

But I was not fated to rest on that day. 'Kovalevskii, we have to finish another matter', the *brigada* told me over lunch. 'If you only knew how the Germans stick their noses into everything that doesn't concern them. They always listen to all sorts of complaints against us Spaniards. But rest easy; we'll get rid of this denunciation.'

This time three of us set out: the *brigada*, López and I, in a car. Along the way they explained the matter to me: we had to find in the settlement of Koptovo, along the Leningrad highway, a certain Fedos'ia Ivanovna, whose cow had been stolen, and because this cow had a German security passport and because the Germans suspected that the Spanish had taken part in the theft, they had turned this matter over to us for investigation.

After a long search, we finally found this woman at twilight. At first she was frightened, and then she cheered up, naively believing that we had actually come to help her. It was bitter to see, for I had known all along that the investigation would be just a comedy. And what transpired confirmed my forebodings. Fedos'ia began to bustle about, explaining in detail how some people had come at night and taken away her cow. She suspected that these were Spaniards, who had more than once come to her to buy milk. 'It's easy to find a cow', she said, 'for its tracks are easy to find in the snow.'

And so, following the tracks through the deep snow, we came to a courtyard where we saw a field kitchen. All of this began to bother the *brigada* – the evidence was all too clear. But he wasn't a Spaniard for nothing and to give up when faced with facts: 'Kovalevskii, this matter is unclear to me and we shouldn't make any hasty decisions, all the more so that we have to think about how we're going to pull out our car, which is stuck in the snow. Order the village elder to call the people together to help us, and we'll go into one of the huts to warm ourselves.' This proved by accident to be the military doctor's quarters. So, the *brigada*, whether he liked it or not, was forced to hear from him the details of how they had brought the cow to the field kitchen and how they had slaughtered it at night. But this was all said, 'between us', so to speak.

Meanwhile, the inhabitants had gathered in the courtyard: they pushed and had nearly gotten the stuck car out of the snowdrift. The excited Fedos'ia tried harder than everyone. But the *brigada* was little interested in the matter of the theft, so he did not consider it necessary to drop into the kitchen, where the beef was being boiled at that time. He headed straight for the freed car in order to depart. The poor woman, coming up to me, whispered: 'Comrade interpreter, I'll show my gratitude to you with butter and eggs, but just get my cow back!' And no matter how difficult it was to disappoint, I could not restrain myself and told her: 'It's too late, auntie, and you should have protected your cow better from these gentlemen!', indicating with my eyes the Spaniards. 'You won't get anything from them.'

Fedos'ia sighed and wrung her hands; but we were already heading back to headquarters. But the *brigada* had evidently been watching me and began to press me: 'Kovalevskii, what did you say to your fellow countrywoman?' 'Nothing', I lied. 'I told her we'd come back another time.' Meanwhile, López was spinning a theory that vindicated the Spaniards. 'First of all', he said, 'the tracks we found resemble more a horse's tracks than a cow's and then, even if the cow was slaughtered at night, it may have been bought. These Russians are always trying to blacken the Spaniards' reputation, so it follows *no es verdad* (it's not true) that the Spaniards stole it.' And this is how the enquiry ended.

But the *brigada* was tired of the Germans' 'intrigues' and when the latter once again requested us to investigate the murder of an accountant, supposedly by the Spaniards, he refused to go and sent me. I arrived at one of Novgorod's remaining monasteries, where homeless Russians had taken shelter. I found the residents there greatly agitated. The excitement was not about the murder, but because they had been ordered to leave the monastery, which had been occupied by the Germans, within three hours. A punctual German sergeant stood at the entrance, with a watch in his hands, to see that the order was carried out.

The murder itself took place as follows: a group of Spaniards had broken into the monastery the previous night. They said that they were looking for some woman (evidently one of loose morals) and they entered all the rooms, without exception. Where they opened the doors in response to their knocking, they went and condescendingly stroked the cheeks of the women who were already in their beds, accompanied by compliments such as *guapa*, *bella* and *preciosa* (pretty), and then would leave for further searches. But the accountant, who lived with his wife, refused to open the door. So, they broke down the door and threw the accountant out of the window. All the residents assured me (perhaps due to caution) that they had seen these Spaniards for the first time and could not give us any more exact information.

What could I do? A heavy atmosphere reigned around us. Everybody was hurrying to pack up their belongings as quickly as possible and to go and look for a new place to live, which given the complete destruction of the city was not an easy thing to do. But what I saw upon leaving upset me even further: a group of soldiers were waiting for the women and threw themselves on them and took away everything of value that they possessed – rings, bracelets and earrings. But I was most indignant with the behaviour of one soldier, who seized from a small girl of 6–7 years a small box with her things and, upon seeing that there was nothing of value, contemptuously threw everything into the snow. The poor girl was bawling her eyes out. I could not restrain myself. Only the presence of the German and his assistance saved me from being beaten by these robbers, and we sent them packing. But having gone on a little farther, I ran into another scene: an old woman, who had been driven from her house, was pulling her modest things with difficulty on a small sled. She had to go up a hill, which was difficult for her. A soldier ran out of a small German detachment that was passing by, harnessed himself to the sled and pulled it up the hill. Knowing of the Germans' strict discipline, this was almost a feat of heroism. This soldier had evidently recalled the mother he had left behind!

Hunting for Partisans

The following day preparations began in the headquarters for our departure for an 'operation'. It was unclear to me what we were supposed to do: I only knew that we were leaving for about 25–30 kilometres from Grigorovo. Foodstuffs were gathered for 7–8 men and the sharpie, López, would be our commissary. The three of them (the *brigada*, the old man Galeote and López) set up late by the stove, talking and putting tins of food, bread and bacon from one sack into another. I repeatedly heard my name mentioned in their conversation and once the *brigada* called me, which he rarely did, and ingratiatingly asked: 'Kovalevskii, we hope that you will give us a lot of help in finding food, won't you? It's easier for you as a Russian.' 'I don't know that we'll be able to get much. After all, everything around us has been destroyed!' 'How about potatoes and milk? After all, we're going where almost nothing has been touched. The main thing is to find chickens and sheep', López added. 'And a calf would be nice too!'

And seeing from the expression on my face that I didn't much care for all these plans, he added: 'Of course, we'll pay or exchange; I remember how during an operation we bought a calf for three marks. And because the local inhabitants have almost no bread, you can get a lot for a loaf of bread, if you use your head.' I foresaw the difficult burden that would fall on my shoulders and not just during the inquiries, searches and hunts for partisans, but in looking for grub for the greedy Spaniards.

We began to load up the supply truck in the morning. We didn't so much load sacks with provisions as we did ammunition: rifles, crates with hand grenades and a machine gun with magazines. The *brigada* had a long conversation with Captain Martínez and he talked even longer on the telephone with the front, into whose rear area we were headed. To crown my surprise, when the people began to gather, there appeared three bicycle riders with their bicycles – our future communications with headquarters. What would these gentlemen do at the height of winter, among the snowdrifts and along the icy highway?

A number of villages were located along both sides of the Leningrad highway on the way to the capital. And it was hard to draw a line where one village began and another ended. Finally, after a good hour of driving, we arrived at the village of Podberez'e, which the Spanish had christened Pobereja. Despite the fact that the village was in the zone of enemy fire, there was not much destruction: two or three huts with fallen-in roofs, although the surrounding fields were pitted with shell holes. The glass in the huts' windows, where any remained, was a complete mosaic from fragments and even simply pieces of paper. We halted at the first hut upon entering the village. What was striking was the absence of homesteads. I don't know if this was always the way it was in the north of Russia, but there was literally not a picket, nor a house, with the hay lying in the fields.

I don't think that the owners were very happily struck by our arrival. But with that humility which is so characteristic of the population of contemporary Russia and which so amazed me from the first day back in the motherland, they accepted us as a necessary evil and even as 'their own'. The best room was set aside for us and there was sufficient room for everyone on the sleeping-benches, which had evidently been built by the Germans.

Our hosts' family was not a large one: a mother and two children. The oldest son was a boy of about 14, who immediately charmed us with his simplicity and eagerness to please. Everybody liked him very much. I believe that one can rarely see such morally healthy young people in Spain. I asked myself why small children here are so charming and nice, as nowhere else, with openness and joy in their entire being, while [Spanish] young people of 10–12 years already strike one by their closed nature and embryonic hypocrisy. The consciousness, which has been inculcated into them by their religious parents, that they belong to a nation beloved of the Lord our God, has killed their childish soul. I, who love children, sought to become closer to them. It's not worth the trouble, so I gave up. One can expect of them only future Lópezes and Martínezes.[1]

But I must return to my reminiscences about the USSR. The Spanish explained the friendly attitude toward themselves as nothing more than the result of their qualities and special services. On the first day they entrusted to me the task of 'borrowing' a sack of potatoes from our hostess and promised to pay well with bread, or at least in money. The trusting woman, who supplied us with potatoes the whole time we stayed with her, was only paid from time to time with a small piece of bread, while the *brigada* did not consider it necessary to give her a monetary reward. And the motive: was she really not satisfied with our leftovers?[2]

We didn't have to stay long in Podberez'e. The *brigada* told us that this was because of our headquarters; we were supposed to be roaming the area, catching partisans and Soviet agents. On the day after our arrival I had to go and make arrangements with the village elder for him to give us two sledges for our trip. This representative of local rule was in a pitiful position: appointed by the Germans, he had to devote his entire time, from morning to evening, to carrying out the often impossible demands of the new lords.

The impoverishment all around was such that it was a difficult problem to procure two sledges for us. But the desired forms of transportation were finally received. Up until the last moment the *brigada* kept the secret, and it was only while getting on the sledge, with all the ammunition, that he said that we had to move it to Nekhotovo.[3] This village, which was four *versts* from Podberez'e, represented in the Spaniards' mind an unsecured zone, to which one must travel armed to the teeth.

The sledges were preceded by two of the bicyclists, while the other one brought up the rear of our detachment. On the first sledge lay a loaded light machine gun, ready at any moment to open a murderous fire into the woods surrounding the road. From the very beginning such a precaution struck me as excessive and a sham. And halfway there, while crossing the railway near a small station, deep in the woods, we actually came across some Germans peacefully strolling along. The Germans looked at us in amazement in reply to our question of whether they had heard anything about partisans in the area and shook their heads in negative reply.

But the complete refutation of our fears was the empty caravan heading toward us, where in almost every sledge there was a Spaniard, hugging in a most tender fashion a broad-shouldered and smiling Russian driver. Some cautionary measures should have been taken, but not the ones the *brigada* had resorted to. To top it off, while continuing our journey along the road, we found in the snow a rifle, lost by one of the love-struck soldiers. After this the *brigada* felt that he had overdone it, and the machine gun was unloaded, while our valorous vanguard of bicyclists abandoned us in order to pre-empt us and ransack the area away from the commanders' gaze and . . . mine!

We made a halt in the first hut in Nekhotovo [Nekokhovo]. In a small and clean room we found a pair of some sort of Spaniards wolfing something down. Observing the formalities, the *brigada* ordered me to ask the owner whether she had seen any partisans and whether or not they had robbed her. To the amazement of both of us, the old woman fell to her knees: 'Have mercy, comrade officers, I haven't seen any partisans and they don't come around here, but for God's sake defend us from these.' And she pointed to the Spaniards sitting at the table: 'They don't' give us any peace and every day they come and ask for something – give them a chicken, give them eggs, or give them some milk, and they took the neighbour's calf. Defend me, and I won't know how to thank you.'

I was not prepared for this reply and the *brigada* even less so. But you can't keep a Spaniard down. He ordered me to tell the woman that he would investigate the matter and we quickly left her. For my part, I added that she should hide anything edible and save it for herself, because these locusts would destroy everything and not even say thank you.

We set out to see the village elder. Along the way our attention was caught by a small building, around which a group of Spaniards had gathered and two or three trucks and bicycles. What was going on? A bicyclist captain, who came out to meet us, explained that this was something of a local club, or more likely a brothel, where you could have a dance and enjoy a good time. And the *brigada* did not even have time to issue the most severe orders to his subordinates not to leave the sledges, when only two of us – he and myself – remained from our small detachment. And when we went to see the village elder we left the machine gun and rifles, along with a crate of hand grenades, unguarded. All of this became the responsibility of the girl-driver and the boy. The precautions along the way and the carelessness and negligence here made for a pretty contrast.

The village elder of Nekhotovo [Nekokhovo][4] had been recommended by the Germans as an always reliable and useful man and the *brigada*, taking upon himself the supervision of the surrounding area, placed great hopes on him as an assistant and informant. It was not clear to me what exactly made this man so zealous and how the Germans paid him. If I'm not mistaken he got absolutely nothing from the Spaniards, so I must think that if he rendered any unconditional services then it was the result of his own anti-communist convictions, or maybe just due to his pettifogging nature.

He sometimes tried so hard in his denunciations that I had to restrain him, and it seemed as though he was ready to give up those whom he personally didn't like, particularly from the other villages. According to him not a single communist remained in Nekhotovo [Nekokhovo] and that the partisans did not even come there, while in two neighbouring villages (Osha and Dolgovo), where there were neither German nor Spanish soldiers, there were communists everywhere. The *brigada* asked me for clarification: 'What do we need general phrases for? We need names, names!'

The village elder scratched his short beard and his little eyes ran back and forth, and then for some reason in a whisper, although there was no one else in the hut but us, began to weave a story. 'First of all, there's the former chairman of the village soviet,[5] Arkashka Davydov, the nephew of Pavel Ivanovich Davydov, whom, of course, you know?' he said to me. 'How the hell should I know any Pavel Ivanovich?' 'Pavel Ivanovich is with them', pointing into the distance with his finger, 'and is a very important personage. He's a former police colonel under the Tsar and went over to serve "them" and now is in charge of their entire intelligence service.' And then, lowering his voice all the way so that I could hardly hear him, he added: 'He's a very dangerous and artful personage. He has crossed the river more than once and has been in Novgorod and Grigorovo while you were there.'

I translated these words to the Spaniard and he even turned pale: 'How can it have happened that a Red spy was among us and it was not reported to us?' The village elder began to whisper: 'People are very afraid of him and it's hard to catch him, as he always goes around disguised and is also a good actor, so it's difficult to recognize him. He came through here not long ago.' The *brigada* got so nervous that without even waiting for the elder to finish speaking, he ran out onto the street to inspect the machine gun that had been left on the sledges under the guard of the drivers.

While he called together in a frenzied voice his subordinates, who had gone over to dance in the hut opposite us, I continued the conversation. 'There's only one way to recognize Pavel Ivanovich, and that's by his gestures. When he speaks he always explains his words with gestures. He, just between us, comrade translator, has an apartment in Osiia, with his daughter, who's married to Odrik.' 'I don't know this Odrik either.'

But the *brigada*'s arrival interrupted our conversation about Pavel Ivanovich's relatives. The first thing my chief began with was a request to tell the informer that the Spanish command would not forget his services and zeal. 'Tell him that, Kovalevskii, but let him only try! So, are there any others in Osiia?' 'Of course, there's a certain Nikitin, the depot chief, who is very devoted to the Soviet regime. And here the main one is the teacher Koz'min.[i] He's missing a leg and is a real villain. Everybody is afraid of him now.'

The *brigada* was, nervous and wrote down all the names on a piece of paper, but evidently not trusting his own notes, urged me on: 'Write this down, Kovalevskii, for God's sake (*por Dios*). See that you don't forget anyone!' And then turning to the village elder [he said]: 'Well, that's enough for now. We'll be spending the night here. And tomorrow we'll leave at dawn and catch all of these suspects unawares.' And having finished, so to speak, the official part of his visit, and said in the most melodious and playful voice of which he was capable: 'Well now, old man, you must put us up in the best hut there is and treat us as befits us.' And then the old man, probably not without regret, left his interlocutors and went off to see about our lodgings. We followed behind him.

While looking for our fellows, we dropped into the hut where they were 'enjoying themselves'. The patrons had already departed and there remained only our 'eagles' and four or five girls. Two pairs were twirling around to the accompaniment of a wheezing gramophone in the spacious room – the 'hall'. The girls were poorly dressed and did not radiate beauty. I, while not letting on that I was Russian, set down a ways off in order to observe this Spanish-Russian *entente cordiale*.[ii] I can't say that the scene was a particularly merry one, particularly when, by the Spaniards' request, one of the girls began to sing, accompanied by a guitar. The song was a very sad one, which had written quite recently. The words and feeling with which the poor girl sang touched me deeply and amazed me. She sang that her motherland had been defeated and that everything around had been destroyed, and that amidst the snows and fires of her enormous country there wander girls who have been abandoned and dishonoured. And what awaits them and where are they to go amidst enemies and the dark night. The girl's voice broke and one could feel that it took a lot of effort not to burst into tears. '*Muy bueno, muy bueno, cantas con mucha alma, Natacha!*' ('Very good, very good, you sing with great feeling, Natasha!'), one of the *Guardia Civil* began to lisp, and tried to reward the girl with a hug and, in order to make an impression, added: '*Este es ruso, tu paisano*' ('He's a Russian, your fellow countryman').

The impression this made on the girls was stunning. 'How is this? Why didn't you say anything? We would never [have begun to sing] this song before

---

[i] A distortion of the surname Kuz'min.
[ii] *Entente cordiale* (Fr.) – a heartfelt agreement.

you. This is for them, who don't understand.' I was terribly sorry for them. As I found out, they were all from Novgorod, without relatives and means of existence. 'Do not judge us harshly', she said. 'Did we really think that we would someday be reduced to this? Most importantly, what will become of us, and we're even afraid to think about it.' And when I was getting ready to leave, they beseeched me almost in unison: 'Come in sometime, without them, because we don't see any Russian people and there's a lot we need to talk about!'

But I was mistaken, assuming that all of our fellow travellers had succumbed to the charms of the fair sex. López and his friend Iglesias were more practical, and when we appeared at the apartment they had already thrown together a sumptuous meal, consisting of potatoes and a young lamb. Where they found the latter remained a secret to me. I only know that in order to procure an extra 'ration' for themselves they did not worry about the means, while their issued rations, consisting of tinned goods, went to enrich the Talaste and other commanders.

At 0300 we left for Osiia, which was 6–7 *versts* distant, although the road was bad and we moved with such precautions that the trip seemed endless. The first hut upon entering the village was that of Nikitin [the depot chief]. We deployed in a skirmish line not quite a half-*verst* away. When we arrived at the hut, the *brigada* ordered us to load and place the machine gun opposite the door to which the *brigada* and I had arrived. I can't call him a coward, for in moments of assumed danger he never allowed anyone (and particularly me) [to be afraid], but all of this had a hysterical character (like the Georgian[6]), which had a great effect on those around him and irritated me no end. 'Why are you howling like an old woman? Be calmer!' I said to him repeatedly, which infuriated him.

With a cry of '*¡manos arriba!*' ('hands up'), we burst into the dwelling, which was even comical, as of course, none of the inhabitants understood Spanish, all the more so the situation inside was quite peaceful. Two of the small house's rooms were filled to the brim with women and children, who had been sleeping side by side on the floor. It was so cramped that there was no place to step without crushing one of the people sleeping. Sleepy and half-dressed, they jumped up from their improvised beds and, by the dim light of a smelly lamp,[iii] one could read the horror on the faces of those we had woken up.

---

iii Author's note. There was almost no kerosene or candles. Therefore people used a lamp made from lard and rags.

'Where's Nikitin?' But the question was superfluous, because there was only one man among the inhabitants. The Spaniard himself saw how out of place was his pose with a revolver in his hand before the frightened women, children and a single man in his undergarments, who had nothing that was either warlike or dangerous. But the *brigada* was not thinking of staying here long. He hurried off under the cover of night to carry out other arrests. He left one of the soldiers to guard the arrested man, with strict orders to shoot anyone trying to run away and to detain anyone who arrived.

But before we had time to leave this house one woman fell at our feet (I don't know why this long outdated custom had taken such hold in the USSR). I assumed that she was going to plead for the arrested man. But it turned out quite otherwise: she implored us for support and assistance, because she was a refugee from Novgorod, with an aged mother and three children, small, smaller and smallest. She had nothing to eat and had already gone hungry for several days.

I gave her what little I could from what was edible. Even the *brigada* was moved and gave her his food, and besides this I promised to 'order' the village elder to regularly issue her a little grain from the village's reserves. In my soul I little believed in success, for I had no right to issue such an order. But it later transpired that the village elder had approved my request halfway and issued her the required food. I so rarely managed to actually ease the sufferings of the dispossessed in this ocean of grief and destruction. In the majority of cases I, more often, against my will, served as a tool of evil than of assistance.

We set off for the local village elder in order to seek out the very dangerous teacher and agent of the Soviet regime. As opposed to the Nekhotovo [Nekokhovo] representative of power, the elder here was a modest man who by no means wanted to quarrel with anyone or denounce someone. He practically begged us not to disturb the teacher, assuring us that there was nothing dangerous about him. But it was useless to plead for leniency with the *brigada*. We took the village elder as a guide and witness and went to arrest Kuz'min.

The same scene was repeated as in Nikitin's home, only more disgusting, because the teacher was a one-legged helpless invalid on crutches. It was clear to me just from how the search was conducted and how rudely they treated the arrested man and how they forced him to part with his family that they would behave ruthlessly toward him. The Spaniards needed some kind of 'scapegoat', while the *brigada* needed some kind of tangible success. We took him away, but López remained in order to conduct a search for weapons. And it was only as we were preparing to leave the village that he appeared with his swag – two lambs and two or three pairs of chickens, but it was quite clear by what means he had acquired them.

The arrest of Arkashka Davydov was not so tragic. I don't know, but there was something in the nature of the arrested lad that took away all the gloom of this process. It was impossible to be solemnly severe with Arkashka. Young and gay, he even disarmed the *brigada*. Matters came to such a pass that we, forgetting our important mission, set down at the table with the 'criminal' in order to share with him a joyfully offered snack. Upon leaving, my stern commander had so softened that he asked me to pass on to Davydov's wife a few soothing words about the fate of her husband. All of this is true, but I can imagine how the Spaniard would have been confused and enraged if he had known that at that same time, in the house across the street, in Oparin's home, the uncle of the arrested man, the fearless Pavel Nikolaevich Davydov, was sleeping.

We had hardly come out onto the street when shots rang out at the other end of the village. It appeared as if the long-awaited moment for Zeiss and his brethren to impart a bit of drama to our expedition had arrived. Without crossfire and without armed resistance by the arrested men and attacking partisans, our expedition would lose its significance and theatricality.

The *brigada*, with his revolver at the ready and followed by his subordinates, headed at a run to Nikitin's house to save the *gendarme* who had been left there. But upon arriving, we did not find the floor covered with bodies or, in general, any kind of change in the peaceful situation. The guard, somewhat confused, sat by the door, while the numerous inhabitants and the 'criminal' huddled in the depth of the dwelling.

What had happened? The Spaniard, trying to impart as much importance as possible to what had gone on, related the following story: some Russian had just entered the building and, at the guard's command to stop and raise his hands, refused to obey and turned around and took off. The *gendarme* opened fire on him, but without result. From my conversations with the inhabitants I was able to learn that such an early guest was Semka Klimov, and that he had run away out of fear, having run into a guard who had threatened him with a rifle and had shouted at him in an unintelligible language.

I explained this to the *brigada*. But the latter, with his suspiciousness, could not agree with such a simple solution of the question. He simply had to complicate the problem. In his opinion, the matter concerned, if not a plot, then at least an attempt to free the arrested Nikitin. And it was only the resourcefulness and valour of the Spaniard that had forced the attackers to run away. For in his imagination Semka was only the vanguard. Thus we immediately set out to search for the unfortunate, but were unable to find him at home. According to his mother, he had gone to the woods for fuel. After this, the *brigada* was faced with a difficult task: to remain in Osiia, in order to wait for and catch Semka, or to return to Podberez'e and take the three arrestees for questioning. He chose the latter, for Captain Martínez needed to open the 'case' of the communists, agents of the USSR and abettors of the partisans, who were making themselves increasingly felt.

Having promised the village elder to return before long, as if the latter found this pleasant, we loaded up, along with the arrestees and two lambs, into our sledges. It cost me a lot of trouble to convince the *brigada* not to tie up the arrested Russians. After all, what could they, being unarmed, do in broad daylight against 7–8 Spaniards with rifles and hand grenades. Not to mention, the main criminal was missing a leg and, deprived of his crutches, was completely helpless.

We had not managed to travel more than half a *verst* when we ran into the culprit behind this alarm, Semyon Klimov. We stopped and here, in the middle of the woods, started an investigation of 'how and why'. We asked why Semka entered someone else's house at dawn. It was clear from the way the culprit kept silent that the matter concerned a woman, one of the numerous 'grass widows' living in Nikitin's hut. I guessed as much there, but due to the confusion of one of the women, young and 'not unpleasant'. I sought to inculcate this idea into my chief as best as I could. No matter how much he liked to create trials, in this case it was all too difficult to 'fabricate' something out of nothing, so he decided to let the culprit go, warning him that he would remain under our observation as a suspicious character. 'Kovalevskii, write down his name, just in case.' I pretended to write something down in my notebook.

Upon our arrival in 'Pobereja' [Podberez'e], we were met with an unpleasant surprise. We found out that during out absence we had been evicted from our apartment. The cook, who had been left to us, came out to meet us and inform us of this unpleasant news. 'How and why? Who had had the temerity to encroach upon the *Benemérito Cuerpo de la Guardia Civil* (the Very Distinguished Corps of the Civil Guard)?[iv]

This is what happened: the 267th Regiment's[7] music chief had been living in one of the village's huts. Unfortunately, this hut was located in our battery's immediate rear and, as one might have expected, a significant number of shells had fallen not far from the 'fife-conductor's' habitat. On the one hand, the latter did not have strong nerves, and on the other he was no stranger to ignoring the interests of others – he simply ordered his lackeys to throw our things out of the hut that he had taken a shine to. The *brigada*'s requests, protests and threats did nothing. Colonel Esparza stood behind the band's chief and even Muñoz Grandes was afraid of him. We had to give in and entertain ourselves in a half-destroyed abandoned hut.

Our quarters were not much to look at. Not only windows, but even frames, were almost non-existent, and one side of the hut had been smashed, and they had somehow patched up the doors with thin boards. We experienced the pleasures of a bombardment on the first night. Sometimes the explosions were so close that one had to hold on tight in order not to fall off one's bunk and the entire hut shook as if in an earthquake. Besides this, it was uncomfortable in that a large family also lived there and the area set aside for us was too crowded: we slept on bunks and in the passageways, and in order to go outside at night one had to move like a tightrope walker.

Everyone cursed the 'fife-conductor': and the only relief we had was that subsequently, for unknown reasons, the enemy switched his artillery fire to the area which we had abandoned. As our old landlady later told us, the brave musician did not find any peace there and often spent the nights sitting in the snow in a hastily-dug trench in the field, which served as a toilet in the daytime. The *gendarmes* were triumphant: the *Benemérito Cuerpo* had been avenged.

We had barely managed to settle into our new quarters when the *brigada*, burning with the desire to serve, ordered us to proceed with interrogating the prisoners. As I have mentioned, there were three of them. The charges against them mainly came down to their membership of the communist party. The legless Kuz'min was also accused of cruelty toward the population and in organizing the partisan movement.

---

iv *Benemérito Cuerpo de la Guardia Civil* (the Very Distinguished Corps of the Civil Guard) is the official name of the institution. Ironically, the Civil Guard is usually referred to as the *Benemérita* (the Very Distinguished).

We began with Nikitin. He either remained silent in reply to all of our questions, or answered evasively, referring to the fact that as chief of a Soviet food store he did not interfere in matters that did not concern him, all the more so in organizing the partisan movement. I don't know what the *brigada* expected from the interrogation; but perhaps he thought he could make his career with this arrest, and became enraged. 'What shamelessness – to deny your participation, as a communist, in the partisan movement. Oh, I'll loosen his tongue for him. López, tie this stubborn Bolshevik's hands behind his back until he makes a full confession. Next.'

The next prisoner was Arkashka Davydov. 'Tell him, Kovalevskii, that if he denies anything that he will be punished and even shot; if he tells us the whole truth, we'll let him go and even compensate him.' What did Davydov say? In a word, nothing. According to his account, only the teacher Kuz'min, as a former party chairman, could offer the necessary information. And the *brigada*, still under the influence of Arkashka's 'charm', did not insist further. The prisoner was not punished and even earned a gracious promise that he would be hired as an informer.

On the other hand, Kuz'min's interrogation was stormy. It continued for 3–3.5 hours. If the teacher, tortured by questions and threats, finally became exhausted, then one can imagine the state that I, who was responsible for translating from one language to another and who, besides this, added my own comments and advice, was in. I believe that without the latter this inquisition would not have led to anything and that it would have continued endlessly.

One should know the Spanish method of conducting an interrogation in order to understand its full absurdity and to feel a nauseating revulsion toward it. Here the matter is not to establish facts, but to demand a confession of guilt and, what is the main thing – repentance. The *gendarme* takes upon himself the rights of a priest during confession and that of a preacher-apostle. I finally shouted: '*Brigada*, this is not a confession, repentance and forgiveness of sins according to the dogmas of the Catholic church, but an interrogation. You've got what you wanted. Let's end it with that!'

And we actually did learn the following: when the 'Reds' were falling back under German pressure and the surrender of Novgorod was expected, the village communist party chairmen were invited to the city in order to hear their instructions. Weapons were distributed to them for the purpose of conducting a partisan war. The teacher received about 200 rifles. He distributed part of them among the villages, while another part remained undisbursed and hidden in the woods. It was hard to get more of a confession. In releasing the teacher from the interrogation, I managed to tell him without anyone hearing that he inform the bound Nikitin of the following: let him fake his 'repentance' and confirm what Kuz'min had already confessed to. After all, why should he suffer tied up, when there was no sense in denying anything. This Nikitin did, and he was rewarded and untied.

Now the *brigada* had the problem of deciding what to do with the arrested individuals. It was not possible to hold them in our quarters. The *brigada* thought to send them all to headquarters for further questioning. I found it difficult to convince him otherwise. 'After all, just what are Davydov and Nikitin guilty of? Of belonging to the Communist Party? And nothing more! The population speaks very highly of them. And what, after all, are we persecuting them for?'

But it was difficult to defend the teacher. Of course, he had not personally taken part as a partisan, but the majority of the population had a poor opinion of him. And it was impossible to leave him in the village. Once the *brigada* had stubbornly decided to send him to headquarters, one had to give in, hoping that the *alférez* G.[urskii] would manage to save him from a bitter fate. At the time I still believed that Captain Martínez had a certain amount of humanity. But the future, as it transpired, had prepared a tragic ending for the lame man. And, it is possible, even for Davydov and Nikitin.

They summoned Davydov and Nikitin again and the *brigada* ordered me to tell them that they were free and could return to their homes. But they had to promise to pass on to us intelligence about the partisans' movements. 'Of course, they are obliged to do this!' And with this they let them go. The Spaniard gave Arkashka the mission on the first day of searching in partisan-held territory, 30 *versts* from his village, in the village of Gory,[8] and to find out in greater detail what was going on. The lame teacher was sent to headquarters by the first passing automobile and the *brigada* devoted a good half-hour to a discussion with Captain Martínez, communicating to him the details of the capture of such an important organizer of the partisan movement.

We began to establish ourselves in our new apartment. It was very crowded and much damaged. The only consolation for the young Spaniards was the fact that there were two pretty girls in the hut, the landlady's daughters, whom they could chase after. But these gentlemen had a very strange way of courting: they hung around these girls like 'imps before matins', devoured them with their lecherous glances and tickled them when they got the chance, while at the same time they made them work for them, giving them their smelly and lice-ridden undergarments and then put the preparation of food on their shoulders.

From early morning until late at night a fire, which eats up an enormous amount of firewood, must burn in a Russian stove, for the greatest pleasure of a Spanish (and not only Spanish) soldier in his free time is to be present while food is being prepared, while looking forward to the coming repast. In order to meet our requirements for firewood, I got permission from the village elder to dismantle one of the huts destroyed by artillery fire. All the Spaniards had to do was to bring back the logs and saw them. But they refused to do this. The girls, hitched up to sleds, had to bring these logs home and then to saw them. The *caballeros*, who considered it an honour to clean someone else's shoes and to sweep the city streets in their own country, considered any work here degrading to themselves.

I had an unpleasant experience at this time. While I was working with the village elder on dismantling the damaged hut, a German patrol that was passing by, noticing that I was speaking Russian, detained me as a disguised Soviet agent. I had to show my documents and photograph in Spanish military uniform in order to disabuse these zealous searchers for spies.

Although the *brigada* and Captain Martínez felt a certain satisfaction with having arrested one of those guilty of organizing the partisan movement in the Novgorod *oblast'*, because this 'criminal' was a legless cripple and thus could not have taken part as an active partisan, his detention did not render the *gendarmes* the desired laurels. 'No', the zealous *brigada* would say, 'our task now is to capture some armed partisan and accuse him of taking part in the murders of Spanish soldiers, which have increased lately. Captain Martínez is very irritated and they are accusing him of not doing anything.'

While listening to him, and knowing Spanish psychology, I began to involuntarily feel fear: if there's no criminal, or even no crime, then you have to create them. And dozens of people had already been arrested in the surrounding villages simply on the suspicion that they had had dealings with the 'Reds', and this was the way it was in the majority of cases: they found someone at six or seven in the evening, sitting under a fence and answering the call of nature, and this was sufficient to 'blow him away'. Nothing more was required: this meant he had been eavesdropping and observing the Spanish army's movements.

While the *Benemérita Guardia Civil* was resting, I was summoned night and day to the villages to interrogate these 'criminals'. To top off this misery, I started to come down with something at this time and often, while lying flat on my back in the sledge, I would conduct interrogations of people who were filed past me. Despite the disgusting nature of this sort of treatment of the population, it was sometimes difficult to hide a smile when the 'case' turned right into a comedy. An old woman, who had just finished milking a cow, was detained with a pail of milk in her hands and accused of associating with the partisans and feeding them. A peasant, who had lit up a hard-to-get cigarette, was accused of signalling the partisans. Another, who was carrying hay for livestock on a pitchfork – this was supposedly a partisan keeping track of his victims.

One case turned into an outright farce. One Spaniard detained and accused a venerable old man of following his every move, evidently in order, to kill him when convenient. What did we find out? The solicitous father, concerned about his daughter, whom the Spaniard was pursuing, considered it necessary to observe the young pair's affair. When, with my assistance, the truth was ascertained, the expansive Spaniard could not disguise his repentance and the accused and the accuser left the court, locked in a close embrace.

What can you say? In a fit of paranoia, one of our sentry guards killed one of his comrades, who had gone out at night to urinate, by the door of his own hut. One could not say that the murderer felt any repentance or pangs of conscience. The word *'accident'* (an unfortunate occurrence) sums it all up. And the murdered man was enrolled in the list of heroes of the *Cruzada* (crusade) who fell at the hands of the barbarians.

More than once, I and the other Russian interpreters, who had come to Russia, asked ourselves the question: is the Soviet regime really so hateful to the Russian people that the enslaved population is only waiting for the moment when it can throw off this yoke, no matter what the price? Or perhaps these are all cock-and-bull stories circulated by the Germans in order to justify their policy of conquest and the future resettlement of Russia? In this case, we who have come here are playing a more than ugly role, betraying our motherland and serving the enemy.

And this doubt caused me much torment. At times it seemed as though the people were defending the country, and not the Soviet regime, and that the people had come to be identified with this communist regime and do not wish for or expect anything better.[9] And those of us, who had arrived from the West, are only sowing death and destruction around us. In this case, all of the émigré press over the past 20 years has lied to us, while creating a bogeyman for the world, and was silent about the blooming of our motherland and its achievements. Yes, at times this seemed almost irrefutable to me. But the voice of experience spoke to me: is this really the truth? To hell with the prattling of the Soloneviches and others, who at one time were connected with the Soviet regime: they would stop at nothing for a colourful turn of phrase in order to justify their flight from the USSR, but do not the deserters at the front report on the dissatisfaction of the population, especially when they express their joy that they would soon be able to work for themselves, and only for themselves, and not for the commune and the state farm? So what of the Nekhotovo [Nekokhovo] elder, who is nothing more than an outright scoundrel, with his denunciations, but why do others, and there are also many of them, do everything they can to help us with their, as they think, liberation?

I'll tell you that at times I'm ashamed that I, an interpreter, am serving the Spaniards and serve with less sincere zeal than these simple people who get nothing from us, the outsiders, except inconvenience. And in serving us they risk everything. That old men, former Tsarist soldiers, help us is hardly surprising, but how can one explain the fact that young people, teenagers of 15–16 years, also have sympathy for us? And for what? And if the Germans (I'm not speaking of the command, but about the soldiers) were able to gain popularity with the population, then the Spaniards, who with their dissipation and thievery have impoverished the population, could only arouse contempt.

The case of the boy from the village of Rogavka[10] will always remain in my memory. During December, when night falls as early as four o'clock, a boy appeared in our Podberez'e. Making the rounds of all the huts in search of the command, he came at last to ours. We ask him where he's from and what does he need. Instead of replying, he hands me a piece of paper, taking it from somewhere deep in his bosom. The following was written: 'Mister commander, two days ago one of your officers and two soldiers were killed in our village by partisans. What do you want us to do? Do we bury them or wait until you come for the bodies? Reply with the messenger? Signature: the Rogavka village elder.'[11]

It was the usual story: the Spaniards, in search of something to eat, or for the sake of amorous escapades, went deep into the woods, far from the front, and there met their deaths. I ask where this 'Rogavka' is, being certain that it is not more than 15 *versts*. But such was not the case! It was actually 30–40 *versts* away.[12] 'How? How did you make it, son?' 'How? I came by foot. I travelled for two days. I left home at dawn yesterday.'[13] 'How did you find us?' 'The Germans showed me: "Go there, where the Spanish are. Our men don't wander around like that."' 'Are there a lot of partisans in your village?' 'There aren't any in our village. They come from the woods. There were 40 of them, but in their camp in the woods there are more, about 120 people.' 'And you're not afraid to come here?' 'What's to be afraid of?' 'But what if the partisans had caught you? They would have killed you.' 'I know they would have killed me, it's true, but I hid the note very well.'

And this boy was no more than 14–15 years old. You have to ask what would make him cover 40 *versts* in order to bring us this news. We didn't give him anything for it. We only gave him supper with what we had. I had to wage an entire battle with the *brigada* in order to wring from him a single box of tinned goods for the messenger. And he did not want to give even that up. The Spanish have a strange conceit that you must do favours for them, 'for the sake of their beautiful eyes'.

He spent the night in our hut and in the morning left for the return trip, having received written instructions for the village elder: to place those killed in coffins and bury them, and to wait for us to gather the necessary detachment, and then we would come for the bodies. I had a long conversation with the boy before he left. He gave me a long list of active communists and partisans, and among the names Novikov,[14] Gavrilov[15] and Trishkov, there figured one Kseniia Vasil'eva and Kuz'mina (fat), who were female partisans and defenders of the communist homeland. And I asked myself: where, in the final analysis, is the truth? Are Kseniia Vasil'eva and fat Kuz'mina right, or the heroic boy, who travelled 40 *versts* alone through the deep woods in order to inform us, foreigners, of the evil deed?

No less than two weeks passed until a Spanish half-company was gathered to make the trip to far-away Rogavka. Upon returning, the detachment's chief thanked me with particular warmth, for the bodies of those killed really had been buried in well-made coffins, and small crosses had even been placed in the hands of the deceased, while those who took part in the expedition had been excellently supplied with food and drink by the village elder. Such was one of the stories of the murder of Spanish soldiers in the USSR. Later on I'll relate a story about a murder of somewhat different type.

But the thirst for laurels, cheap ones, of course, gave the zealous *brigada* no peace. Visits to Nekhotovo [Nekokhovo] by the ever-ready-to-denounce village elder, increased in frequency. But these denunciations had yet to offer, one may say, grounds for accomplishing 'feats'. 'Oseja' (Osiia) had been cleared of communists, but there remained the neighbouring village of Dolgovo. Despite all his ingenuity, the volunteer informer was unable to communicate interesting information regarding the remnants of communism in this village. Finally, giving in to the Spaniard's insistence, it seemed as though he had located a criminal. 'There's a certain Vas'ka Nikolin, who goes by the nickname of Pomazok, who at one time was a party member. Although he's young, he's an active communist.' 'Kovalevskii', the *brigada* began, 'you're terribly non-energetic. The captain and I are disappointed in you. You must act! Ask him where we can find this Pomazok and we'll go and arrest him!'

We left our headquarters, as always, before dawn, in order to descend upon the village and catch the 'criminal' by surprise. Maybe we'll get lucky and manage to come across some 'real' partisans, the dream of Zeiss and Captain Martínez.

I must admit that the road to the village was horrible. One must think that it was completely impassable in autumn and spring, for the village was located among bogs. And even now, in the winter, when everything had frozen through, the slender trunks of the trees, which paved the way, bent into the half-frozen mud, forcing those of us who were sitting in the sledges to bob up and down and hang on to each other so as not to fall out. According to the instructions of the Nekhotovo [Nekokhovo] village elder, upon arriving at the village, we paid a call on the forester and learned details about Pomazok from him. 'You know, comrade interpreter, the matter is not worth it.' 'How? Why?' 'Because this Pomazok is not a serious man, and one might even say, if you'll forgive the expression, an idiot. I don't know for sure if he was a party member, but that he's a hooligan and a skirt-chaser I have no doubt. And you won't find him in his apartment right now, but somewhere among the broads and young girls!' I did not disappoint the *brigada* beforehand, but the forester's prediction was fully justified.

We didn't find him at home. 'Who knows where he's wandering, but most likely at the flax butter press', said his mother. Off to the butter press we went. It was late at night. The *brigada* deployed all of his forces according to the rules of military strategy. They surrounded the little hut, that is to say, the factory, and the main forces forced their way into the press door. As always, passing everyone by, the *brigada* broke in with his revolver in hand. A half-darkness reigned inside, because a rather large forcing bed was illuminated by a lamp from melted fat and a wick made out of rag.

From the first glance one could understand that this was a complete women's kingdom. This entire frightened [group] ran away where they could – into the dark corners or hiding behind the sacks and millstones of this improvised factory. 'Where's Pomazok?' We saw the pitiful figure of a boy and by the light of a pocket lamp one could see the face, distorted by fear, of someone who was almost a child. The *brigada* was obviously ill at ease. 'Is this really him?' 'As you can see, there's no one else.' 'Let him follow after us.'

On the following day the interrogation of the 'criminal', as one could have expected, yielded nothing. It was not difficult to convince my chief to set Pomazok free, particularly when referring to the fact that the boy, as a skier, might be very useful to us while conducting reconnaissance among the neighbouring villages and in the woods. But it was not only this that aroused Zeiss's indulgence. López discovered that the arrested boy had a great knowledge of and capacity for seeking out food. I don't know in what international language they came to an agreement on this question, but in only a single day López 'captured a rich harvest' from the population. Lambs, chickens and even butter were present from now on at our modest table. Thus the trip to Dolgovo was recognized as not without success.

Just one small circumstance put somewhat of a damper on the *brigada*'s radiant mood: again, some woman, already quite old, threw herself in tears at the *gendarme*'s feet, imploring him to defend her from being robbed. One Spanish soldier, whom she called Ivan (Juan), had killed her chickens with a rifle. This Juan appeared before the *brigada*. He turned with a stormy look to the soldier, ordering him first of all to take off his hat. It appeared that this was an augury of future harsh punishments. To the surprise of both of us, the woman fell on her feet. 'What now?' The old woman now tearfully implored him: 'Don't punish Ivan too harshly. He's a good boy, just a little mischievous.' I translated this phrase to Zeiss. He only shook his shoulders: 'Ach, I'll never understand these Russians!' This is where the matter ended, for the time being. But before long 'Ivan' and the old woman once again appeared on the stage.

Captain Martínez was not satisfied with our truly fruitless searches for partisans, and he was ready to take part himself in the capture and execution of these killers of Spanish soldiers. And finally an unexpected opportunity presented itself. He swooped into 'Pobereja' without warning us, with a detachment on twenty sledges. He started out with reproaches.

> You don't see a damn thing, while at the same time they are killing the valorous sons of Spain before your very eyes! The division headquarters has received news that the partisans in a small village in the woods not far from Dolgovo, attacked Spaniards, killing one and seriously wounding another. And so I'm riding with a detachment to search out these partisans and to punish the village which hides them. Kovalevskii, get some guides and take us to that village in the woods!

I was most struck by the presence of a new person in the captain's suite. A young man, but already a professor of international law, Señor Castiella[16] was not a military man and held no rank, but he wore the uniform of a German soldier. This high-ranking sponger had a very strange role. It seemed that given his civilian status, if he had wanted to see the '*Cruzada* against the barbarians' up close, then his place would have been at division headquarters, or even of a regiment, but not among the *Guardia Civil*, where the methods of dealing with the population were not always fitting for a distinguished professor. But I little knew the Spanish then. Subsequent events showed that what is impossible in any kind of barely civilized and cultured country is possible in Spain. Later on, with his chest festooned with innumerable orders, he was the Spanish minister of foreign affairs for a long time. He left behind a 'pleasant memory'.

I once again took the forest watchman in Dolgovo and we drove deeply into the woods on the lead sledges. I asked the driver to go as quickly as possible, so as to have time before the captain's arrival to find out how things lay and just how much the village was responsible for the Spaniard's murder. Upon entering a small hut on the edge of the village, I saw in the vestibule the coffin with the murdered Spaniard (with a cross in the hands of the deceased). I moved further on. In a spacious front room I saw a bed with a wounded man. The owners, with fearful faces, surrounded him. One may imagine my amazement when I recognized in the prone Spaniard 'Ivan'. I had to move fast. 'Tell me, quickly, how the partisans attacked you.' 'What partisans? They were Germans. A German patrol took us, who were dressed in Russian sheepskin coats and caps for partisans and opened fire. I shouted "*Spanien, Spanien*",ᵛ but it was too late. When they saw that we were Spaniards, they brought us to the village, which was not far away, and promised to inform our people.'

The captain arrived and was deeply disappointed. The denouement was not the one he (and probably Señor Professor) wanted. He sought to trip up 'Ivan' in his testimony, but the latter stubbornly refused to change what he had said. I took advantage of the time and hurried off to find the village elder, whom I advised to entertain the arrivals as well as possible. In these villages, in the depths of the Novgorod *oblast*'s forests, far from the battlefields, there remained, if not plenty, then at least a sufficiency of food: livestock, pigs and poultry. Only bread was missing. Raids by 'Ivans' and their like could not seriously undermine their economy. They really showed us a good time. I thought that with this everything was over. But alas, I still did not know Spaniards well, Captain Martínez in particular.

We had not yet travelled half a *verst* on the return trip from the village, when the captain halted the column of sledges and, calling me, ordered me to lead the people into the village of Dolgovo, while he, under the pretext of issuing some kind of orders, turned around, followed by the sledge with López. I believe I don't have to go into detail to say why he did this. With the arrival of night he caught up with us beyond the village of Dolgovo, with his sledges weighed down with goods.

But let's return to us. We had only just reached Dolgovo and the boys hurriedly left their sledges and scattered among the huts, some in order to eat once again, and some to chase after girls, but most importantly – to get warm, for by evening the frost had grown harder. I remained by myself next to the sledge, alongside the coffin of the deceased and 'Ivan', who was helplessly lying still. The poor man was especially susceptible to the cold. But help arrived unexpectedly: the old woman, who had complained about him not so long ago, ran out and, upon seeing 'Ivan' began to howl, seeing what was wrong with him. 'Shameless people, to leave their comrade out in the cold.' And turning to the wounded man, she asked: 'What do you want, Ivan, to eat something, or perhaps some tea?' She began to hurry and returned with a warm blanket, maybe the only one she had and, while we waited in Dolgovo, and did not move from the sledge, giving him tea and food and

---

ᵛ   *Spanien* (Ger.) – Spain.

pouring tears over her 'unfortunate Ivan' like for her own son. The *brigada* was right: Russians are hard to understand.

But we had little time to rest on our laurels in 'Pobereja'. A note arrived from headquarters – red alert: a large group of partisans, the remnants of the Soviet 88th Division, which had been routed by the Germans, had infiltrated the front-line area in order to get through to the 'Reds'.[17] It was possible that they would decide on seeking out isolated groups of Spaniards, employing the cover of night and the support of the population.

There was no end to the *brigada*'s panicky concern. Each day, with the onset of twilight, he would send out a patrol to roam through the village, with orders not to move from the Novgorod–Leningrad highway, and to shoot at any suspicious figure. As a result of this, it was precisely at this time that the *Benemérito* killed his own comrade, who had gone out to urinate.

But the note said something else, more unpleasant: the *Guardia Civil* detachment must finally capture at least one 'real' armed partisan and thus justify its existence. We were given to understand that given such paltry achievements to date, there could be no question of decorations and advancement for the officers of this corps. The *brigada* was in a rage. I had to tell him that while sitting in 'Pobereja' we could not hope to catch any kind of partisans, because only regular units could break through here and attack the Spaniards, having first routed Colonel Esparza's regiment. One must catch partisans in 'no man's land' (*tierra de nadie*), by moving to 'Oseja', Dolgovo and even Rogavka. Of course, that required a risk, or, as the saying goes, in for a penny, in for a pound. This would not be playing the fool or the comedy that we were now playing out.

Zeiss turned red, his self-esteem and pride stung (oh, this Spanish self-esteem and pride!), and immediately issued an order to get ready to set out. 'We will not return to "Pobereja" without our quarry, and if we are not successful there, Kovalevskii, then it will be your fault. The captain and I are both beginning to lose our faith in you. What are you, after all, an interpreter for, if you can't or don't want to do anything?' It would seem that it was my turn to be insulted, but I was actually quite pleased to leave the unbearable 'Pobereja' with its semi-starved existence and nighttime bombardments.

They chose 'Oseja' as a more populated, richer and more hospitable village. And they were not mistaken. The village elder put us six men (the first echelon included only six men, without López) up with a family which accepted us very hospitably. They 'threw' us such a dinner on the first day, the likes of which I had not eaten in 20 years of emigration. What wasn't there: pies, open-topped pastries and marinated mushrooms; for the second course we had a suckling pig and horseradish, and then blancmange from cranberries, nor were sweet buns absent from the tea. I asked myself how all this could have been preserved . . .

The Spaniards had become so completely relaxed that, to top it off, the landlords had two daughters, very pretty ones. All a Spaniard needs is something that looks like a woman, for without them he will simply wilt. I was quite unpleasantly struck by one circumstance. From my first appearance Zina, the younger of the two daughters, blurted out to my face: 'This means that you must be Kovalevskii, Vladimir Ivanovich?' I was taken aback. The sister burst out laughing: 'We know all of you Aleksandr Aleksandrovich Tringam and Konstantin Andreevich Goncharenko, and others.' 'Where from?' 'Kolia Zotov[vi] told us everything and described everyone in detail.[18] That's why we made no mistake in guessing who you were.' 'Why', I thought, 'do we need such openness here, where the "Reds" are so close by and may be here tomorrow?' But I was mistaken, for the 'Reds' came that very night, and this is how it happened.

[vi] Author's note. Kolia Zotov was one of the youngest interpreters and a corporal; he was wounded six or eight times in the Spanish Civil War and walked with a limp; as opposed to I. Perchin, he was loved by all for his friendliness and responsiveness to the needs of the population.

Denouement

The darkness of low truths is dearer to me
Than the deception which elevates us.

A.S. Pushkin, 'Hero'

Having stuffed ourselves, and in the most beatific mood, we lay down to sleep. The *brigada* did not even concern himself with placing people on guard duty in shifts. Moreover, everyone undressed as if they were home and immediately passed into the sleep of the blessed. As the Spanish say, *como si nada hubiera pasado* (as if nothing had happened). I don't know how long I slept. I woke up, awakened by a loud conversation in the next room. Dressing hastily, I went out. The agitated landlords and half-dressed daughters are having a vigorous conversation with some teenager. It was clear that they were arguing amongst themselves about something. They became quiet when I appeared.

'What's the matter?!' The boy, somewhat confusedly and, perhaps, frightened, quickly began to speak, getting mixed up under the reproachful gaze of the landlords. 'Armed partisans have come to our hut!' 'Are there many?' 'I don't know'. 'Have they been there long?' 'They've only just arrived. I ran away while they were eating and drinking, to let you know. I don't want them to punish us.' I was undecided for only a few seconds: what is to be done? The *brigada* and the Spaniards joined in on our conversation. Upon finding out what the matter was, Zeiss began to rush about: 'Quickly. Bring the machine gun and rifle and let's attack them! Elder, Kovalevskii, how many are there and how are they armed?' Not knowing how many 'Reds' there were somewhat took the wind out of his sails: 'What if there are a lot of them? There are only six of us, counting the driver and the barber.'

I burst out laughing. 'What are you laughing at?' 'Do you really not find it funny what the barber is going to do?' 'Nonsense! Ask the landlord if there are any Spaniards or Germans, foragers perhaps, in the village that can support us.' 'There are no Spaniards, but there are 5–6 Germans who arrived in the village the other day and who are living almost opposite us', was the reply. 'Let's go quickly, and let the landlord show us where they live.'

We found the Germans, led by a sergeant, but they did not express a particularly great desire to accompany us, referring to the fact that they were not here to fight the partisans. I gave up on this and firmly set out behind the boy to the other end of the village, to the hut where we found the 'Reds" refuge. 'Where are you going? What about me?' the *brigada* shouted hysterically, and with his revolver in his hand he tried to catch up with and head me off. I think that in this case it was not only a feeling of vanity to be first that moved the Spaniard. The fear that I would go over to the enemy aroused him to be brave.

From far off we could see the hut where the newcomers were: only its windows were illuminated. Everything around was in darkness. A plan of attack was quickly worked out: to cordon off the hut (and this was with six people) and set up the machine gun opposite the door, which threatened to cut down any one who came out. Fortunately, they were slow in doing this; otherwise they would have killed the owner, the boy's father, who came out of the hut. From him we learned that there were only six of them, three of whom were armed with rifles and the remainder with revolvers and hand grenades.

What do we do? Attack? But how? If we toss hand grenades into the window it's unlikely that they would land inside, and then they might harm the wife and her children. The commander did not hesitate long in making a decision: 'Kovalevskii, go to the door and propose to "them" that they surrender voluntarily in light of their hopeless situation and our overwhelming superiority in men (?!) If they are stubborn, threaten to burn the hut down. We will back you up from afar with machine guns and rifle fire!' I well knew that this machine-gun and rifle fire would more likely be directed against my back than at the partisans hiding in the hut.

So I went. At first the landlady replied. Then a man's voice. I passed on the proposal to surrender. I suggested that the besieged toss their weapons out of the window. Five minutes passed, but there was no answer, so the *brigada* decided to begin preparations for setting fire to the hut. First of all, they tossed a hand grenade in front of the window in order to scare them. This had no result. They extinguished the light inside and were as silent as the grave. The hut was connected with the cow-shed by the same straw roof and it was this roof that they decided to torch so that the smoke would force the besieged to come out.

To my great surprise, the straw quickly burst into flames, despite the thick layer of snow, and the flames enveloped the barn from all sides. We again proposed that they surrender, because in any event the denouement would have to come. The partisans must already be feeling the smoke. And at that perilous moment an aircraft appeared in the cloudless sky of the chilly night and, attracted by the fire of the burning hut, began to rain down a hail of bullets on us. It was an apocalyptic picture: *'confusión'* in Spanish, for it was hard to say who was attacking and who was defending. One must suppose that panic and indecisiveness reigned in the hut, which doomed the arrivals.

What was more simple? To throw open the door and finish me off with a blow from a rifle butt and flee – the nervous *brigada*, with his driver and barber would in all likelihood not have had time to fire, and even if they had the time they would not likely have hit the partisans running away, and it's possible that the Russians would have even managed to capture the machine gun. Quantitatively, they were our equals, but qualitatively superior. But the moment was missed and, wheezing from the smoke, they could do nothing better than to throw their weapons out of the window: revolvers, grenades and rifles. The Spaniards threw themselves like a pack on them to gather up the 'trophies'.

But the door opened and six stocky Russians, dressed in quilted sheepskin coats and with their hands raised, came out of the hut. I don't know, but I think my companions looked more scared and nervous than did the partisans. With their rifles at the ready and their fingers on the trigger, one might expect the 'victors' to open fire on their captives at any moment, all the more so that during these minutes I was trying as best I could to save something of the owners' property for them. But I was not able to do much, as the fire was spreading too rapidly. The *brigada* pulled me from the site of the fire almost by force: *'Deja eso, deja esas tonterías'* ('Leave it, drop all this nonsense'). And we walked along the road to the elder's hut, accompanying our 'booty'. I don't know where he came from, but the German sergeant arrived at the interrogation with a half-dozen of his fellow countrymen and their interpreter from among the Russian peasants.

Who were these prisoners? Three of them were privates. One was a battalion commander, one a captain, and finally the political commissar. The latter did not admit this, but the Germans' interpreter assured us that one could unmistakably spot a commissar by the star on his sleeve.[1] We didn't find any money when searching the prisoners, only old watches, penknives, pencils and other knickknacks. The plenitude of glass-like material caught our attention.[2] The prisoners were the remnants of the Soviet 88th Division, who on their long journey[3] found a shot-down aircraft and gathered up this burning[i] material for illumination.

We took a small diary from the captain, where he marked the way covered and what remained to do in order to break through to 'their people'. Aside from this, each of them had a page with the names and addresses of each of his comrades, in the event that one of them could manage to avoid death. Aside from the captain, whom I particularly wanted to save (but actually doomed), the list read as follows: Ivan Novikov,[4] Aleksei Ziganov,[5] Timofei Borovenko,[6] Ivan Vagin,[7] and Veniamin Belolipetskii.[8] All of them were from northern provinces (*oblasts*, in Soviet parlance), except for the captain, who was from Chernigov province.

It seemed to me that since the Russians were in military uniform, with rank insignias, there was no question of their not belonging to the Soviet 88th Division, and thus there could be no question of treating them as partisans (that is, shooting them). Nor could I see that the *brigada* had any intention of killing them, all the more so that they had practically surrendered without a fight. But for some reason the Germans, who had not taken part in capturing them, cried out in unison: '*Schießen, schießen!*' ('Shoot them, shoot them!'). I sought to explain my point of view to both them and the Spaniards and think that I would eventually have succeeded in doing so, for it would undoubtedly have been pleasant for Zeiss to present such valuable booty to headquarters, when there suddenly arose interference from where I least expected it.

The interpreter, who insulted the prisoners under interrogation in all sorts of ways, called me a secret Bolshevik who, having treacherously 'come to an understanding' with the communists, was defending them. He sought to compromise me in obscene German (it's possible that he was also a former prisoner of war) in the eyes of his masters. The Spaniards did not understand much, but by the gestures of this degenerate, who even dared to grab me by the throat, and the Germans, who were brutally looking at me, guessed that I was being accused of treason. Knowing the Spaniard's suspicious nature, and in particularly taking into account the *brigada*'s dislike for me, I believed that to continue to defend my fellow countrymen was no longer safe for me, and since this could do the prisoners no good, I had to save myself.

---

[i] A mistake by someone who was starting to forget his native language. This should be 'combustible'.

Playing on the *brigada*'s vanity that we had actually captured the Russians and that for us to appear at headquarters empty-handed would be more than shameful, I convinced him that they should leave us Spaniards at least one alive, namely the captain. I don't know if the eventual victims understood this back and forth. If they understood only a part, then their psychological condition was horrible. The Germans took the doomed men away and one of the Spaniards went with them as a witness. I sat down next to the captain and, while calming him down, said that for the moment I had managed to save him and was sure that at division headquarters it would be easy for the senior Russian interpreter [Gurskii] to defend him. I did not speak of the fate of his comrades, but I think he guessed where the Germans had taken them.

He asked for a smoke. I don't smoke myself and turned to the *brigada* for a cigarette. And it seemed as if he, being in a good mood because of the day's 'good luck', was preparing to carry out the captain's request. But on this day some kind of cruel fate hung over our Russian. The door burst open and our excited 'spy' burst in, waving his rifle and shouting something. To be frank, I assumed, no matter how unlikely, that the 'Reds' had attacked the village.

But that was not it! The Germans, not being satisfied with shooting their[ii] prisoners, whom they were conducting unarmed, decided for considerations of sadism, to burn them alive. Having lead them up to the burning hut (the residents were afraid to put out the fire out of fear of repressions), the barbarians pushed their victims forward. But they decided to risk it: the battalion commander turned around and with one blow grabbed the rifle from the hands of the sergeant and took off running. The others followed his example. As the Spanish 'spy' told us *'confusion'* broke out, which was aggravated by the fact that the aircraft appeared again and began to fire on the participants of this drama from above. The result: of the five prisoners being led to death, three got away and two were killed. One of the latter, as Ibanez[9] proudly assured us, was killed by him.

Upon hearing this dramatic story, panic arose among the Spaniards sitting in the hut. Spanish panic is a particular kind of panic, bordering on hysteria, where the ability to reason is stifled and a man turns into an animal.[10] Then it's too much too expect logic in actions. And this is the way it was in 'Oseja'. Immediately, and without speaking among themselves, they threw themselves on the still-living captain and, tying his hands behind his back,

---

ii Author's note. Actually, 'our' prisoners.

pushed him out of the hut. The prisoner looked with horror all around, as if expecting salvation from somewhere. I wanted to tell him in brief what had happened, but the *brigada* interrupted me hysterically, and waving his revolver, shouted: '*¡Ni una sola palabra! ¡Ni una sola!*' ('Not a word, not a single word!').

Martínez, the greedy Spaniard, was so cruel that he forced the Russian to take his boots off. This was sufficiently eloquent to give the captain to understand what was awaiting him. So they led him to the 'scene of the crime'. Only a pile of charcoal remained where the hut had been. The end was approaching for the doomed man. Even now, nearly ten years later,[11] his plea still rings in my ears: 'Save me, Russian! I'm still so young and want to live! Save me. What are you killing me for, what have I done? After all, I was defending my homeland!' But a bullet in the back of the head from the ruthless Martínez put an end to the captain's sufferings.

During my long life (at the time I was nearly 50 years old), a good quarter of which I served as a soldier and took part in battles and combat clashes and, therefore, was present at mass murders and death, often of my best friends. And I've killed myself, as a machine-gunner, often not knowing whom. During the civil war of 1917–21 my enemies were also Russians and their death before my eyes left me almost indifferent. But this death, in the deep forests of the Novgorod *oblast'*, of a man who was alien to me in every way, and who perhaps was born after I left the motherland, of another culture and living with quite different interests – this death shook me to the depths of my soul.

Why is this so? Repentance for the fact that I went to my motherland with foreigners? A lack of conviction that I was defending a 'just cause?' Or the result of old age? Or, finally, did I have the right at my age, having lived, been worn out and disappointed in everything and not expecting anything from life, but chiefly tired, tired of life and wanderings and betrayed illusions, to kill (after all, I essentially killed those three Russians who had surrendered to me) a life just beginning, full of faith and ideals, perhaps not entirely understood, but without a doubt ideals? I don't believe in the Christian view of atonement through repentance and senselessly beating one's chest '*Mea culpa, mea maxima culpa!*'[iii] But more likely, with the analytical view of an observer of one's own soul, I must bitterly note that I am falling lower and

---

iii A Catholic prayer of repentance: 'My guilt, my great guilt'.

lower. And my line of conduct is moving further and further from the best ideals of humanity.

What else can I say about the episode with the Russian soldiers? The morning, which did not waste any time in coming after such an eventful night, was repulsive. The German sergeant had the shamelessness to appear with a request to give him one of the revolvers from our 'booty'. The *brigada* flat out refused to share his 'booty' with such an unworthy accomplice and only agreed to give him a rifle in exchange for the one carried off by the Russian commandant, in order to save the German from punishment for losing his weapon. We also agreed to cover up from our own officers everything that had happened, while limiting ourselves only to mentioning the capture and execution of the partisans. The *brigada*, in parting, turned his back to him, not even wishing to shake his hand.

But I did not know that this 'tragedy in the forest' would bring in its wake a comedy that is possible only among Spaniards in modern Spain. In the spirit of *Don Quixote*? Oh, no! There we had insanity, valour and a lack of interest for oneself. Here there was meanness, cowardice, immeasurable vanity and covetousness. I'm afraid that to say that these were the dregs would be to say too little!

Upon returning to 'Pobereja', the *brigada* dedicated nearly the entire day to talking on the telephone with Captain Martínez. Having received thanks from the captain, he rubbed his hands with pleasure. 'Only', he admitted to me with a guilty smile, 'you were right, Kovalevskii, it would have been more effective to present the commanders with live partisans; of course, there are their weapons, but it's not the same thing!'

The days passed and soon the Christmas holidays were approaching, and I nursed the secret hope that they would recall us to headquarters for a rest. But this was not to be! On 21 December the brigade came running with his *conferencias*[iv] by telephone and announced: 'Do you have materials on the partisans, Kovalevskii? Tomorrow the Captain himself is arriving at dawn, with a detachment of soldiers on sledges for hunting partisans!' I only thought: 'We've become the "flavour of the month!" This is something akin to "Marlborough is ready for the campaign".'

They arrived. From the very first I disappointed the captain as to the possibility of easily catching 'partisans'. 'First of all', I said, 'it is necessary

---

iv *Conferencias* (Sp.) – here: conversations.

to leave the car in Dolgovo or "Oseja" and to penetrate into the woods on sledges 30 or 40 kilometres as far as Rogavka.' His answer was simple: 'Isn't it possible to catch them somewhere closer?' 'Yes, Captain! The partisans have a fortified camp not so far away, but it has to be taken by storm!' '¿*Asalto?* ('By storm?') Isn't there a way to avoid all of that?' And the 'brave' captain even turned pale. I only shrugged my shoulders. We finally decided, leaving the car in Dolgovo, to carry out a takeoff[12] on the village of Gory,[13] halfway from Rogavka. And then we'll see. All the more so as there's a good informant in Gory, the forester K.

We set out and went deep into the swampy woods. I was surprised that Captain Martínez, in setting out on this expedition, had gathered up all the others previously arrested by us: the lame teacher Kuz'min, Nikitin and Davydov. An evil fate brought the latter together with our train when we were already leaving the village of 'Oseja'. Sensing something bad, I cursed openly, telling Arkashka: 'What the hell did you cross our path for? This won't turn out well!'[14] He, who in his naiveté, had been seduced by the captain's gentle conduct, only looked at me in amazement.

We arrived in Gory at night. It was a large village and complete untouched. They quartered me together with the captain and a German lieutenant. Of course, Professor Castiella was in Martínez's suite. This meant that one could expect some kinds of adventures allowing gain or medals. The family which opened its doors to us consisted of a mother and her two daughters, one of which, a girl of 4–5 years, was a charming child. The captain played nursemaid to her the whole time, sang songs, and jokingly asked the mother to give him this 'treasure' to take to Spain with him. I don't know if the poor mother believed this lisping, while furtively drying her tears, mourning the unknown fate of her two sons, cadets[15] in the Red Army.

And I was barely able to dissuade this same 'gentle' captain the next morning not to arrest and torment with questions this unhappy mother and gracious host, who had the temerity, as he assured me, to go out into the yard for some reason. In his opinion, she had gone out to turn him over to the partisans. Subsequent events showed me that he was pursuing another end, which he fully achieved the following night, fortunately, far from the hospitable Russian family. That which is impossible in any other cultured state is possible in Spain.

Forestalling the captain, I set out in the morning to meet with the forester K., in order to find out about partisan concentrations. The forester turned out to be an agreeable man and while we were drinking tea he laid out the entire picture for me: the partisans' nearest camp, between the villages of Zaklin'e and Sherkovo, was four *versts* from here. He did not think that there were more than forty people there now, which one could calculate by the amount of livestock which they periodically requisitioned from the population. 'Are they armed?' 'Two or three machine guns.' He knew the way well and their flank could always be turned.

When the captain and a German officer arrived, I laid out the situation to them. I immediately noticed the captain's hesitation. 'Kovalevskii, I would not like', the captain said, 'to attack the camp, as that might cause heavy losses, and for me it would be sufficient to catch two or three live partisans and one or two dead ones.' I could not help asking: 'Whose? Theirs or ours?' and, leaving the gentlemen officers to confer, went out, slamming the door. They called me in again a few minutes later. Upon entering I see the *brigada*, spreading his hands and heard a snatch of conversation: 'That Russian is worth all of us, but his character . . . ', and on that note the [conversation] broke off.

They finally decided to follow my instructions. I got into the first sledge with the forester and the German, and we set out. The train of forty sledges stretched out in a long line. It was already after midday when we arrived at the place where we were supposed to unload and go deep into the woods along a narrow cutting. The partisan camp was located a *verst* or *verst* and a half away. The German officer and I penetrated quite deeply into the woods and, on the advice of the forester, prepared to deploy our forces. But they did not arrive. We and 8–9 men of the vanguard wandered mournfully among the ice-covered tree trunks, up to our knees in snow.

We finally got orders to return to the sledges. The captain, with the look of a naïve girl, informed us: 'I've changed my mind, and besides it's late. We're going back. You, Kovalevskii, will bring up the rear of our train!' I exchanged glances with the forester, and he only looked down, whispering 'This means it's all over with me!' Perchin, whom the captain had brought with him from headquarters, now headed up the train. I thought: 'Well, this means that I can expect all kinds of unexpected tricks of the lowest sort.'

We covered the road back faster, bypassing the village of Torzhi. It was growing dark and there still remained 2–3 *versts* to Dolgovo. All of a sudden we turned somewhere to the left. The forester said: 'They've taken the wrong road'. The German officer shouted and halted the train, wanting to inform the captain of his mistake. But the latter only waved his hand and laughed, as if to say 'right'. 'Where are we going?' 'To Tatino', the Russian said, 'a small railway station where the Germans are working now to repair the line.'

We pass three of four huts. Our 150 men, not counting the drivers, are stamping our feet in place. The captain, of course, established himself in a hut with a German engineer. The *'Honorable'*ᵛ professor-sponger completes the company. The remaining hungry soldiers wander around like spirits, not knowing where to put themselves. And night, a long and wintry one, has already fallen. The lucky ones, including myself, made our way into one of the huts, full of workers and German soldiers and, while standing up, leaned against the door, and dozed after an exhausting day.

Suddenly I'm called to the captain. I thought: 'What the hell does he need me for if he's got Perchin?' 'Kovalevskii, ask the German commandant where we can shoot our captured partisan.' 'Which prisoner?' 'Kuz'min, the teacher.' Now they've done it! I go to the German. The commandant categorically declares that they are not in the habit of shooting anyone at night in order to avoid accidents and causing panic. And if it pleases the Spanish captain to go his own way, then he can do it, where he wants and how he wants.

I transmit the reply. The captain smiles good-naturedly: 'Such fussiness! Anyway, Kovalevskii, could you please trouble yourself to get a final testimony from the condemned? Perhaps he would like to repent before his death.' 'Spare me, spare me, Captain, Perchin is better for this sort of thing.' 'Why no, after all, you . . . ' But I did not hear the end and, waving my hand, went out. They told me later that Perchin had 'heard the confession' of the poor teacher for a good hour before they took the unfortunate man out to be executed.¹⁶

I spent a horrible night: parts of my body swelled up and I was panting from the stuffy heat and crowding in the room into which 25–30 people had been packed. At dawn a noise and some kind of excitement woke me from my half-sleep. What now? There were the excited faces of some and the derisive faces, full of disbelief, of others. 'The partisans have attacked and the Captain is wounded!' 'Where? When? And why only the Captain?' 'We don't' know, we don't know!'

I go out into the yard. The drivers are quietly preparing to depart by their sledges. The German and Spanish patrols are peacefully idling between the

---

ᵛ   *Honorable* (Sp.) – esteemed.

few huts. I ask around: 'Was there a fight?' The Germans only look with amazement. The loquacious López is declaiming among his comrades: 'During the night the Captain went out on the hut's balcony to urinate, when a shot rang out, wounding him in the foot, but he had the presence of mind to shoot back. A Spanish patrol also supported him with its fire. They say they killed a partisan.'

Perchin was walking by and I beckoned to him and ask him. He avoids looking me in the eye and prattles something that he has learned: 'The Captain has been wounded. Partisans. The corpse is there, in the woods!' I go in the direction where I expect to find the corpse. A German who has been standing watch there says that there is no corpse and only the headless remains of a Russian executed ten days ago. At that moment they were already loading the 'hero' himself onto the sledge. Suffering, but with the humble look of a martyr suffering for truth. The role was played brilliantly. Only a halo was missing in order to be inscribed among the saints. Our eyes meet and he closes his eyelids from exhaustion. It's repulsive. What can a man's meanness and falsity lead to?

I can further relate something about this tragicomedy: before departing for Dolgovo, the [captain] gave the drivers ten rubles!! (for forty people) for their services and at the same time handed Nikitin and Arkashka Davydov over to the Germans to be shot, as punishment for the 'attempt' against his person.

Decorations were distributed a little bit later: six German Iron Crosses for feats and the destruction of a group of partisans and their headquarters (?!). In first place was the 'hero', Captain Martínez, who was wounded in the fighting, then Professor Castiella (now the Spanish ambassador to Peru),[17] who was no less valorous, followed by *brigada* Zeiss, López and Perchin, nor was the captain's orderly forgotten.[18] The Spaniards wrote one of the glorious pages in their history with this 'feat'. The Blue Division's '*Cruzada*' put into the shade with its feats the conquest of Mexico and Peru!

In this lies the tragedy of modern Spain. Less than ever before and less than any other people, is the Spaniard under the Franco regime capable of feats, but he continues to live in the glorious past and there are no boundaries to his ambition to be the 'chosen' people.

And heroes *a la* Captain Martínez are created. It's doubtful that they can fool anyone, but you have to ask whether they believe in these modern Pizarros and Cortés?[19] I doubt it. For they have long ago lost their faith in man and . . . in God. In a word, to use their expression, *confusion*.

Endotes

Introduction: 'White, Blue and Red': Russian Emigrants, The Spanish Blue Division and the USSR

'The Ongoing Defeat': Officers as Taxi Drivers

1. Panoramic works about the civil war in Russia include: J.D. Smele, *The 'Russian' Civil Wars, 1916–1926. Ten Years that Shook the World*. Oxford, New York, 2015; M.D. Steinberg, *The Russian Revolution, 1905-1921*. Oxford, 2017, pp. 99–121; M. Aust, *Die russische Revolution: Vom Zarenreich zum Sowjetimperium*. Munich, 2017, pp. 156–201; A. Jevakhoff, *La guerre civile russe: 1917–1922*. Paris, 2017.
2. A. Kröner, *The White Knight of the Black Sea. The Life of General Peter Wrangel*. The Hague, 2010; A. Kuznetsov, *Russkii Flot na Chuzhbine*. Moscow, 2009, p. 104; A. Pinti, 'Revolución rusa y primera oleada migratoria (1917–1923)', *Stvdivm. Revista de Humanidades*, 23 (2016), pp. 195–226.
3. B. Bruno, 'Lemnos, l'île aux Cosaques', *Cahiers du Monde Russe*, 1 (2009), pp. 187–230; K.M. Ostapenko (edited by V.E. Koisin and A.A. Konvalov), *Lemnosskii dnevnik ofitsera Terskogo kazach'ego voiska, 1920–1921 gg*. Moscow, 2015; University of North Carolina at Chapel Hill, Louis Round Wilson Library, Rare Book Collection, Andre Savine Collection (hereafter UNC-CH/Savine); G.F. Voloshin, V.K. Mironovich, V.V. Polianskii, P.S. Savchenko, V.V. Sakhanev and S.M. Shevliakov (eds), *Russkie v Gallipoli. Sbornik statei, posviashchennyi prebyvaniiu 1-go Armeiskogo korpusa Russkoi armii v Gallipoli*. Berlin, 1923.
4. A. Shmelev, 'Gallipoli to Golgotha: Remembering the Internment of the Russian White Army at Gallipoli, 1920-3', in J. Macleod (ed.), *Defeat and Memory: Cultural Histories of Military Defeat in the Modern Era*. Basingstoke, New York, 2008, pp. 195–213.
5. UNC-CH/Savine. P. Pashkov, *Ordena i znaki otlichiia Grazhdanskoi voiny 1917–1922 godov*. Paris, 1961, pp. 24–5.
6. Columbia University Rare Book and Manuscript Library, Bakhmeteff Archive, Mitrofan Ivanovich Boiarintsev Papers (hereafter BAR Ms Coll/Boiarintsev), Box 1. M.I. Baoarintsev, 'Epokha 1937–1965 gg.', pp. 33–4.
7. P. Robinson, *The White Russian Army in Exile, 1920–1941*. Oxford, 2002, pp. 99–100.
8. E. Chinyaeva, *Russians Outside Russia: The Émigré Community in Czechoslovakia, 1918–1938*. Munich, 2001, pp. 121–30; S.V. Mironenko, *Putevoditel'. Fondy Gosudarstvennogo arkhiva Rossiiskoi Federatsii po istorii belogo dvizheniia i emigratsii*. Tom 4. Moscow, 2004, p. 607; V.G. Chicheriukin-Meingardt, 'Drozdovtsy posle Gallipoli', in R.G. Gagkuev (ed.), *Drozdovskii i drozdovtsy*. Moscow, 2006, p. 634.
9. On the press and other emigrant cultural output, see A. Zelenin, *Iazyk russkoi emigrantskoi pressy (1919–1939)*. St. Petersburg, 2007.
10. P. Robinson, 'Zemgor and the Russian Army in Exile', *Cahiers du Monde Russe*, 46:4 (2005), pp. 719–37 (especially pp. 720–21).

11. L. Manchester, 'How Statelessness can Force Refugees to Redefine Their Ethnicity: What can be Learned from Russian Émigrés Dispersed to Six Continents in the Interwar Period', *Immigrants and Minorities*, 34:1 (2016), pp. 70–91.
12. M. Housden, 'White Russians Crossing the Black Sea: Fridtjof Nansen, Constantinople and the First Modern Repatriation of Refugees Displaced by Civil Conflict, 1922–1923', *The Slavonic and East European Review*, 88:3 (2010), pp. 495–524; C. Gouseff, *L'exil Russe. La fabrique du réfugié apatride, 1920–1939*. Paris, 2008.
13. M. Esch, *Parallele Gesellschaften und soziale Räume. Osteuropäische Einwanderer in Paris, 1880–1940*. Frankfurt a. M., 2012; R.H. Johnston, *New Mecca, New Babylon: Paris and the Russian Exiles, 1920–1945*. Montreal, 1988; A. Jevakhoff, *Les Russes Blancs*. Paris, 2011.
14. G. Cardona, *El gigante descalzo. El ejército de Franco*. Madrid, 2003, p. 113. The author adds that Franco supposedly then decided to subscribe to a French anti-communist publication put out by Russian émigrés.
15. N. Katzer, *Die Weisse Bewegung in Russland. Herrschaftsbildung, praktische Politik und politische Programmatik im Bürgerkrieg*. Cologne, 1999, pp. 495–532.
16. V. Volkov, 'Kharakter i perspektivy Vtoroi mirovoi voiny v otsenke russkoi voennoi emigratsii', in I. Beliakova (ed.), *Russkoe zarubezh'e i Vtoraia mirovaia voina: Kul'turolog. chteniiia 'Russkaia emigratsiia XX veka' (Moscow, 28–29 marta 2011 g.): Sbornik Dokladov*. Moscow, 2013, p. 15; UNC-CH/Savine. 'Informatsionnyi list Alekseevtsev', *Vestnik Obshchestva Gallipoliitsev*, 38, 24 August 1936, pp. 6–7.
17. Iu.S. Tsurganov, 'Istoriia antibol'shevistskoi emigratsii v gody Vtoroi mirovoi voiny v dokumentakh Gosudarstvennogo arkhiva Rossiiskoi Federatsii', in K. Aleksandrov, O. Shevtsov and A. Shmelev (eds), *Trudy II mezhdunarodnykh istoricheskikh chtenii, posviashchennykh pamiati professora General'nogo shtaba general-leitenanta Nikolaia Nikolaevicha Golovina. Belgrad, 10–14 sentiabria 2011 goda. Sbornik statei i materialov*. St. Petersburg, 2012, p. 290.
18. M. Aizpuru, 'Ciudadanía e immigración: los exiliados rusos en España, 1914–1936', *Ayer*, 78 (2010), pp. 171–93.

'It's Strangely the Same': General Franco's Russian Soldiers

1. C.G. Kruger and S. Levsen (eds), *War Volunteering in Modern Times. From the French Revolution to the Second World War*. Basingstoke, 2011; N. Arielli and B. Collins (eds), *Transnational Soldiers: Foreign Military Enlistment in the Modern Era*. Basingstoke, 2013.
2. V.K. Abdank-Kossovskii, 'Rossiiskie ofitsery v izgnanii', *Voenno-Istoricheskii Zhurnal*, 2 (1996), pp. 91–2; R.C. Austin, *Founding a Balkan State: Albania's Experiment with Democracy, 1920–1925*. Toronto, 2012, pp. 146–56.
3. J.A. Hutchins, *The Wrangel Refugees: A Study of General Baron Peter N. Wrangel's Defeated White Russian Forces. Both Military and Civilians, in Exile*. MA Thesis, University of Louisville, 1972, p. 145; A.V. Okorkov, *V boiakh za Podnebesnuiu. Russkii sled v Kitae*. Moscow, 2013.
4. L.E. Giovine Gramatchicoff, *Aporte de los inmigrantes rusos al desarrollo del Paraguay*. Asunción, 2009.
5. Vladimir Vladimirovich Bogoiavlenskii, the son of an Orthodox prior, became one of the most successful Finnish breakers of Soviet radio codes. After 1944 he took up service in Swedish radio intelligence. V. Nikitin, *Sostiazanie s burei. Finskaia radiorazvedka protiv SSSR*. St. Petersburg, 2020, pp. 70, 96, 106 and 286.

6. D. Porch, *The French Foreign Legion. A Complete History of the Legendary Fighting Force*. New York, 2010, pp. 385–6. Ch. Kohler, *Die Fremdenlegion. Kolonialismus, Sőldnertum, Gewalt 1831-1962*. Paderborn, 2013, pp. 35–6.
7. M. Ballenilla y García de Gamarra, *La Legión 1920–1927*. Lorca, 2010, pp. 86–8, 111, 364. See also M. Daranas, 'Los feligreses de la Santa Rusia', *ABC*, 6 September 1942, pp. 3–4. The Russians constituted a completely insignificant percentage (0.13 per cent in 1930) of the number of foreigners in the Spanish Legion, which was in contrast to the multiplicity of Portugese, Germans, Latin Americans and French. As opposed to the Foreign Legion, the sub-units of which had almost no contact with French units, the Spanish Legion regularly cooperated with troops sent from the mother country, which fed governmental fears regarding the Bolshevik or Social-Revolutionary 'infection'.
8. A.A. Pchelinov-Obrazumov, 'Obraz ispanskoi respubliki (1936–1939) v presse rossiiskoi politicheskoi emigratsii', *Naucnye vedomosti Belgorodskogo gosudarstvennogo universiteta*, (2013) 1 (144), vol. 25, pp. 44–51.
9. E. Traverso, *A sangre y fuego. De la guerra civil europea, 1914–1945*. Buenos Aires, 2009; N. Katzer, 'Der Weisse Mythos: russischer Antibolschewismus im europäischen Nachkrieg', in R. Gerwarth and J. Horne (eds), *Krieg im Frieden. Paramilitarische Gewalt in Europa nach dem Ersten Weltkrieg*. Göttingen, 2013, pp. 57–93.
10. UNC-CH/Savine. N.A. Ragozin, 'Ruka Providenija', *Morskie Zapiski. The Naval Records*, XII:3 (1954), p. 33.
11. X.M. Núñez Seixas, *¡Fuera el invasor! Nacionalismos y movilización bélica durante la Guerra Civil española (1936–1939)*. Madrid, 2006, pp. 180–9, 245–61.
12. J. Keene, *Luchando por Franco. Voluntarios europeos al servicio de la España fascista, 1936–1939*. Barcelona, 2001; Dz. Kin, 'Srazhaias' za Franko: russkie beloemigranty na storone natsionalistov', *Neprikosnovennyi zapas. Debaty o politike i kul'ture*, 1 (82) (2012), pp. 207–28; C. Othen, *Las Brigadas Internacionales de Franco*. Barcelona, 2007.
13. S.S. Balmasov, *Russkii shtyk na chuzhoi voine*. Moscow, 2017, p. 438.
14. M. Raeff, *Russia Abroad: A Cultural History of the Russian Emigration, 1919–1939*. Oxford, 1990, pp. 38, 84, 152.
15. Russian State Public Historical Library (GPIB). A. Kersnovskii, 'Nikakikh Ispantsev', *Tsarskii Vestnik*, 521, 4 Oct./21 Sept. 1936, p. 2.
16. A.K. 'Ispanskie Dela', *Tsarskii Vestnik*, 527, 6 Sept./24 Aug. 1936, p. 3.
17. M. Skorodumov, 'Nikakikh Ispantsev', *Tsarskii Vestnik*, 524, 25 Oct./12 Oct., p. 5; M. Skorodumov, 'O Don Kikhotstve!', *Tsarskii Vestnik*, 527, 15 Nov./2 Nov., pp. 2–3.
18. In 1940 Kersnovskii was drafted into the French army and he wrote his wife in sorrow that he did not wish to die for another country. He was seriously wounded, after which he endured the German occupation and died in a Paris attic in 1944. In the autumn of 1941 Skorodumov began to collaborate with the German authorities, while creating a Russian factory security group (*Russische Werkschutzgruppe*). For more about him, see A.A. Samtsevich, *Marsh smerti Russkogo okhrannogo korpusa*. Moscow, 2019.
19. Staritskii family archive. Biographical note; J. Clarà, *El partit únic: La Falange i el Movimiento a Girona (1935–1977)*. Girona, 1999, p. 298.
20. Columbia University, Rare Book and Manuscript Library, Bakhmeteff Archive, Michael Schatoff Papers, Box 1, Folder 'REM-Koreiskii, Iur.-MS'. Iu. Koreiskii, 'S Vostoka na Zapad. Iz Istorii RNNA', pp. 19–20.
21. Cited in K.K. Semenov, 'Litsom k solntsu: uchastie beloemigrantov v Grazhdanskoi voine v Ispaniii (1936–1939)', in N.F. Gritsenko (ed.), *Ezhegodnik Doma russkogo zarubezh'ia imeni Aleksandra Solzhenitsyna*. Moscow, 2010, p. 49.

22. A.V. Okorokov, *Russkie dobrovol'tsy*. Moscow, 2004, p. 109.
23. A.P. Iaremchuk II (ed. by V.N. Azar-Azarovskii), *Russkie dobrovol'tsy v Ispanii, 1936–1939*. San Francisco, 1983, pp. 26, 81. According to Shinkarenko's data, twenty-seven Russians served in this *tercio* in the spring of 1938. Stanford University, Hoover Institution Archives, Nikolai Vsevolodovich Shinkarenko Memoirs (HIA/Shinkarenko), Box 4, Chapter VI. 'Cuesta de la Reina (oktiabr' 1937 goda). I posledui-ushchee', p. 83-A.
24. 'Iz pisem iz Ispanii', *Vestnik gallipoliitsev*, no. 46, 15 April 1937, p. 19.
25. UNC-CH/Savine. 'Russkie belye voiny v ispanskoi grazhdanskoi voine'. Translated from the Spanish journal *Historia y Vida*, 69 (December 1973). *Informatsionnyi biulleten' Otdela Obshchestva gallipoliitsev v S.A.S.Sh-kh*, 156 (August–September 1976), p. 5.
26. It happened that the insulted volunteers went home. For example, Shinkarenko crossed the border the first time together with a captain from the 8th Ulan Regiment and the famous pilot Leonid Aleksandrovich Kushlianskii. The latter asked the Spaniards to take him into their air force but was harshly refused. The vexed Kushlianskii set off immediately back to Paris.
27. There were other examples as well, although overall they were fewer. Shinkarenko wrote that they treated the Russians with respect only in the *Zumalacárregui tercio*. In the middle of July 1937 Polukhin informed Fok that he was satisfied with his material state and had established himself well, although he did not yet know whether or not the Spaniards had recognized his officer's rank. M.E. Kol'tsov, *Ispanskii dnevnik*. Moscow, 1957, pp. 531–2.
28. Of course, different things were said in public: UNC-CH/Savine. *Ispanskie pis'ma o voinstve*. Berlin, 1939.
29. Keene, *Luchando por Franco*, pp. 290–4; Othen, *Brigadas Internacionales*, p. 168.
30. Russian State Military Archive (RGVA), fond 35082, opis' 1, delo 8, list 209. Leaflet 'Inostrannye soldaty internatsional'nykh brigad!', 1937.
31. M. Ibarra Alonso, 'Guerra civil española y contrarrevolución. El fascismo europeo bajo el signo de la Santa Cruz', *Ayer*, 109 (2018), pp. 289–90. During the First World War Torkom was a Colonel and representative with the French General Staff. K. Gomon, 'Voenno-politicheskie sobytiia v Azerbaidzhane posle oktiabr'skogo perevorota 1917 v Petrograde', in Sh.N. Kamalova (ed.), *Azerbaidzhanskaia Respublika – 100. Istoriia, politika, kul'tura; sbornik statei*. St. Petersburg, 2018, p. 176.
32. National Parliamentary Library of Georgia, Tbilisi. N. Dzhavakhishvili, 'Ispanskaia grazhdanskaia voina i gruzinskaia emigratsiia: (1936–1939)', *Gruzinskaia diplomatiia: ezhegodnik nauchno-issledovatel'skogo tsentra istorii gruzinskoi diplomatii Tbilisskogo gosudarstvennogo universiteta im. Ivane Dzhvakhishvili*. Tbilisi, 2003, vol. 10, pp. 469–80 [in Georgian].
33. Pr. M. Tsouloukidze, 'La lute nationale en Espagne', *Kartlossi. Organe du nationalisme intégral géorgien*. 2–3 (1937), pp. 15–18 [in Georgian].
34. G. Mamulia and R. Abutalybov (eds), *Za svobodu i nezavisimost' Kavkaza. Prometeevskoe dvizhenie v sekretnykh dokumentakh i materialakh uchastnikov, nabliu-datelei i protivnikov*. Paris/Baku, 2020, pp. 132, 134–5.
35. Stanford University, Hoover Institution Archives, Petr Panteleimonovich Savin Papers (HIA/Savin), Box 1, Folder 'Gibel' generala Millera'. P.P. Savin, 'Gibel' generala E.K. Millera (ne vymysel, a istoricheskaia byl')', pp. 3, 8. See also Miller's letter to General Fidel Dávila in November 1936, quoted by Ibarra Alonso, *Guerra civil*, p. 280.
36. V.V. Markovchin, 'Nesostoiavshiisia soiuz: ROVS i grazhdanskaia voina v Ispanii', in *Izvestiia Iugo-Zapadnogo gosudarstvennogo universiteta. Ser. 'Istoriia i pravo'*, 1 (22), vol. 7 (2017), pp. 96–101.

37. V.V. Markovchin, 'Russkii polkovnik, ispanskii serzhant', in *Izvestiia Iugo-Zapadnogo gosudarstvennogo universiteta. Seriia 'Istoriia i pravo*, 2 (23), vol. 7 (2017), pp. 135–40.
38. State Archive of the Russian Federation, (GARF), fond R5853, opis' 1, delo 67, list 285. Lampe to Shinkarenko, 23 July 1939.
39. Keene, *Luchando por Franco*, p. 295; Othen, *Brigadas Internacionales*, pp. 169–71; Iaremchuk II, *Russkie dobrovol'tsy v Ispanii*, pp. 2–3; Semenov, *Litsom k solntsu*, pp. 59–61; A.A. Pchelinov-Obrazumov, *Grazhdanskaia voina v Ispanii, 1936–1939 gg. i rossiiskaia politicheskaia emigratsiia*. Candidate dissertation, Belgorod State University, 2015, p. 134. See also the detailed description by K.K. Semenov, *Russkaia emigratsiia i grazhdanskaia voina v Ispanii, 1936–1939 gg*. Moscow, 2011, pp. 144–5.
40. B.S. Permikin (ed. by S.G. Zirin), *General, rozhdennyi voinoi. Iz zapisok, 1912–1959 gg*. Moscow, 2011, pp. 144–5.
41. J.S. Ciechanowski, 'Polish Military Presence in Spain in the 20th Century', *International Journal of Military History*, 98 (2020), pp. 173–4.
42. The article contains facts that are distorted and exaggerated: supposedly the 'Union of Russian Officers' had dispatched a 'composite detachment' of ninety-seven men. See 'Belobandity i katorzhniki – podkrepleniiia dlia Franko', *Pravda*, 70 (7036), 12 March 1937, p. 5.
43. P.A. Jordan, *Stalin's Singing Spy: The Life and Exile of Nadezhda Plevitskaya*. Lanham, 2016, pp. 144–5. The coda of Skoblin's life rang out in September 1937, when he helped the Bolsheviks kidnap Miller, after which he was immediately removed from Paris. Skoblin was stabbed to death during a flight from France to Spain and his corpse thrown out somewhere over the Pyrenees. According to other data, he was liquidated immediately upon landing, or perished during a Francoist bombing raid in October 1937. Whatever the truth, Spain played the final grim chord in his fate.
44. Iaremchuk II, *Russkie dobrovol'tsy v Ispanii*, p. 18; Savin, 'Gibel' generala E.K. Millera', p. 12.
45. K.M. Aleksandrov, *Generalitet i ofitserskie kadry vooruzhennykh formirovanii Komiteta osvobozhdeniia narodov Rossii, 1943–1946 gg*. Doctoral dissertation, St. Petersburg Institute of History, 2015, p. 189. By the end of the 1930s Denikin's word was no longer decisive for anyone, except for a small group of friends. During the years of the Second World War his influence, due to his 'defencism', became even more attenuated and immediately upon the conclusion of the war he had a falling out with the ROVS regarding 'defeatism'. Thus, never having recognized the Bolsheviks as a creative force, which was typical of the 'defencists', he remained misunderstood, as did his principles. A.I. Denikin (ed. by A.S. Kruchinin), *Na strazhe russkoi gosudarstvennosti: izbrannye stat'i, rechi, pis'ma*. Moscow, 2014.
46. HIA/Shinkarenko, Box 7. Romanova to Shinkarenko, 1 December 1937; Lampe to Shinkarenko, 27 March 1938.
47. The National Library of Latvia (hereafter LNB). 'Parizhskie ogni (ot nashego parizhskogo korrespondenta)', *Dlia vas. Ezhenedel'nyi illiustrirovannyi zhurnal (Riga)*, 35 (28 August 1938), pp. 15, 24.
48. UNC-CH/Savin 'Grazhdanskaia voina v Ispanii', *Chasovoi*, 185 (February 1937), p. 10; Keene, *Luchando por Franco*, pp. 298–9.
49. N. Belogorskii, 'Privet ispanskim "Kornilovtsam". San Jago! Espana!' *Chasovoi*, 172 (August 1936), p. 3. A certain part of Shinkarenko's epistolary heritage was released in a very small edition. N. Belogorskii (ed. by A.S. Emel'ianov and others), *Belaia Pesnia Ispanii*. Kursk, 2018.
50. N. Belogorskii, 'Chudo Al'kasara', *Chasovoi*, 176, 15 October 1936, pp. 3–5.
51. 'Russkii dobrovolets iz Ispanii (iz pis'ma)', *Chasovoi*, 173, 1 September 1936, p. 5.

52. 'Pis'mo iz Ispanii', *Vestnik Gallipoliitsev*, 47, 20 May 1937, p. 11. By the 'First Campaign' is meant the First Kuban' 'Ice March' in February–May 1918, Those who took part became the military exile's elite.
53. 'Pis'ma iz Ispanii', *Gallipoliiskii vestnik*, 51, 15 September 1937, p. 29.
54. Keene, *Luchando por Franco*, p. 298.
55. 'Pis'ma iz Ispanii', *Galilipoliiskii vestnik*, 51, 18 August 1937, pp. 9–10.
56. Academic Library of the State Archive of the Russian Federation (NB GARF). Iu.F. Semenov, 'Mirovaia Revoliutsiia', *Signal. Organ Russkogo natsional'nogo soiuza uchastnikov voiny*, 1, 20 February 1937, p. 2.
57. Al. Am., 'In Spain. Towards Bilbao', *Kartlossi. Organe du nationalisme intégral géorgien*, 2–3 (1937), p. 18 [in Georgian].
58. 'Zverstva ispanskikh fashistov', *Pravda*, 13 September 1936, p. 2; 'Belyi terror v Ispanii', *Pravda*, 21 July 1939, p. 2.
59. 'Naglyi vyzov fashistov vsemu rabochemu klassu', *Pravda*, 6 August 1936, p. 1.
60. Ragozin, 'Ruka Provideniia', pp. 35, 44.
61. HIA/Shinkarenko, Box 4. Chapter II. 'Pulia v golovu', pp. 23–4.
62. See his service record, Archivo General Militar, Segovia (AGMS), 2262.
63. HIA/Shinkarenko, Box 4, Chapter IV. 'General Franco i naznachenie v Legion', pp. 50–2; Keene, *Luchando por Franco*, pp. 304–05; Alonso Ibarra, 'Guerra Civil española', pp. 289–90; V.V. Markovchin, 'Na sluzhbe Ispanii: missiia generala Shinkarenko', in *Izvestiia Iugo-Zapadnogo gosudarstvennogo universiteta. Seriia 'Istoriia i pravo'*, 22 (2017), pp. 135–44.
64. CRAI Biblioteca del Pavilló de la República (Universitat de Barcelona). Collection of Jose Luis Infiesta Perez FP (Infiesta) 3/2, J.L. De Mesa Gutierrez, *Los Rusos blancos en la guerra 1936-1939*, p. 8.
65. Iaremchuk II, *Russkie dobrovol'tsy v Ispanii*, pp. 43–4; C.D. Eby, *Comrades and Commissars: The Lincoln Battalion in the Spanish Civil War*. University Park, PA, 2007, pp. 212–16.
66. 'Iz pisem iz Ispanii', *Galipoliiskii vestnik*, 60, 1 June 1938, p. 29.
67. N.N. Platoshkin, *Grazhdanskaia voina v Ispanii, 1936–1939*. Moscow, 2005, p. 358; A.H. Landis, *The Abraham Lincoln Brigade*. New York, 1967, pp. 276, 279.
68. P.N. Carroll, *The Odyssey of the Abraham Lincoln Brigade: Americans in the Spanish Civil War*. Stanford, CA, 1994, pp. 155–6; R. Baxell, *Unlikely Warriors: The British in the Spanish Civil War and the Struggle Against Fascism*. London, 2012, p. 268; C. Nelson and J. Hendricks (eds), *Madrid, 1937: Letters of the Abraham Lincoln Brigade from the Spanish Civil War*. New York, 1996, p. 204.
69. The collective cross of the Order of St. Ferdinand (*Cruz Laureada de San Fernando*) was awarded to the *tercio*'s 2nd Company as a subunit. *Diario Oficial del Ministerio del Ejército*, 261, 20 November 1941, p. 586; HIA/Shinkarenko, Box 3, Chapter XVI. 'Iz Frantsii v Ispaniiu. V dva razdel'nykh priema'. Two additional pages with no numbers; 'Pamiati russkikh v Ispanii', *Gallipoliiskii vestnik*, 88, 1 October 1940, p. 19.
70. P. Kemp, *Mine Were of Trouble*. London, 1957, p. 43.
71. Koreiskii, 'S Vostoka na Zapad. Iz istorii RNNA', pp. 20–1.
72. UNC-CH/Savine. V. Abdank-Kossovskii, 'Russkie emigranty v riadakh ispanskoi osvoboditel'noi armii. (K 20-I godovshchine zaversheniia grazhdanskoi voiny)', *Vozrozhdenie: literaturno-politicheskie tetradi* 90 (June 1959), p. 101.
73. In April 1939 the Gallipoli Union in Prague sent a congratulatory letter to General Franco. See the reply from Franco's headquarters of 9 May 1939. GARF, fond R-5759, opis' 1, delo 65, listy 138–139.

74. Columbia University, Rare Book and Manuscript Library. Bakhmeteff Archive. Anton Antonovich Kersnovskii Papers (BAR Ms Coll/Kersnovskii), Box 1. Letter to parents, 827, 5 April 1939. K.M. Aleksandrov was kind enough to point out this source.
75. Medal no. 1 was awarded to Franco during a meeting in October. 'Russkie dobrovol'tsy v Ispanii', *Novoe slovo*, 19, 7 May 1939, p. 3.
76. Iaremchuk II, *Russkie dobrovol'tsy v Ispanii*, pp. 177–8.
77. Archivo General Militar, Ávila (AGMAV) 6205/119. As for Boltin's efforts on behalf of his comrades, which continued until 1940, see the detailed correspondence in AGMAV 24017/2.
78. For exact figures, see Alonso Ibarra, *Guerra civil española*, p. 272.
79. Semenov, *Russkaia emigratsiia*, p. 103; Othen, *Brigadas Internacionales*, p. 175.
80. Testimony of Vladimir Dvoichenko. See J. De Urbino, 'Rusos blancos en San Sebastián', *Unidad*, 30 June 1941, p. 3.
81. N. Boltin, *Memoria*. Madrid, 19 April 1940. AGMAV, 24017/2. In another source Boltin maintained that there were ninety-six volunteers. J.L. De Mesa Gutiérrez, *Los rusos blancos en la Guerra, 1936–1939*, p. 11.
82. Many French, Canadian and American volunteers were actually émigrés from Eastern Europe or the children of refugees or migrants. Thus, Russians did not constitute an important part of the International Brigades. R. Skoutelsky, *Novedad en el frente. Las brigadas internacionales en la guerra civil*. Madrid, 2006, pp. 168–173. As for the ethnic makeup of the Russian volunteers who fought for the Republic, see K.K. Semenov, 'Pervyi opyt antifashistskoi bor'by – beloemigranty v armii Ispanskoi respubliki', in K.K. Semenov and M.I. Sorokina (eds), *Rossiiskaia emigratsiia v bor'be s fashizmom. Mezhdunarodnaia nauchnaia konferentsiia*. Moscow, 2015, pp. 59–60.
83. Semenov, *Russkaia emigratsiia*, p. 122.
84. GARF, fond R-5853, opis' 1, delo 67, listy 380–382. Shinkarenko to Lampe, 12 May 1939.
85. 'Ispanskii uzel', *Golos Rossii. Ezhenedel'naia obshchestvenno-natsional'naia gazeta*, 30, 19 January 1937, p. 1.
86. R. Stradling, *The Irish and the Spanish Civil War, 1936–1939: Crusades in Conflict*. Manchester, 1999; J.S. Moen and R. Sæther, *Tusen Dager: Norge og den Spanske Borgerkrigen, 1936–1939*. Oslo, 2009; P. Glazer, *Radical Nostalgia: Spanish Civil War Commemoration in America*. Rochester, New York, 2010; M. Møller, *De Glemtes Hær: Danske Frivillige i den Spanske Borgerkrig*. Copenhagen, 2017; M. Merriman and W. Lerude, *American Commander in Spain: Robert Hale Merriman and the Abraham Lincoln Brigade*. Reno, 2020.
87. P. Robinson, *The White Russian Army*, p. 225.
88. 'Rastlenie russkoi dushi', *Signal. Organ Russkogo natsional'nogo soiuza uchastnikov voiny*, 3, 20 March 1937, p. 1.
89. Cavalry Captain Vladimir Filippovich Bazilevich, a St. George's Cross recipient, one of the participants of the 'Ice March' and a veteran of Gallipoli, was unable to find himself in exile. At one time he thought of joining the French Foreign Legion, but finally ended up performing odd jobs in Paris. He renounced his former views and became a 'returnee' (a person willing to repatriate to the USSR), then went to fight for the Spanish Republic. He distinguished himself in the fighting and received Soviet citizenship, but did not have time to take advantage of it – he perished in 1937. L. Khurges, *Moscow-Spain-Kolyma: Iz zhizni radista i zeka*. Moscow, 2012, pp. 215–18.
90. J.C. Jiménez, *Memorias de un combatiente de la Brigada Internacional*. Granada, 1938; P. Sawicki, *La narrativa española de la Guerra Civil (1936–1975). Propaganda, testimonio y memoria creative*. Alicante, 2010, p. 77.

91. Tringam's fellow officer, upon seeing his photograph in *Chasovoi*, took heart and wrote an article which ended with the words: 'Let us not bow down to him, for he does not expect that, but to the bright banner that burns in his heart'. 'Fotograficheskaia kartochka', *Gallipoliiskii vestnik*, 74, 1 August 1939, p. 33.
92. Stanford University. Hoover Institution Archives. Ob'edinenie Chinov Kornilovskogo Udarnogo Polka Records. Copy on a microfilm (HIA/OCKUdP), Box 1, Folder 1. Colonel Kondrat'ev to Staff Captain Iaremchuk, 24 April 1938.
93. LNB. 'Parizhskie ogni (ot nashego parizhskogo korrespondenta)', *Dlia vas. Ezhenedel'nyi illiustrirovannyi zhurnal (Riga)*, 25 (18 June 1939), pp. 5, 12.
94. LNB. 'Parizhskie ogni (ot nashego parizhskogo korrespondenta)', *Dlia vas. Ezhenedel'nyi illiustrirovannyi zhurnal (Riga)*, 27 (2 July 1939), p. 12.
95. The Solzhenitsyn Russian Home Archives Abroad (hereafter ADRZ), fond 55, opis' 1, delo 17, list 11. Circular letter for I Department of ROVS, No. 1361/7, 29 March 1940.
96. GARF, fond R-5759, opis' 1, delo 76, list 101. Nazarov to Dobrokhotov, 27 February 1944.
97. The right hand is placed horizontally to the heart, with the palm facing down. 'Istoriia Rossiiskogo imperskogo soiuza-ordena: 1929–2009', *Impertsy. 80 let RIS-O. 1929–2009*. No publisher, pp. 16–17.
98. N. Dzhavakhishvili, 'Grazhdanskaia voina v Ispanii i gruzinskaia emigatsiia (1936–1939)', *Literaturnaia Gruziia*, 1–6 (2007), pp. 163–73.
99. Stanford University. Hoover Institution Archives. Globus Publishers Records (HIA/Globus), Box 7. Staff Captain Iaremchuk II, 'Poslednie tuchi rasseiannoi buri (lichnye vospominaniia dobrovol'tsa Ispanskoi voiny)', p. 17.
100. J. Sanz y Díaz, *Por las rochas del Tajo. Visión y andanzas de guerra*. Valladolid, 1938, p. 102.

'Sandcastles': Russian Émigrés and Operation Barbarossa

1. O. Beyda and I. Petrov, 'Stakeholders, Hangers-On and Copycats. The Russian Right in Berlin in 1933', *Illiberalism Studies Program Working Papers*, 6 (April 2021); M. Kellogg, *The Russian Roots of Nazism: White Emigres and the Making of National Socialism, 1917–1945*. Cambridge, 2005.
2. I. Petrov, "Vse samochintsy proizvola...": podlinnaia biografiia Sergeia Taboritskogo', *Neprikosnovennyi zapas. Debaty o politike i kul'ture*, 122 (2018), pp. 162–89.
3. K. Brüggemann, 'Max Erwin von Scheubner-Richter (1884–1923) – der "Führer des Führers"?' in M. Garleff (ed.), *Deutschbalten. Weimarer Republik und Drittes Reich.* Vol. 1, Cologne 2008, p. 129; T. Weber, *De Adolf a Hitler. La construcción de un nazi.* Madrid, 2018, pp. 328–33.
4. Robinson, *The White Russian Army*, p. 219.
5. B.A. Khol'mston-Smyslovskii, *Izbrannye stat'i i rechi*. Buenos Aires, 1953, p. 6.
6. F.L. Sinitsyn, 'Sovetsko-germanskoe ideologicheskoe protivoborstvo na okkupirovannoi territorii SSSR: natsional'nye i religioznye aspekty'. Doctoral dissertation, Institute of Russian History, RAN, 2017, p. 107.
7. See several mentions of the émigrés in Alfred Rosenberg's diary: I. Petrova (ed.), *Politicheskii Dnevnik Al' freda Rozenberga, 1934–1944 gg.* Moscow, 2015.
8. For a contemporary overview, see C. Hartmann, *Operation Barbarossa: Nazi Germany's War in the East, 1941–1945*. Oxford, 2018; X.M. Núñez Seixas, *El frente del Este: Historia y memoria de la guerra germano-soviética (1941–1945)*, Madrid, 2018.
9. 'Eintragung im Kriegstagebuch des Wehrmachtführungsstabes im OKW über die Ziele und Methoden des in der Sowjetunion zu errichtenden faschistischen

Okkupationsregimes, 3. Marz, 1941', in E. Moritz (ed.), *Fall Barbarossa: Dokumente zur Vorbereitung der faschisten Wehrmacht auf die Aggression gegen die Sowjetunion (1940/41)*. Berlin, 1970, pp. 285–7.
10. At the end of October 1938, under pressure from the Germans and following lengthy consultations and discussions, the ROVS's II (German) section, was transformed into the 'independent' Association of Russian Military Unions (ORVS).
11. GARF, fond R-5796, opis' 1, delo 3, list 142.
12. M. Shkarovskii, *Die Kirchenpolitik des Dritten Reiches gegenüber den orthodoxen Kirchen in Osteuropa (1939–1945)*. Münster, 2004, p. 117; M.V. Shkarovskii, *Natsistskaia Germaniia i Pravoslavnaia tserkov': natsistskaia politika v otnoshenii Pravoslavnoi tserkvi i tserkovnoe vozrozhdenie na okkupirovannoi territorii SSSR*. Moscow, 2002, p. 248.
13. A. Dallin, *Deutsche Herrschaft in Russland, 1941–1945. Eine Studie uber Besatzungspolitik*. Dusseldorf, 1958, p. 123; Núñez Seixas, *El frente del Este*, pp. 87–9.
14. J. Baur, *Die russische Kolonie in München, 1900–1945: Deutsch-russische Beziehungen im 20. Jahrhundert*. Wiesbaden, 1998, p. 295; O. Beyda, 'Re-Fighting the Civil War: Second Lieutenant Mikhail Aleksandrovich Gubanov', *Jahrbücher für Geschichte Osteuropas*, 66:2 (2018), pp. 254–6.

'German Prohibitions, Spanish Needs': Émigrés in the Blue Division

1. On the formation of the Blue Division and the vicissitudes of fate of its participants, see: X. Moreno Julià, *La División Azul: sangre española en Rusia, 1941–1945*. Barcelona, 2004; X.M. Núñez Seixas, *Camarada invierno. Experiencia y memoria de la División Azul (1941–1945)*. Barcelona, 2016; idem, *The Spanish Blue Division on the Eastern Front, 1941–1945. War, Occupation, Memory*. Toronto, 2022.
2. O.I. Beyda, *Frantsuzskii legion na sluzhbe Gitleru, 1941–1944 gg*. Moscow, 2013, pp. 273–95.
3. On the role of Russian émigrés in several of the foreign legions, see: D. Alegre Lorenz, *Experiencia de guerra y colaboracionismo político-militar: Bélgica, Francia y España bajo el Nuevo Orden (1941–1945)*. PhD Thesis, Autonomous University of Barcelona, 2017, pp. 45–6, 58, 110, 228.
4. *Akten zur Deutschen Auswärtigen Politik, 1918–1945*. Serie D: 1937–1941, Vol. XIII. 1. *Die Kriegsjahre. Sechster Band, Erster Halbband. 23 June bis 14 September 1941*. Göttingen, 1970, p. 69; Politisches Archiv des Auswärtigen Amtes, Berlin (PAAA). Sammlung der Berichte, Madrid 553/3, Folder 761, report by Heberlein. 'Russische Freiwillige'. Madrid, 22 July 1941.
5. HIA/Globus, Box 1. A. Gabrieli [A.P. Iaremchuk II], *S ital'ianskoi armiei v Rossii. Moia posledniaia (chetvertaia) voina*, pp. 83–4.
6. AGMAV 2005/3/2/18; 2005/3/2/2/21. Letters from N. Boltin. Madrid, 28 June 1941 and 3 July 1941.
7. 'España, en pie contra el comunismo', *ABC*, 29 June 1941, p. 3; J. Miquelarena, 'Los rusos blancos van a llegar cuando esté barrida "esa basura"', *ABC*, 3 July 1941, p. 5.
8. USC Shoah Foundantion Institute. Testimony of Demetrius Dvoichenko-Markov (b. 1921), VHA interview code 12666, 21 March 1996, Washington DC. Interviewer: Esther Finder. 34:12–34:54.
9. 'Carta abierta a Jaime de Urbino', *Unidad*, 3 July 1941, p. 3.
10. AGMAV 2005/3/2/33. Letter of M. Ali Gurski. Madrid, 23 June 1941. His request, which was supported by General Aranda, was finally granted (Moreno Julià, *La División Azul*, p. 454, n. 132).

11. HIA/Shinkarenko, Box 6. Chapter XII. 'V Ispanii. O godakh voiny, v kotoroi ia ne uchastvoval. I besplodnye popytki, kotorye ia delal, chtoby priniat' v nei uchastie', pp. 171–2.
12. AGMAV 2005/3/2/3. 'Relación de los voluntarios rusos con expresión de sus empleos y antecedents', n.d. [July 1941]; Moreno Julià, *La División Azul*, pp. 97–8, 454, n. 133; Iaremchuk II, *Russkie dobrovol'tsy v Ispanii*, pp. 365–9, 372. There are a few photographs in G. Morales and L.E. Togores, *La División Azul: las fotografías de una historia*. Madrid, 2009, pp. 45–9.
13. A. Gabrieli [A.P. Iaremchuk II], *S ital'ianskoi armiei v Rossii*, pp. 83–4; O. Beyda, '"Rediscovering Homeland": Russian Interpreters in the Wehrmacht, 1941–1944', in A. Laugesen and R. Gehrmann (eds), *Communication, Interpreting and Language in Wartime: Historical and Contemporary Perspectives*. Cham, 2020, pp. 131–52.
14. PAAA, R105187, Bl. 205030. Auslandsbriefprüfstelle Wien to OKW Ausl. VIII— Intercepted mail. Major General Zhdanov to D.A. Marchenko, 16 September 1941.
15. GARF, fond R-5759, opis' 1, delo 55, list 48. Zinkevich to Dobrokhotov, 15 September 1941.
16. Bundesarchiv – Militararchiv Freiburg (BArch Freiburg), RW 4/331, Bl. 169–174. 'Rede bei Zusammenkunft weissrussischer Emigranten', 25 May 1943.
17. V.I. Goldin, *Rokovoi vybor: Russkoe voennoe zarubezh'e v gody Vtoroi mirovoi voiny*. Arkhangel'sk/Murmansk, 2005, p. 427.
18. The teenager Konstantin A. Iniushin (1926–?), who was probably left without his parents, served in Spanish units and enjoyed the protection of one lieutenant, who took him back to Spain. In May 1944 he joined the ranks of the Spanish Foreign Legion, studied to be a mechanic and tractor driver and, following demobilization, worked in Laracha (Northern Morocco) performing agronomic work. F.J. Tortosa Anton, 'El "legía" que surgió del frío', *La Legión*, 540 (2017), pp. 38–9.
19. Central State Archive of St. Petersburg (TsGA SPB), fond 9788, opis' 1, delo 31, list 21. Sicherheitspolizei und SD, Aussenstelle Puschkin. 'Vermerk', 7 November 1942.
20. V.J. Hall, *'For a Better Spain and a Fairer Europe': A Re-Examination of the Spanish Blue Division in Its Social, Cultural and Political Context, 1941–2005*. Thesis for the Degree of M. Litt. National University of Ireland, Maynooth, 2005, pp. 64–6.
21. G.P. Lamsdorf, 'My, russkie natsionalisty, khoteli ispol'zovat' nemtsev', *Nasha strana*, 2771, 14 May 2005, p. 3.
22. A Finn by birth, young Walter (Ivan?) Iamsia left with his parents for the USSR and resided in the Leningrad region in the village of Koshelevo. In 1938 his father fell victim to the Great Terror and was shot. In 1941 his younger brother was killed in a bombing raid. Iamsia went over to the enemy and remained with the Spanish mess hall in Pushkin. He knew the language and became an assistant to a lieutenant who took him back to Spain. He was living in Ciudad Real in the spring of 1944. His subsequent fate is unknown. See 'Un muchacho ruso en Ciudad', *Lanza. Diario grafico de la tarde*, 22 April 1944, p. 3. Moreover, young Boris was taken to Santiago de Compostela by an artillery lieutenant, where he was adopted in 1944 by an artisan and given a new name. See 'Mañana será bautizado un niño ruso', *El Compostelano*, 7 June 1944.

'The Young Lady is **Mucho** *Beautiful!': Spaniards on the Russians, Russians on the Spaniards*

1. Núñez Seixas, *The Spanish Blue Division*, pp. 226–38; J. Guzmán Mora, *Visiones de Rusia en la narrativa española. El caso de la División Azul*. PhD Thesis, Universidad de Salamanca, 2016.

2. The instructions on the immediate execution of political commissars upon their capture was in effect until May 1942. F. Römer, *Der Kommissarbefehl. Wehrmacht und NS-Verbrechen an der Ostfront 1941/42*. Paderborn, 2008.
3. For a comparison with the occupation practices carried out by the Italians in Ukraine and along the Don, see: X.M. Núñez Seixas, 'Unable to hate? Some comparative remarks on the war experience of Spanish and Italian soldiers on the Eastern front, 1941–44', *Journal of Modern European History*, 16:2 (2018), pp. 269–89.
4. T.P. Filippova and N.G. Lisevich, '"V grudi moei chto-to szhalos", i s etoi tiazhest'iu ia i zhil vsiu voinu'. Iz vospominanii uchenogo-entomologa K.F. Sedykh', *Vestnik arkhivista*, 1 (2015), p. 235; '"Tochnymi dannymi o poteriakh 250-i ispanskoi divizii my ne raspolagaem". Spravka Glavnogo razvedyvatel'nogo upravleniia General'nogo shtaba Vooruzhennykh sil SSSR ob uchastii ispanskikh voennykh formirovanii vo Vtoroi mirovoi voine. 1946 g', *Istoricheskii arkhiv*, 2 (2015), p. 76.
5. X.M. Núñez Seixas, 'Good Invaders? The Occupation Policy of the Spanish Blue Division in Northwestern Russia, 1941–1944', *War in History*, 25:3 (2018), pp. 361–86.
6. B.N. Kovalev, 'Akty ChGK (Chrezvychainoi gosudarstvennoi komissii) o prestupleniiiakh Goluboi divizii pod Novgorodom (1941–1942 gg.)', *Vestnik Novgorodskogo gosudarstvennogo universiteta*, no. 73, vol. 1, 2013, pp. 88–92.
7. Núñez Seixas, *The Spanish Blue Division*, pp. 183–6; V.N. Kovalev, *Dobrovol'tsy na chuzhoi voine. Ocherki istorii Goluboi divizii*. Velikii Novgorod, 2014, pp. 330–4.
8. V.M. Tsypin, *Gorod Pushkin v gody voiny*. St. Petersburg, 2010, pp. 78, 84, 255, 271.
9. B.N. Kovalev, *Pribaltiiskii sled na Severo-Zapade Rossii, 1941–1944 gg.: prestupleniia voennykh i paramilitarnykh formirovanii: nauchnyi doklad*. St. Petersburg, 2020, pp. 32–3.
10. Museum of Russian Culture, San Francisco, California. The Manuscript Collection, Box 2, Folder 4. Untitled memoirs of E.V. Bogacheva-Baskakova, 1970, p. 17 (30).
11. Ibid., p. 22 (35).
12. Ibid., p. 24 (37).
13. M. Shkarovskii, *Tserkov' zovet k zashchite Rodiny: religioznaia zhizn' Leningrada i Severo-Zapada v gody Velikoi Otechestvennoi voiny*. St. Petersburg, 2005, pp. 159, 344, 564.
14. D.S. Likhachev, *Vospominaniia*. St. Petersburg, 1995, p. 311.
15. Naturally, it was easier for Petrov to recall and overemphasize precisely the role of the Spaniards, and not the fact that he spent about the same amount of time with a German unit, convincing the Germans of his loyalty and was valued by them as a useful translator, all about which he preferred not to go into detail following the war. TsGA SPB, fond 9788, opis' 1, delo 31, list 21. Sicherheitspolizei und SD, Aussenstelle Puschkin, 'Daniel Petrow', 7 November 1942.
16. V. Rudinskii, 'Ispantsy Goluboi Divizii', *Nasha Strana*, 2827, 8 September 2007, p. 5; V. Rudinskii, 'Kapli pravdy v more lzhi', *Nasha Strana*, 2887, 6 March 2010, p. 7; N. Kazantsev, 'Patriarkh russkoi zarubezhnoi publitsistiki', *Nasha Strana*, 2921, 6 August 2011, p. 1.

'Bygone Natures': *Russians on Russians and About Themselves*

1. A.V. Elpat'evskii, *Golubaia diviziia: voennoplennye i internirovannye ispantsy v SSSR*. Moscow, 2015, pp. 109–19; V. Chicheriukin-Meingardt, *Po sledam drozdovtsev . . .* Moscow, 2016, pp. 134–5; B.N. Kovalev, *Ispanskaia diviziia: soiuznik Tret'ego reikha. 1941–1945 gg.* St. Petersburg, 2020, pp. 336–53.

2. D. Ridruejo (X. M. Núñez Seixas, ed.), *Los Cuadernos de Rusia: diario 1941–1943*. Madrid, 2013, pp. 189–90 (entry of 30 September 1941).
3. M. Torra Puigdellivol, *Ideals i desenganys. Cartes des de Rússia a un germà (1941–1942)*. Barcelona, 2013, pp. 67, 83–4.
4. P.N. Luknitskii, *Leningrad deistvuet: frontovoi dnevnik*, book 3. Moscow, 1968, pp. 488–90.
5. L. Fabritsius, *Sem'ia Belago. Roman*. Toronto, 1984, pp. 7–11.
6. B. Filippov, *Izbrannoe*. London, 1984, pp. 151–3, 155–7.
7. E. Errando Vilar, *Campaña de Invierno*. Madrid, 1943, p. 144.
8. "Svershilos". Prishli nemtsy!', in O.V. Budnitskii (ed.), *Ideinyi kollaboratsionizm v SSSR v period Velikoi Otechestvennoi voiny*. Moscow, 2012, pp. 138–9, 146–8, 156; N. Lomagin (ed.), *Neizvestnaia blokada. Dokumenty, prilozheniia*, vol. 2. St. Petersburg, 2004, pp. 464–70.
9. I. Bratyshenko, 'Ispantsy, nemtsy, balalaika: iz vospominanii', *Chelo: al'manakh*, 18:2 (2000), p. 83.
10. V.S. Rudinskii, 'S ispantsami na Leningradskom fronte', *Pod belym krestom*, 3 (September 1952), p. 13.
11. AGMAV 5347/4; Central Armed Forces Museum. Archival Fund (TsMVS RF-DF). 4/47. 762/2. A. Tringam, 'Sluzhba moia v Goluboi divizii', pp. 1–4.
12. B.N. Kovalev, 'Russkie emigraty i ispanskaia Golubaia diviziia na Vostochnom fronte: ot pervoi do vtoroi voiny', in P. N. Bazanov et al. (eds), *Zarubezhnaia Rossiia XX vek: Slepukhinskie chteniia–2016. Trudy Mezhdunarodnoi nauchnoi konferentsii*. St. Petersburg, 2018, p. 296; B. Kovalev, 'Na sluzhbe Franko. Kollaboratsionisty v "Goluboi divizii"', *Rodina*, 4 (2013), p. 109. On Nikolai Krivosheia, see his file in AGMAV 4569/15.
13. S. Pardo Martínez, *Un año en la División Azul*. Valladolid, 2005, p. 133; L.A. Palacio Pilacés, *Tal vez el día. Aragoneses en la URSS (1937–1977), el exilio y la División Azul*. Vol 1. Zaragosa, 2013, p. 552.
14. Georgii Gustavovich (Eduardovich) Shebeko (1894–1942) was born in St. Petersburg. In July 1914 he graduated from the Nikolaevskoe Cavalry School as a cadet and was sent as a cornet to the 2nd Life Guards Pavlograd Hussar Regiment. He fought in the First World War and suffered a concussion in the fighting and was decorated several times and became a cavalry staff captain. He took part in the Russian Civil War (perhaps with Bermondt-Avalov in the Count Keller Hussar Regiment). He lived as an émigré in Germany. In 1924 Shebeko joined the Spanish Legion in Morocco, and six years later was granted Spanish citizenship. He also married a Spanish woman. Shebeko took part in the Spanish Civil War and was wounded and decorated. From July 1941 he was a lieutenant in the 1st Company of the Blue Division's mobile reserve battalion. He was killed in March 1942 during the fighting for the village of Zemtitsy, where units of the 2nd Shock Army surrounded the Germans in the village and the Spanish rushed to their aid. He was buried in Grigorovo and later reinterred in the Spanish sector of the German military cemetery in the village of Pankovka, near Velikii Novgorod. He was posthumously awarded the Iron Cross, Second Class.
15. A. Gabrieli [A.P. Iaremchuk II], *S ital'ianskoi armiei v Rossii*, p. 118.
16. UNC-CH/Savin. *Gallipoli. Iubileinyi al'manakh-pamiatka, izdannyi k 35-letiiu prebyvaniia v Gallipoli Russkoi armii, 1920–1955*. Hollywood, 1955.
17. Stanford University. Hoover Institution Archives. N.A. Tsurikov Papers, Box 3. 'S chest'iu pavshie v Ispanii'. *Gallipoli, 1920–1950 gg. K tridtsatiletiiu vysadki 1-go Armeiskogo korpusa v Gallipoli*, p. 14.

18. UNC-CH/Savine. 'K tridtsatipiatiletiiu ostavleniia Kryma', *Informatsiia Glavnogo pravleniia Obshchestva gallipoliitsev* 14, 30 November 1955, p. 17; *Informatsiia otdela Obshchestva gallipoliitsev vo Frantsii*, 7, December 1958, p. 1.
19. A. Inglis, *Australians in the Spanish Civil War*. Sydney, Boston, 1987; H. Wehenkel *D'Spueniekämpfer: Volontaires de la Guerrre d'Espagne partis du Luxembourg*. Dudelange, 1997; M. Derby, *Kiwi Compañeros: New Zealand and the Spanish Civil War*. Christchurch, 2009.
20. S. García de Pruneda, *La soledad de Alcuneza. Historia de espuela y de espada*. Madrid, 1961.
21. Polkovniik D.S. Frank, 'Deti – Belye voiny', *Nashi vesti*, 380 (July–September 1980), p. 10; K.K. Semenov, 'Vernut'sia domoi!? Beloemigranty v riadakh ispanskoi divizii na Vostochnom fronte', in Iu.A. Nikiforov and D.V. Surzhik (eds), *K 74-letiiu nachala Velikoi Otechestvennoi voiny. Na grani katastrofy. Mezhdunarodnaia konferentsiia (Moskva, Tsentral'nyi muzei Velikoi Otechestvennoi voiny 1941–1945 gg., 22–23 iiunia 2016 g)*. Vol. 2. Briansk, 2017, p. 47; 'Nezabytye mogily', *Chasovoi*, 614 (September–October 1978), p. 19; K.K. Semenov, 'Russkaia sektsiia Ispanskogo radio kak instrument antisovetskoi bor'by', *Elektronnyi nauchno-obrazovatel'nyi zhurnal 'Istoriia'*, 8: 10 (2017), available at: https://history.jes.su/s207987840001993-1-1 (site consulted on 19 November 2021).
22. His chief novel, *Man at War*, was supposed to come out in the spring of 1940, but the world war changed these plans, and the manuscript, which was kept with a female émigré in Berlin, was destroyed in an air raid. In the 1960s Shinkarenko published at his own expense the novel *Yesterday* in Madrid. Readers may evaluate his work for themselves: N. Belogorskii, *Marsova maska: roman*. Moscow, 2014.
23. HIA/Shinkarenko, Box 3. Chapter XVI. 'Iz Frantsii v Ispaniiu. V dva razdel'nykh priema', p. 248.
24. Abdank-Kossovskii, 'Russkie emigranty', pp. 99, 101.
25. 'XXV-letie russkogo dobrovol'cheskogo otriada v Ispanii', *Chasovoi*, 432 (May 1962), p. 25.
26. TsMVS RF-DF. 4/47. 762/1. A. Tringam, 'Kratkaia istoriia uchastiia russkikh emigrantov v grazhdanskoi voine v Ispanii za beluiu ideiu', pp. 6–7.
27. 'Alas, in today's Spain they are trying to forget the heroism of General Franco's soldiers and the executioners of the 1930s enjoy complete freedom of action to demoralize the country, which was for many years an oasis of Christian civilization and order in a Europe in turmoil'. Review of Marc Augier's (*Saint Loup*) book about the Blue Division, *Chasovoi*, 616 (January 1979), p. 21.
28. UNC-CH/Savine. 'Al'kazar'. A.A. von Lampe (ed.), *Puti vernykh*. Paris, 1960, p. 204.
29. Russian State Library (RGB). N. Kremnev, 'Madridskii voennyi muzei', *Suvorovets*, 21 (31 May 1952), p. 3.
30. UNC-CH/Savine. N.N. Protopopov, 'Belaia armiia za rubezhom', *Kadetskaia pereklichka*, 37 (December 1984), p. 123; V. Granitov's address. *Kadetskaia pereklichka*, 66-67 (November 1999), pp. 208–09.

'The Riddle of a Life': Vladimir Ivanovich Kovalevskii

1. AGMS. Trasf. 82, 113. Letter from V. Kovalevskii to the Provincial Head Office of the Militia, San Sebastián. 15 January 1944.
2. As maintained by C. Garay and J.L. Orella, without citing sources. See idem and idem, 'Poddannye traditsii. "Belye russkie" v ispanskoi "Rekete" i drugikh voinskikh chastiakh natsionalistov v 1936–1939 gg', in O.V. Aurov (ed.), *Russkii sbornik: SSSR*

i grazhdanskaia voina v Ispanii 1936–1939 gg. Moscow, 2016, p. 364. However, his name is not found in a list of nearly seventy White Russian officers who came to Paraguay between 1924 and the beginning of the 1930s and took part in the Chaco War (Gramatchicoff, *Aporte de los inmigrantes rusos*).
3. Iaremchuk II, *Russkie dobrovol'tsy v Ispanii*, p. 172.
4. Columbia University. Rare Book and Manuscript Library, Bakhmeteff Archive, Evgenii Eduardovich Messner Papers, Folder 'Memoirs 'Moi vospominaniia – Na chuzhbine', VI. E.E. Messner, 'Glava T – V Evrope'. Additional page VI–259.
5. TsMVS RF-DF. 4/47. 762/1. A. Tringam, 'Kratkaia istoriia', p. 1.
6. AGMS. Frasf. 82, 113. Sworn statement by V. Kovalevskii. 18 January 1944; E. Herrera Alonso, *Los mil días del Tercio Navarra: biografíoa de un tercio de requetés*. Madrid, 1974, pp. 251–2.
7. Grenader [N.N. Boltin], 'Pis'ma iz Ispanii', *Chasovoi*, 234 (1 May 1939), p. 4.
8. TsMVS RF-DF. 4/47. 763/1. V.I. Kovalevskii, 'Kak dralas' "Navarra"'. Opisanie boia 7–8 ianvaria 1939 g. Sektor Monterubio – Ekstremadura', pp. 3–4, 6.
9. Iaremchuk II, *Russkie dobrovol'tsy v Ispanii*, p. 368; V.V. Markovchin, 'Russkie ispantsy: vek XX', *Izvestiia Iugo-Zapadnogo gosudarstvennogo universiteta. Seria 'Istoriia i pravo'*, no. 2 (23), vol. 7, 2017, pp. 120–1; K.K. Semenov, *Russkaia emigratsiia i grazhdanskaia voina v Ispanii 1936–1939 gg.*, p. 146; K. Semenov, '"Biali" rosjanie przeciwko czerwonej Hiszpanii. Rosyjska "bialia" emigracja w czasie wojny domowej w Hiszpanii (1936–1939)', *Glaukopis*, no. 32, (2015), p. 24.
10. TsMVS RF-DF. 4/47. 762/1. A. Tringam, 'Kratkaia istoriia', p. 5.
11. *Boletin Oficial del Estado*, 6 October 1939, p. 5.604.
12. Finnish National Archives (Kansallisarkisto). T6572/24. Paamajan/Vapaaehtoistomisto, 1939-1940. Telegram, Madrid to Helsinki, 11 December 1939, 13:30; C.-F. Geust, 'Valkoiset emigrantit ja Stalinin sotilaat', *Sotahistoriallinen aikakauskirja*, 31 (2011), p. 110. The documents were made available thanks to the kind help of Dr Carl-Fredrik Geust.
13. Bibikov, who had lived in France for 15 years and went to college before joining the Francoist side in 1936, settled permanently in Spain after returning from Russia, since that country was 'the sole corner in the old Europe where a man can spiritually rest'. He moved in 1946 to the Galician coastal city of A Coruña, where he worked as an administrative assistant, and wrote about philosophy and arts in Spanish, and even poems. See his interview in *La Noche*, 20 February 1952.
14. 'San Sebastián se manifiesta contra la Rusia soviética', *La Voz de España*, 26 June 1941, p. 1.
15. De Urbino, 'Rusos blancos en San Sebastián'.
16. Local officials and Falange representatives warmly welcomed this small group of wounded and recovering patients. A few days later the wounded were visited by the Falangist leader Dionisio Ridruejo, who had also returned from Russia a few weeks earlier. 'El paso de heridos y repatriados de la División Azul', *Unidad*, 18 May 1942, p. 1; 'Regreso de voluntarios', *La Voz de España*, 19 May 1942, p. 2; 'El regreso de los héroes', *La Voz de España*, 20 May 1942, pp. 1, 5.
17. AGMAV 6237/41, 5537/28, 24017/2. Request by Vladimir Kovalevskii to the Guipúzcoa Militia Provincial Head Office, San Sebastián, 8 February 1944. Registration form in the Blue Division, 20 June 1941; report by Nikolai Boltin, Madrid, 12 February 1942; AGMS, Trasf. 82. 113. Medical Report. San Sebastián. 24 January 1944.
18. It is possible that in San Sebastián, or in the village of Suances in nearby province of Santander, there exists unconfirmed information that in 1962 he was promoted to the rank of captain in the *Requeté* and retired to Bilbao. See J. Barruso and P. Sagarra, *Por*

el Zar y por la Patria. Rusos blancos en la guerra civil española y la II Guerra Mundial, 1935–1945. Madrid, 2019, p. 122.
19. V.[ladimir] K.[ovalevskii], pervoprokhodniik 'rekete', 'Kak dralas' 'Navarra'! (Ocherk iz boevoi istorii Ispanskoi grazhdanskoi voiny)', *Chasovoi*, 471 (September 1965), p. 8. The published text is stylistically distinct from the existing original.
20. E. Crespo, 'Rusos blancos en la Guerra de España', *Historia y vida*, 69 (December 1973), pp. 128–36; UNC-CH/Savin, 'Russkie belye voiny v grazhdanskoi voine', p. 6.

'A Tale of a Manuscript', or There and Back Again

1. HIA/Globus. Box 7. [V.I. Kovalevskii], 'Siniaia diviziia i pokhod v Rossiiu'.
2. Vladimir Nikolaevich Azarenko-Zarovskii was born in 1925 in Yugoslavia, to an émigré family. Having received his education in the Grand Duke Konstantin Konstantinovich First Russian Cadet Corps in Belaia Tserkov', he continued to study at Heidelberg University. During 1944–5 he joined General Andrei Vlasov's army (ROA), which had been gathered from Soviet prisoners of war, collaborators and émigrés. In 1949 he emigrated to the United States, where he died in 1984. Aside from the 'Globus' publishing house, he founded a Russian library in San Francisco. A.A. Khisamutdinov, *Russkoe pechatnoe slovo v Kalifornii*. Vladivostok, 2017, pp. 92–6.
3. TsMVS RF-DF. 4/47. 763/3. Kovalevskii, 'Pokhod na Rossiiu'.
4. TsMVS RF-DF. 4/47. 763/2. Kovalevskii, 'Pokhod na partisan', pp. 21–2.
5. There is a note by Azar with a list of matters and questions in Madrid, in which Iaremchuk is mentioned; one of the points states: 'Manuscript about the Blue Division'. – HIA/Globus, Box 3, a file with pictures and a manuscript page under the title 'V Madride'.

'The Mirror of Trauma': The Russian View of Spanish Warfare

1. K.G. Kromiadi, *'Za zemliu, za voliu!' Vospospominaniia soratniika generala Vlasova*. Moscow, 2011; D.P. Karov, 'Nemetskaia okkupatsiia i sovetskie liudi v zapiskakh russkogo ofitsera Abvera, 1941–1943 gody', in K.M. Aleksandrov (ed.), *Pod nemtsami. Vospominaniia, svidetel'stva, dokumenty. Istoriko-dokumental'nyi sbornik*. St. Petersburg, 2011, pp. 383–429; R.V. Zavadskii (Oleg Beyda, ed.), *Svoia chuzhaia voina. Dnevnik russkogo ofitsera vermakhta 1941–1942 gg*. Moscow, 2014; O.I. Beyda, '"Mesiats v Germanskoi Armii". Iz vospominanii D. Khodneva', in D.A. Zhukov and I.I. Kovtun (eds). *Posobniki. Issledovaniia i materialy po istorii otechestvennogo kollaboratsionizma*. Moscow, 2020, pp. 384–422.
2. E. Scherstjanoi (ed.), *Rotarmisten schreiben aus Deutschland. Briefe von der Front (1945) und historiche Analysen*. Munich, 2004; A. Peri, *The War Within. Diaries from the Siege of Leningrad*. Cambridge, MA/London, 2017; J. Hellbeck (ed.), *Stalingradskaia bitva. Svidetel'stva uchasniikov i ochividtsev: po materialam Komissii po istorii Velikoi Otechestvennoi voiny*. Moscow, 2018.
3. As to the often improvised role of translators during war, see J. Baigorri-Jalón, 'War, languages, and the role(s) of interpreters', in *Les liaisons dangereuses: Langues, traduction, interpretation*. Beirut, 2010, pp. 173–204.
4. G. Corni, *Raccontare la Guerra: la memoria organizzata*. Milan, 2012; J. Echternkamp, 'Mit dem Krieg seinen Frieden schliessen: Wehrmacht und Weltkrieg in der Veteranenkultur (1945–1960)', in T. Kühne (ed.), *Von der Kriegskultur zu der Friedenskultur? Zum Mentalitatswandel in Deutschland seit 1945*. Münster, 2000, pp. 80–95.

5. B. Cabanes and G. Piketty (eds), *Retour à l'intime au sortir de la guerre*. Paris, 2009.
6. 'A true war story is never moral. It does not instruct, nor encourage virtue, nor suggest models of proper human behavior, nor restrain men from doing the things men have always done. If a story seems moral, do not believe it. If at the end of a war story you feel uplifted, or if you feel that some small bit of rectitude has been salvaged from the larger waste, then you have been made the victim of a very old and terrible lie. There is no rectitude whatsoever. There is no virtue. As the first rule of thumb, therefore, you can tell a true war story by its absolute and uncompromising allegiance to obscenity and evil.' M.A. Heberle, *A Trauma Artist: Tim O'Brien and the Fiction of Vietnam*. Iowa City, 2001, p. 37.
7. On this incident, see J. Garcia Hispán, *La Guardia Civil en la División Azul*. Alicante, 1991; J.N. Núñez Calvo, 'La Guardia Civil en la División Española de Voluntarios', *Aportes*, 61 (2006), pp. 86–118.
8. A. Hill, *The War Behind the Eastern Front. The Soviet Partisan Movement in North-West Russia, 1941–1944*. London/New York, 2005, pp. 47–68; S. Meddoks, 'Prestupleniia i nakazanie: karatel'nye otriady v Leningradskoi oblasti, 1941–1944 gg', in O. Budnitskii and L. Novikova (eds), *SSSR vo Vtoroi mirovoi voine. Okkupatsiia. Kholokost. Stalinizm*. Moscow, 2014, pp. 26–48.
9. P. Gavrilov, "Naselenie stanovitsiia ne za nas, a protiv nas': partizany Leningradskoi oblasti, sovetskaia identichnost' i natsistskaia okkupatsiia', *Neprikosnovennyi zapas. Debaty o politike i kul'ture*, 13:3 (2020), pp. 70–95.
10. B. Musial, *Sowjetische Partisanen 1941–1944: Mythos und Wirklichkeit*. Paderborn, 2009, pp. 351–3.
11. On the collaborators' motives, see J. Burds, 'Turncoats, Traitors and Provocateurs: Communist Collaborators, the German Occupation, and Stalin's NKVD, 1941–1943', *East European Politics and Societies and Cultures*, 2017 (published online at: https://doi.org/10.1177/0888325417742486 (site consulted on 19 November 2021).
12. On the concept of the 'spaces of violence', see J. Baberowski, *Räume der Gewalt*. Frankfurt a.M., 2018.
13. B. Kovalev, 'Ispanskaia Golubaia diviziia i evreiskoe naselenie na severo-zapade SSR (1941–1944)', in I. Al'tman and A. Zel'tser (eds), *Voina, Kholokost i istoricheskaia pamiat': materialy XX Mezhdunarodnoi ezhegodnoi konferentsii po iudaike*. Vol. IV. Moscow, 2013, pp. 32–46.
14. N.N. Nikulin, *Vospomininiia o voine*. St. Petersburg, 2008 (2nd ed.), p. 9.
15. J. Keene, 'Un ruso blanco en la División Azul: Memorias de Vladimir Kovalevski', *Labour History: A Journal of Labour and Social History*, 117 (November 2019), pp. 231–2.
16. A. Zakharov, 'Ispanskaia grust', *Neprikosnovennyi zapas. Debaty o politike i kul'ture*, 137 (2021), pp. 274–8; E. Zinov'eva, 'Knizhnyi ostrov', *Neva*, 5 (2021), pp. 233–5; K. Kotel'nikov, 'Russkii v Goluboi divizii', *Diletant*, 24 September 2021 (published online at: https://diletant.media/articles/45327487/ (site consulted on 19.11.2021).
17. 'New Publications Feature Russian and Eurasian Collections At Hoover'. *Hoover Library and Archives News*, Monday, 19 April 2021 (published online at: https://www.hoover.org/news/new-publications-feature-russian-and-eurasian-collections-hoover (site consulted on 19 November 2021).

The 'Blue Division' and the Campaign in Russia

Preface

1. *Ut desint vires, tamen est laudanda voluntas* ('Let there not be enough strength, good will should nevertheless be lauded') – a Latin aphorism presented here as a quotation from Ovid's *Pontian Letters*.
2. The author is speaking here of the Cold War's fronts, that is, about the people living in the USSR.
3. The sick Kovalevskii was sent to the military hospital in Grigorovo on 27 February 1942, and from there to a rear-area hospital in the Cologne area, where he remained until demobilized. He returned to Spain on 17 May 1942.

June 1941. San Sebastián

1. This is inaccurate. The USSR was not the same as the Russian Empire: the latter was not a totalitarian state, while the former did not exist in 1914, when Russia entered the war against Germany.
2. Following its defeat and occupation in April 1941, the territory of Yugoslavia was divided between neighbouring countries. The partition was legally confirmed at a meeting of the German and Italian foreign ministers in Vienna on 21–22 April. The main beneficiaries were Germany and Italy, while Hungary, Bulgaria and Albania were also present. An independent Croatian state was formed, as was the independent state of Montenegro, under the aegis of Italy. Ethnic cleansings and mass murders of Serbs and Jews began to be conducted in some of the newly-formed territories. We were unable to find any information regarding a Soviet protest. J. Tomasevich, *War and Revolution in Yugoslavia, 1941-1945: Occupation and Collaboration*. Stanford, CA, 2001, pp. 61–4.
3. Kovalevskii is not exaggerating, but he is most likely speaking about the attitudes among the Russian diaspora. German analysts, who studied the press of the Russian émigré organizations in 1940, noted that the 'defeatists' and 'defencists' were highly skeptical of the Hitler-Stalin pact and did not believe that it would last for long. Archiv des Instituts fur Zeitgeschichte (IfZ-Archiv), Munich, MA 128/2. Dr Kurt Krupinski, 'Die Emigrantenpresse', end of 1940, p. 7.
4. The fate of the Polish state was decided on 23 August 1939, when the USSR and the Third Reich signed a non-aggression pact. The Soviet Union and Nazi Germany were, *de jure*, not allies; cooperation and trade were conducted *de facto*. E.E. Ericson III, *Feeding the German Eagle: Soviet Economic Aid to Nazi Germany, 1933–1941*. Westport, CO, London, 1999, pp. 69ff.
5. This is an obvious mistake. The invasion by German armies of the USSR took place early on the morning of 22 June 1941, and not 23 June. The German ambassador in Moscow, Count Werner von der Schulenburg, received a telegram from Berlin with the text of the note about the declaration of war against the USSR. It was only two hours after the start of military operations that the note was handed by Schulenburg to Viacheslav Molotov. Personally, Schulenburg was very much against the start of a war with the USSR and had undertaken diplomatic efforts to change the situation. I. Fleischhauer, *Diplomatischer Widerstand gegen 'Unternehmen Barbarossa'. Die Friedensbemühungen der Deutschen Botschaft Moskau, 1939–1941*. Berlin, 1991, pp. 347–9; L.P. Schmidt and K.D. van Weringh, *Friedrich-Werner Graf von der Schulenburg. Diplomat und Widerstandskämpfer*. Moscow, 2012.

6. An obvious mistake. The Wilhelminian empire, or the Second Reich, existed from 1871 to 1918. Nazi Germany, as is known, called itself the Third Reich.
7. Angelo Brunetti (1800–49) was an Italian politician who was known in his time for his speeches in defence of the rights of Jews.
8. Both European public opinion and German officers were alike in imagining that the Wehrmacht would hold a victory parade in Moscow in the autumn. X.M. Núñez Seixas, *El frente del Este: Historia y memoria de la guerra germano-soviética (1941–1945)*. Madrid, 2018, pp. 37–8.
9. On 24 and 25 June demonstrations were held, organized by the Spanish Falange, in the capitals of some provinces and important towns. According to data from German consuls, a significant number of Falangist activists and supporters gathered at some demonstrations, while there were fewer attendees at others. A demonstration took place in San Sebastián on 25 June, during the latter part of the day and, judging from the photographs published in the local press, there were few attendees. X.M. Núñez Seixas, *Camarada invierno. Experiencia y memoria de la División Azul, 1941–1945*. Barcelona, 2016, pp. 60–1; idem, *The Spanish Blue Division on the Eastern Front, 1941–1945: War, Occupation, Memory*, Toronto 2022, p. 37; 'San Sebastián se manifiesta contra la Rusia soviética', *La Voz de España*, 26 June 1941, p. 1.
10. On 25 June instructions on the immediate organization of recruitment were sent out to all the provincial chiefs of the Falange (*Falange Española Tradicionalista y de las JONS*, FET). It was at first recommended to choose volunteers from among the best Falangists, taking into account their military training and moral and political qualities, and to also open the doors to officers possessing the 'Falangist spirit'. They were to be between 20 and 28 years of age, with preference to be given to those with experience in the army and proficiency with weapons; they also had to undergo a medical examination. A correlation of 75 per cent and 25 per cent was established beforehand between veterans and politically reliable volunteers. Regular military were given 48 hours to enroll, while Falangists had until 2 July. If several military candidates were competing for one position, then the best trained were to be picked. At the same time, instructions with a demand to send lists of volunteers were dispatched to the General-Captaincy and units stationed in Morocco. Subsequent orders increased the allowable proportion of sergeants and specialists who could be taken into the army. In those places where there was a shortage of volunteers, their number could be compensated by recruiting regular soldiers.
11. Nikolai Nikolaevich Boltin (1881–1954), the 'dean' of Russian émigrés in Spain. Because of his French mother, he sometimes showed off by signing his name 'Baron Boltin de Courcel'. He graduated from the Corps of Pages in 1901 and was assigned to the Cavalry-Grenadier Life Guards Regiment, although he soon resigned and worked in the agricultural ministry; the reason for such a move is unclear, and in emigration the cavalry grenadiers, for some reason, did not want to associate with him. During the First World War he served in the 2nd Pskov Life Dragoon Regiment as a colonel. From May 1918 he headed an underground officers' organization in Smolensk, and then in Belorussia. He was arrested in April 1919 but escaped and served in the Armed Forces of South Russia from the summer of 1919. He was evacuated from Novorossiisk. He was engaged in commerce while an émigré in France. During the Spanish Civil War he became one of the organizers of the Russian detachment in Franco's army and he served in the *Doña María de Molina tercio* of Carlist volunteers (*requetés*). He was wounded and continued to serve in the 55th Division. After 1939 he received the rank of honorary colonel in the National Militia and was under the protection of the Falangist chief Raimundo Fernández-Cuesta. He was the organizer

of a song-and-dance troup made up of Russian red berets. In 1940–1 he represented the interests of his comrades-in-arms before the Spanish military authorities. He was one of the very few veterans of the civil war who did not fight in the Blue Division, although he took part in talks to form a Russian detachment in the Italian army. He knew how to make an impression, spoke French and Spanish fluently, and was distinguished by slyness. He married a Spanish woman from San Sebastián. He died in Madrid and was buried with military honours. Archivo General Militar de Ávila (AGMAV) 6205/119; 'Polkovnik N. N. Boltin', *Chasovoi*, 348 (11), (December 1954), p. 18. Here and subsequently, in compiling information on Russian émigrés, besides Spanish and Russian documents, the following works are used: S.S. Volkov, *Russkaia voennaia emigratsiia: izdatel'skaia deiatel'nost'*. Moscow, 2008; V.V. Markovchin, 'Russkie ispantsy: vek XX', *Izvestiia Iugo-Zapadnogo gosudarstvennogo univesiteta* 7: 2 (2017), pp. 106–34 (Ser. 'Istoriia i pravo'); K.K. Semenov, *Russkaia emigratsiia i grazhdanskaia voina v Ispanii 1936–1939 gg.* Moscow, 2016, pp. 142–52; A.P. Iaremchuk II, *Russkie dobrovol'tsy v Ispanii, 1936–1939 gg.* Edited by V.N. Azar-Zarovskii. San Francisco, 1983, pp. 365–73.
12. Anton Profof'evich Iaremchuk II recalled: 'General Franco ordered the enrollment of Russian officers at the same rank they held in the Russian army. [. . .] The Spanish leadership summoned us in the morning and informed us that a colonel, the German military attaché with the embassy, wished to see us. A number of people went to see him. He declared, with a look of embarrassment on his face, that there was a Hitler order forbidding White Russians from serving in the ranks of the German army in the war against the USSR. It was as if a bucket of cold water had been poured on our heads . . . An exception was made for a few Russians who had served as officers in the Spanish Legion. It was later determined that the Germans approved of these officers' participation because they were from Little Russia [Ukraine] and the thick-headed Germans imagined that they must be Ukrainians independence fighters and later demanded that they be sent back to Spain, but the commander of the "Blue Division", General Muñoz Grandes, replied that "I have no Russian officers serving with me, only Spanish officers". The Germans were forced to swallow the pill . . . '. Stanford University. HIA. Globus Publishers Records, Box 1. A. Gabrieli [A.P. Iaremchuk II], 'S ital'ianskoi armiei v Rossii. Moia posledniaia (chetvertaia) voina', pp. 83–4.
13. On 30 June 1941 the Germans confirmed general directives on the recruitment of foreigners. The volunteers, while dressed in German uniforms, were to serve in national legions. In creating these units, an ethnic hierarchy, in accordance with racial theory, was strictly observed.
14. The author is speaking of the National Militia as part of the Spanish Falange (FET), in which all of the Francoists' party militias were united from April 1937. The militia was reorganized in July 1940 and put under army command, thus finally ceasing to be the Falangists' autonomous 'storm troopers'. Officers who had the task of the military training of youth were taken into the militia's ranks. The militia was abolished at the end of July 1941. The Franco Guard (*Guardia de Franco*) became its legal successor and was subordinated to the FET. It consisted of veteran Falangists and radicals, as well as some former soldiers.
15. Twenty-eight men set out, not counting Sergei Ponomarev and Igor Perchin. Anton Iaremchuk wrote that thirty-five Russian émigrés enrolled in the division in Madrid, 'nearly the entire male population of our colony'.
16. Aleksandr Vladimirovich Bibikov (1906–77) was born in Vladimir and was a sailor by profession. He left Russia while still a teenager. He served in the French Foreign Legion. He took part in the Spanish Civil War from 15 July 1937 in the ranks of the

Spanish Foreign Legion. He fought at Tereul, on the Ebro, and in Levante, and was wounded twice. He settled in Madrid in 1939 and wrote programmes for the Spanish radio; he later moved to San Sebastián, where he became a provisional sergeant in the headquarters of the National Militia in Guipuzcoa. In July 1941 he joined the Blue Division and served in an anti-tank group and in October he transferred to the 3rd Battalion of the 269th Infantry Regiment. In July 1942 he returned to Spain and lived in San Sebastián. He moved then to A Coruña at the end of the 1940s, and finally to Madrid in the middle of the 1950s, where he worked for Spanish radio. AGMAV 5531/7, 4497/51.

17. Such were the initial conditions, as reported by the San Sebastián press. 'Banderín de enganche para luchar contra el comunismo', *La Voz de España*, 1 July 1941, p. 1.
18. The success of the recruitment campaign was heavily dependent on which region the enrollment was conducted. On the whole, such cities as Madrid, Seville and Valencia, as well as those areas that remained under the control of the Spanish Republic until the end of the war (Levante and Murcia), where there were Falangist-inclined students and allies of Franco who had not managed to take part in the war, supported the recruitment campaign. Two hundred and fifty-seven volunteers signed up in Guipuzcoa in June-July 1941, with another 346 later; they were, for the most part, city dwellers (San Sebastián most of all). This province delivered the largest number of Basque volunteers to the Blue Division, among which the urban lower classes clearly predominated: workers and tradesmen – 38 per cent; day labourers – 7 per cent; white-collar workers – 26 per cent and; students – 8 per cent. I. Fernández Vicente, *El proyecto fascista en el País Vasco, 1933–1945*. PhD Thesis, University of the Basque Country, 2019, pp. 345–6, 350–1.
19. Preference was theoretically given to Falange members, and they were even taken from the party's branches. In practice, party membership was not a mandatory condition for being accepted. It is difficult to calculate exactly the percentage of Falangists, but among the first contingent it did not exceed 20–25 per cent of the overall number who left for the front.
20. The overall number of deserters from the Blue Division was much lower than Kovalevskii maintains. They 'screened' the volunteers beforehand and the division's intelligence section later kept track of the soldiers' attitudes. The first party of volunteers was distinguished by a high level of ideological solidarity; finally, it was physically difficult to desert. One can believe that in two years of service by the 250th Division, the number of deserters varied from 80 to 100 men, that is, barely 0.2 per thousand of the number of military personnel. X. M. Núñez Seixas, *The Spanish Blue Division*, pp. 69–70.
21. Similar enthusiasm was noted in the Wehrmacht's other foreign legions. The political leadership of the Wehrmacht's French Legion (*Légion des Volontaires Français contre le Bolchévisme*) was particularly impatient to take part in the capture of Moscow; partly due to this, the Legion's training turned out to be very rudimentary, and the 638th Regiment suffered heavy casualties in the winter of 1941. D. Ridruejo, *Los cuadernos de Rusia: diario 1941–1943*. Edited by X. M. Núñez Seixas. Madrid, 2013, pp. 156–67. (Diary notes, 17 and 19 September 1941); O. Beyda, '"La Grande Armée in Field Gray": The Legion of French Volunteers Against Bolshevism, 1941', *The Journal of Slavic Military Studies*, 29:3 (2016), pp. 500–18.
22. According to an order of 25 June, the deadline for enrolling regular soldiers was 48 hours, while the enrollment of Falangist recruits was to be completed on 2 July. On 28 June the army quota was increased (three-quarters of the junior specialists and technical personnel), while the percentage shortfall of local volunteers was covered

through the regular army. On 8 July the volunteers' vanguard left for Germany, with the main body following on 13 July. X. M. Núñez Seixas, *Camarada invierno*, pp. 62–4.

23. An interview with Vladimir Dvoichenko, the third émigré serving in the Militia in San Sebastián, was carried in the Falangist daily *Unidad* ('Unity'). At that time he was already 57 years old and he had managed to serve in four wars (the Russo-Japanese War and the First World War, and two civil wars, in Russia and Spain). Three days later Bibikov or Kovalevskii appeared at the paper's office in order to thank the editor for mentioning the émigrés.

24. During the first period of Francoism's existence in Spain, the image of the 'Russian' was practically indistinguishable from the image of the communist enemy, and this impression was strengthened by the propaganda that began after the anti-Republican uprising. The White émigrés who fought in the Francoist ranks noted that many of their Spanish comrades found it difficult to distinguish between these two concepts. X.M. Núñez Seixas, *¡Fuera el invasor! Nacionalismos y movilización bélica durante la guerra civil española (1936–1939)*. Madrid, 2006, pp. 245–61; idem, *Spanish Blue Division*, pp. 15–16.

Burgos

1. Pavel Ivanovich Rashevskii (1898–1944) was born in St. Petersburg and served as a captain in the Russian General Staff and was a topographer. He was in France by 1926. From September through October 1936 he fought in the ranks of the *Virgen del Pilar tercio* of Aragonese red berets, from whence he transferred to the *Doña María de Molina tercio*, where he received the rank of sergeant. He distinguished himself in the fighting and was severely wounded in the lung in November 1936. In September 1937 Rashevskii put in a request to allow him to travel to France and Germany; his daughter, Natal'ia, who knew little about his fate (as noted by the Spanish consul in the city), lived in Toulouse. During the trip he disappeared: they said in the '*Doña María de Molina tercio* that he had been demobilized 'in light of his unworthy behavior and an unquenchable thirst for spirits'. Iaremchuk wrote in September 1938 that Rashevskii was thrown into prison in Irun and that 'the Germans dug up information that he was linked with French intelligence – the 2nd Bureau – and the matter might end in a trial'. Nonetheless, he later turned up again. In May 1941 Rashevskii was awarded the medal 'Suffered for the Fatherland' (*Medalla de Sufrimientos por la Patria*) and was listed as a sergeant. He was enrolled in the Blue Division into the First Section of the division staff. Whether he was in prison in Spain or in France, or whether he had been arrested before leaving for the front, still remains unknown. He died in Pamplona. AGMAV 4346/100. Diversa documentacion en AGMS. CG/R3; 'Russkie belye voiny v ispanskoi grazhdanskoi voine / per isp. zhurn. *Istoriia i zhizn*. 1973, no. 69, Dec, *Informatsionnyi biulleten' Otdela Obshchestva gallipoliitsev v S.A.S.Sh-kh*, 156, August–September 1976, pp. 4–5.

2. The author is probably speaking about Lieutenant Ismael García-Romeu (pseudonym *Tirolaipi*; 1918–99), from Barcelona and a veteran of the Civil War, whose eccentricity and bravery in battle won him a particular reputation in the division. He is often mentioned in his fellow soldiers' memoirs. He had one eye, so it is possible that Kovalevskii is confusing the captain with the lieutenant.

3. The author is speaking of Captain José Fernández Rodríguez, who on 1 August took up the command of the 4th Machine-Gun Company and served there until 11 June 1942.

4. The author is speaking here of Colonel Pedro Pimentel Zayas (1893–1963), a cadre officer who made a career in Africa, as an officer in the Spanish Foreign Legion and a teacher in the military academy in Zaragoza. In 1936 he took an active part in the uprising of the army units stationed in Africa; he later moved to the peninsula, commanding Legion subunits. Pimentel occupied the position of commander of the 262nd Infantry Regiment until May 1942. Upon returning to Spain, he was promoted to lieutenant general. He commanded one of the military districts and at the end of the 1950s had a seat as member of the Cortes (consultative assembly set up by the Franco regime).
5. Here the author is speaking of Tartarin from Tarascon, a literary figure invented by Alphonse Daudet in his 1872 novel *The Unusual Adventures of Tartarin from Tarascon* (*Les aventures prodigieuses de Tartarin de Tarascon*).

On the Road to Germany

1. The manifestations of hostility on the part of the French population and the Spanish Republican refugees did not cease throughout the volunteers' entire journey from Hendaye to Alsace. The division's trains encountered a similar reaction later on. A number of incidents took place: rocks and bottles were thrown at the train and fights broke out during layovers. The accompanying Germans often played the role of passive observers. On this note, the volunteers of the Walloon Legion saw a similar picture on the way to Poland in the middle of August 1941. Rostislav Vadimovich Zavadskii noted in his diary: 'The Dutch greet our train with their fists. It's clear that the inhabitants' attitude is similar to that of the Belgians.' Various reports from the Second Section of the division staff for 19–22 July 1941 are available in Grafenwöhr: AGMAV 20052/2; R.V. Zavadskii, *Svoia chuzhaia voina. Dnevnik russkogo ofitsera 1941–1942 gg.* Edited by O.I. Beyda, Moscow, 2014, p. 76.
2. The author is speaking here about nurses from the German Red Cross (*Krankenschwestern*).
3. This is the city of Strasbourg, which had been incorporated into the Third Reich after 1940.
4. The exchange of photographs and addresses sometimes grew into epistolary relations with the German 'military godmothers' (*madrinas de Guerra*), whom the Spanish often idealized. Kovalevskii overstates the significance of these relations. The division's soldiers were often not capable of reading the addresses written on the back of the photographs, insofar as the German girls used the gothic script *Fraktur*.

Camp Grafenwöhr (Bavaria)

1. Kovalevskii's positive attitude toward the division's sergeants is in contrast to the picture created by the Falangist volunteers, many of whom despised the sergeants, ascribing to them a lack of education, coarseness and insufficient devotion to Falangist ideals. On the contrary, many of the army's younger officers, who made their career during the war years, although they shared the basic values of the Franco regime, were not particularly fond of the volunteers from among the middle-class urban dwellers – to their way of thinking, the latter were *señoritos*, that is, from rich families. D. Ridruejo, *Cuadernos de Rusia*, pp. 76–8, 280–94 (Diary notes, 30 July, 13 and 14 November); X.M. Núñez Seixas, *The Spanish Blue Division*, p. 68.
2. The Spanish soldiers repeatedly complained about the German rations they received during their training, as well as the harsh, spartan conditions in which they had to eat.

The Spaniards were distressed by the shortage of wine and tobacco, and the dishes, such as pearl barley, struck the Iberians as strange. X.M. Núñez Seixas, *Camarada invierno*, pp. 66–7.
3. The author is speaking of the 262nd Battalion.
4. This is Major Angel Enríquez Larrondo.
5. This may be Lieutenant José M. Vicente Izquierdo, a native of Burgos and a graduate of the Zaragoza Infantry Academy, who subsequently (1 August) assumed command of a company in transport group 250, and who was then transferred to the 269th Infantry Regiment's second battalion. He was wounded in the foot in March 1942 and was sent back to Spain. AGMAV 4499/4.
6. The Spanish army proved incapable of supplying the formation with transport, thus the Blue Division was forced to move to the front by foot and on horses, similar to the majority of the Wehrmacht's infantry units. The formation disposed of 5,610 horses, which had been seized by the German army in the Balkans; following a long journey, the animals arrived at Grafenwöhr in horrible condition. This, together, with many of the stable hands' lack of experience, as in the case with Kovalevskii, became the source of constant problems in the division.
7. Agustín Muñoz Grandes (1896–1970), was an officer who served in Morocco and the commander of the Spanish Republic's storm guard, was the first commander of the Blue Division and Spanish minister of defence at the end of the 1950s. He enjoyed a certain popularity among the soldiers. He was close to the Falangists (general secretary of the party from August 1939 to March 1940) and loved populist gestures: he would wander *incognito* along the front line, handing out cigarettes to the privates, or he sometimes chewed out the commanders in front of their subordinates. His value as a military strategist was highly controversial.
8. The Blue Division contained a significant number of sergeants and provisional junior lieutenants who had received their ranks for their military service and, after taking special courses, remained to serve in the army after 1939. They shared the basic postulates of Francoism, consolidated by military experience; that is, Catholicism and a traditional view of the social order. During training their relations with the Falangists often proved to be quite strained. According to German evaluations, these officers' technical training left something to be desired; on the other hand, Kovalevskii rates this group positively.
9. The author is presumably speaking of Sergeant Mariano Alonso Tomillo (1920–2008), who served in the 262nd Infantry Regiment's battalion headquarters and who also fought in a special operations company (*Compañía de Operaciones Especiales*). He was mustered out with the rank of colonel. The incident in question does not figure in his personnel file. AGMAV 4439/23.
10. The author is presumably speaking of Sergeant Marcelino Cortés García (1915–?), who came from the 24th Infantry Regiment in San Sebastián and who was appointed to serve in the 262nd Infantry Regiment's 1st Battalion. There is not much more information in his personnel file. AGMAV 4191/43.
11. Homosexuality in the army and incidents related to it are usually taboo in memoirs. One may count on the fingers of one hand the accounts and diary entries in which this subject is not passed over in silence. There were also such incidents in the Blue Division, which became the subjects of investigation and involved punishment. About seventy courts martial took place before the end of 1941, involving officers, sergeants and soldiers; two officers were discharged from the army. X.M. Núñez Seixas, *The Spanish Blue Division*, p. 144.

12. In this case, Kovalevskii is most likely speaking of field experience. The Spaniards' training period (5–6 weeks) was short in comparison with the standard course for the German units (three months), but nevertheless the command considered that the training had passed in good time. The desire of the volunteers to get to the front as quickly as possible, the fact that many of them had the military experience of 1936–9, as well as the necessity of making good losses at the front, influenced the shortening of the training cycle.
13. Friction arose during training due to the differences in the German and Spanish military cultures, which was exacerbated by the fact that many volunteers did not readily submit to military discipline. Complaints by the German commanders and liaison headquarters (*Verbindungsstab*) within the division only increased as time went on.
14. The author is speaking here of the German 7.92mm MG34 machine gun (*Maschinengewehr 34*).
15. The author is speaking here of the Degtiarev DP-27 machine gun, in the Red Army since 1928.
16. This corresponds to the German opinion. Reports from the German liaison office with the division and from other German observers on the repulsive treatment of horses reached the Wehrmacht high command and even as far as the Nazi leaders. The problem was partly due to the lack of junior officers and cavalry soldiers, whom Muñoz Grandes asked about in the army ministry from August 1941. At the beginning of October, Field Marshal Wilhelm von Leeb's adjutant, Major Baron Robert von Griessenbeck, wrote with horror in his diary about the Spanish reinforcements and their treatment of horses, calling them an 'insane mob'. X.M. Núñez Seixas, *Camarada invierno*, pp. 66, 116–18; Iu. M. Lebedev, *Po obe storony blokadnogo kol'tsa*. St. Petersburg, 2005, p. 86.
17. On 31 July the main part of the division was quartered in the Kramerberg camp, in the center of a complex of training camps, for taking the oath to the 'commander of the German army, Adolf Hitler in the cause of the struggle against communism' and in the name of 'God and your Spanish honour', under the flags of Germany and Spain. The text of the oath was the same as in the Wehrmacht one, although the term *Führer* had disappeared and it was added that the Spaniards' loyalty to Hitler applied only to the Eastern Front. Besides Muñoz Grandes, Generals Conrad von Cochenhausen (the commander of the XIII Military District) and Friedrich Fromm (the commander of the Replacement Army [*Ersatzheer*]), presided at the ceremony. In his speech, von Conchenhausen mentioned the 'crusade against the Bolsheviks' and the defense of European civilization from 'Jewish-Marxist power' several times.
18. This was not a mere coincidence. The hymn was written by the composer Dmitrii Stepanovich Bortnianskii, to the poem by Mikhail Matveevich Kheraskov, in 1794. This hymn was the unofficial national anthem of the Russian Empire before the adoption of 'God Save the Tsar' in 1833. In Germany Bortnianskii's melody was used for the German song 'I Pray for the Power of Love' (*Ich bete an die Macht der Liebe*), to the words of the German poet Gerhard Tersteegen. In time the church hymn became a traditional part of military ceremonies (*Großen Zapfenstreich*) and the music was performed as a march in the German Wehrmacht. Only in May 1944 was the march replaced by 'The Heavens Sing the Praises of the Almighty' (*Die Himmel rühmen des Ewigen Ehre*) by Ludwig van Beethoven. R. Absolon, *Die Wehrmacht im Dritten Reich: 19 Dezember 1941 bis 9 Mai 1945*, vol. VI. Boppard am Rhein, 1995, p. 799; R.-D. Müller, *Hitlers Wehrmacht 1935 bis 1945*. Munch, 2012, p. 38.

On the Road to Russia

1. Three weeks earlier a group of Spanish officers had left for various subunits on the Eastern Front in order to acquaint themselves with German methods of conducting combat operations. Before long the group returned. On 20 August the first convoy, consisting of six trains, left. The division departed for the front in several echelons (66 trains and a column of 200 motorized transport vehicles) over the course of five days.
2. At the end of July 1941 the organization of the Spanish volunteer division (*División Española de Voluntarios*) had been moved to the Wehrmacht model. In accordance with the initial Spanish model, there were four regiments in the division: three front-line and one reserve, which was to remain in Germany. Now the latter had been allocated among the front-line units. A mobile reserve battalion (the 250th Battalion) had also been created, consisting of a headquarters and three companies (two infantry and one mixed), which was located in the nearby rear and ready to enter the fighting in the event of necessity. Thus the Blue Division was officially transformed into the Wehrmacht's 250th Infantry Division (*Spanischen Freiwilligen Division*). Its original four regiments had been reduced to three and each of them consisted of three battalions and two additional companies; the 262nd Infantry Regiment (Colonel Pedro Pimentel), the 263rd Regiment (José Vierna), and the 269th Regiment (José Martínez Esparza). The commander of the fourth, reformed regiment, Miguel Rodrigo, became the deputy division commander. The division also contained an artillery regiment and signals battalion and engineer battalions; an anti-tank group; intelligence and medical sections; the quartermaster and veterinary assistance; a military police section (consisting of soldiers from the Civil Guard), which carried out the functions of a field *gendarmerie*; military mail service; a headquarters and general staff. The overall number of soldiers in the division reached 18,000.
3. Kovalevskii exaggerates the influence of the Falangist cadres in the Blue Division's internal hierarchy. The majority of the FET's leaders who had signed on as volunteers became ordinary soldiers. Of course, they retained a certain status among their comrades and in some units there developed a sort of 'double hierarchy' parallel to the army one: this was the case in the 2nd Anti-Tank Company, which consisted to a significant extent of such commanders as Agustín Aznar, Enrique Sotomayor and Dionisio Ridruejo, all of them members of the Falange prior to the civil war (*Old Guards*). The professional soldiers were jealous of the party 'bigwigs' (*señoritos*).
4. Kovalevskii is speaking of the Blue Squadron (*Escuadrilla Azul*, or the *15. Spanische Staffel*), which was part of the Luftwaffe in Army Group Centre and which consisted of several dozen pilots from the Spanish air force, as well as ground personnel. About 100 pilots (in four intakes) passed through the squadron. J. Fernández-Coppel, *La escuadrilla azul: los pilotos españoles en la Luftwaffe*. Madrid, 2007.
5. An obsolete Russian unit of distance, equaling to 1.068km.
6. This is the Polish town of Sejny. It had the same name under the Russian Empire and was part of the Suwałki governate.
7. The number of those who 'had foot problems' and who complained of blisters and pain in their feet became a serious problem for the division from the moment it advanced to the front. According to the military doctor, Bernardino Lopez Romeo, from 8 through 28 September alone 2,177 soldiers applied for aid, 'the majority of whom suffered from foot problems to various degrees; others were simply tired from the hard march, as well as some who had come down sick'. At the same time, the state of the troops' morale had 'decreased notably': the soldiers who approached the doctors 'were full of complaints – in a word, they were dispirited. After only a few days since the beginning

of the march, many of them already looked downcast: torn clothing, unkempt hair, beards, and even lice'. *Hospital de campaña 250. Memoria. Desde el día 8 de septiembre al 1 de octubre de 1941*. Private Archive of Mr. Carlos López del Río. Boiro/Madrid.
8. From the French word for truck.
9. Strictly speaking, Kovalevskii is incorrect: it is accepted to number the second wave of emigration from the time following the Second World War and up to the 1960s. People who left following the October Revolution, or who left with the White army in the beginning of the 1920s, are usually consigned to the first wave of emigration. Thus the authors listed here were most likely representatives of the late first wave.
10. Ivan Luk'ianovich Solonevich (1891–1953) was a Russian writer, commentator and social activist. He escaped from the USSR in the 1930s and was quite active in emigration. He was a theoretician and convinced defender of the monarchy, and the author of books about the USSR (*Russia in a Concentration Camp*). By the summer of 1941 he was cooperating with Nazi propaganda. He was the editor of the papers *The Voice of Russia* (in Bulgaria) and *Our Country* (in Argentina).
11. Grigorii Zinov'evich Besedovskii (1896–1963) was a Soviet diplomat and adviser with the Soviet embassy in France. He fled from the embassy in 1929 and received political asylum. He became involved in émigré affairs and wrote for the newspapers *Rebirth* and *The Latest News*.
12. Sergei Vasil'evich Dmitrievskii (1893–1964) was a Soviet diplomat and adviser with the Soviet embassy in Sweden. He fled the embassy in 1930 and became a non-returnee. He immigrated to Paris and took part in the 'Young Russia' movement and worked in various émigré publishing houses. He later returned to Sweden.
13. These are very precise impressions that coincide with what other of the division's soldiers wrote. The population of former eastern Poland, which was occupied by the Soviets at the end of September 1939, was subjected to severe repressions, lived through the deportations of so-called anti-Soviet elements and the executions of representatives of the Polish elite. The Poles were under the impression that the local Jews sympathized with the Soviet regime, which only poured oil on the fire of traditional anti-Semitism. F. Ackerman, *Palimpsest Grodno. Nationalisierung, Nivellierung und Sowjetisierung einer mitteleuropäischen Stadt 1919–1991*. Wiesbaden, 2011, pp. 93–127.
14. The Spaniards often called in on the small towns and villages along the division's route on Polish, Belorussian and Lithuanian territory. They established contacts with the peasants and trade arose, exchanging food for equipment. In some cases the volunteers encountered Poles who had returned from Argentina following a few years of emigration and who spoke Spanish. X.M. Núñez Seixas, *The Spanish Blue Division*, p. 197.
15. This mental trait was characteristics of many émigrés: Tsarist Russia had not existed for more than 20 years, however the new geographical and political borders were actively rejected by them as not real.
16. In post-war memoirs by the division's soldiers one often encounters passages that the Poles, Lithuanians and Spanish shared the same Catholic values. They often wrote about the Masses which the Blue Division's chaplains held, or about Polish priests in modest little village churches. Religious unity did not interfere with periodic marauding and instances of swindling the civilian population.
17. In September 1941 Leib Reizer, a Jew who had escaped from Grodno, travelled through the Belorussian village of Radun' in the company of Dutch drivers from the Todt Organization. Reizer asked one peasant woman whether there were any Spaniards in the village. 'Yes, they were here', she replied [. . .] 'They tried to make themselves understood with the aid of gestures and asked about "fats" (butter), "cluck, cluck" and "oink, oink" (that is, chickens and pigs), offering in exchange shirts, scarves, socks and

the like.' According to data from the German liaison staff, not all cases were requisitions or exchanges and there was thievery. L. Reizer, *In the Struggle. Memoirs from Grodno and the Forests*. New York, Jerusalem, 2009, p. 96; Bundesarchiv-Militararchiv (BA-MA). Freiburg im Breisgau. RH 26-250/2. The military diary of the liaison staff, entries for 26 August and 1 and 6 September 1941.

18. On the eve of the invasion of the USSR, the Wehrmacht received instructions on how to treat Soviet prisoners of war, according to which it was not required to observe the norms of the Geneva Convention. Part of the prisoners were to die, while hard labour to complete exhaustion awaited the others. By May 1942 nearly half of the Red Army soldiers captured by the Germans had died. Long columns of Soviet prisoners of war, wandering in the rear, made an enormous impression on the Spaniards; they often mention this in their diaries and post-war recollections. Some volunteers felt compassion for the prisoners, while others, quite the opposite, found in their horrible condition confirmation of propaganda stereotypes and the theory of 'subhumans'. X.M. Núñez Seixas, *The Spanish Blue Division*, pp. 156–7; K. Streit, *Keine Kameraden. Die Wehrmacht und die sowjetischen Kriegsgefangenen 1941–1945*. Stuttgart, 1978.

19. Grodno (today Hrodna, Belarus) was located along the then-extant ethnic boundary, where Polish Catholics coexisted with Orthodox Belorussians, Lithuanians and Jews (the majority of the latter spoke Yiddish) without problems. In September 1941 nearly 30,000 Jews resided in the city, of which only 2 per cent survived the Holocaust.

20. Kovalevskii, despite his traditional anti-Semitism, does not use the disparaging term 'Yids', which was usually employed by Russian anti-Semites in speaking about Jews. He employed the neutral term 'Jews', which was possibly conditioned by the fact that his memoirs were written after 1945.

21. Judging from the reference to 'crimes', Kovalevskii held to the popular theory about the Jewish origins of Bolshevism and, what was typical for anti-Semites, exaggerated the role of the Jews in the October Revolution. Anti-Semitism was almost the norm for officers of the Russian imperial army. J. Frankel, *Crisis, Revolution, and Russian Jews*. Cambridge, et al. 2009; S. Goldin, *Russkaia armiia i evrei, 1914–1917*. Moscow, 2018; J.D. Klier, *Imperial Russia's Jewish Question, 1855–1881*. Cambridge, 1995; H. Rogger (ed.), *Jewish Policies and Right-Wing Politics in Imperial Russia*. Los Angeles, Berkeley, 1986.

22. The Spaniards arrived during a 'transition period' in the fate of the Grodno ghetto. From the beginning of the occupation at the end of June 1941, the German authorities limited the Jews' rights and introduced forced labour. This was accompanied by the random murders of individuals. In the beginning of July 1941 about 100 leading members of the Jewish community were shot outside of town. When the Spaniards arrived in Grodno the Germans forced the Jews to carry distinguishing badges, to take part in forced labour and to yield the road to Wehrmacht soldiers. A significant number of Jews belonging to the middle class and professions was exterminated. However, at the time the Spaniards appeared the Jews had not yet been driven into the ghetto, which the Germans began to create in September. It was divided into two ghettoes: they held qualified workers in the first one and those who were not 'beneficial' in the second. Ghetto No. 1 was located in the central part of the city, around a large synagogue, and accommodated about 20,000 people. Ghetto No. 2 was located 2 kilometres away and approximately 7,000–8,000 people were kept there. By the beginning of November 1941 both ghettoes had been completely established and the Jews ended locked up within their confines. The situation rapidly worsened. Ghetto No. 2 was destroyed in November 1942 and Ghetto No. 1 in January–March 1943. In March 1943 the Jewish community in Grodno ceased to exist. X.M. Núñez Seixas, *Camarada invierno*,

pp. 302–08; F. Ackerman, *Palimpsest Grodno*, pp. 115–27; L. Chapnik, 'The Grodno Ghetto and Its Underground: A Personal Narrative', in *Women in the Holocaust*. Edited by D. Ofer, L.J. Weitzman. New Haven, London, 1998, pp. 109–19; Y. Arad, *In the Shadow of the Red Banner: Soviet Jews in the War against Nazi Germany*. New York; Jerusalem, 2010, pp. 221ff; P. Polian, *Svitki iz pepla. Evreiskaia zonderkommando v Aushvitse-Birkenau i ee letopistsy – rukopisi chlenov zonderkommando, naidennye v peple u pechei Osventsima*. Edited by Z. Gradovskii, L. Langfus, Z. Levental', Kh. German, M. Nadzhari and A. Levit. Moscow/Rostov-on-Don, 2013, pp. 160–2, 196.

23. This phrase makes us assume that Kovalevskii was a witness to several cases of degrading Jews, although he does not supply any details. The employment of the indefinite term 'repressions' speaks to an incorrect understanding of violence: they punished the Jews not for violating the rules established by the occupiers – they were the victims of lawlessness.

24. This should be Zhitomlia.

25. Nikolai Evgen'evich Krivosheia (1897–1970) was from Lugansk and served as an artillery captain in the Russian army. He graduated from the Poltava Cadet Corps and was a cadet in the Mikhailovskoe Artillery School in St. Petersburg. From November 1917 he served in the Volunteer Army and took part in a raid by Colonel Chernetsov's partisan detachment. He participated in the First Kuban' ('Ice March') Campaign and transferred to the 1st Light Artillery Battalion. He was a St. George's cavalier. He served as a staff captain in General Markov's battery in the Markov Artillery Battalion. He was evacuated with the Russian army in 1920 and was in the camp at Gallipoli. As an émigré in Paris he worked as a driver. He was a board member of the Gallipoli Society in Paris. In February 1937 he joined the 'Zumalacárregui' *requeté tercio* in San Sebastián and from there, already a lieutenant, was sent to command the Russian detachment in the 'Navarra' *tercio*. Following the war he received Spanish citizenship and received the post of honorary junior lieutenant in the second 'Duke of Alba' (*Duque de Alba*) *tercio* in the Spanish Foreign Legion. In the summer of 1941 he volunteered for the Blue Division and served as a translator in the headquarters of the 262nd Infantry Regiment. He took part in the fighting and in October 1943 was wounded several times by shrapnel and was evacuated to a hospital in Krasnogvardeisk, from where he was sent to Riga. He returned to Spain in December 1943, where he continued to serve in the Legion. From July 1969 until his death from a stroke in April 1970 in Madrid, Krivosheia was registered with the translator's section of the General Staff of the Spanish army. In April 1970 he was forced to confirm his knowledge of Russian before a tribunal. He had a brother, Vasilii, who died in Melilla in September 1964 in an accident: he was a cadet in the Poltava Corps and served in the Markov Division's artillery throughout the Russian Civil War. He served five years in the French Foreign Legion. Under Franco he served in the *Doña María de Molina tercio*. He was a Sergeant in the Spanish Foreign Legion and a translator in the Blue Division. AGMAV 4569/15 and his service record in AGMS 3809; *50 let vernosti Rossii. 1917–1967. Izdanie markovtsev-artilleristov*. Paris, 1967, pp. 20, 70, 74, 289; 'Nezabytye mogily', *Chasovoi*, 461 (11) (November 1964), p. 23; 'Nezabytye mogily', *Chasovoi*, 535 (1) (January 1971), p. 23; 'Popravka', *Chasovoi*, 537 (3) (March 1971), p. 24.

26. By the time the division arrived at Vilnius a ghetto had already been created there. A Spanish rear-area hospital was located in the city, through which a large number of soldiers who passed through it, often described Vilnius as a 'European' city because, as opposed to Russia, there was a large number of Catholic churches in it. X.M. Núñez Seixas, *The Spanish Blue Division*, pp. 98–9.

27. This is an obvious mistake. Molodechno is not part of Lithuania and is located not far from the capital of Belarus, Minsk.
28. *Oblast'* means 'region' in Russian, a type of administrative division. 'In July 1941 a large number of prisoners of war had accumulated in the collection points and in the transit camps located in the ground forces' area of responsibility, for which no funds had been allocated for their maintenance. In connection with this, general-quartermaster's order no. 11/4590 was issued on 25.07.41 for the freeing of Soviet prisoners of war from a number of nationalities (Volga Germans, inhabitants of the Baltic States, Ukrainians, and then Belorussians). However, by OKW order no. 3900 of 13.11.41, further action of this order was suspended. In all during this period 318,770 men were freed, of these 292,702 in the OKH's zone and 26,068 in the OKW's zone. In all, there were 277,761 Ukrainians among those freed.' G.F. Krivosheev, P.D. Burikov and V.V. Gurkin, 'Velikaia Otechestvennaia bez grifa sekretnosti', *Kniga poter'. Noveishe spravochno izdanie.* Moscow, 2010, pp. 320–1.
29. That is, the idea of an independent Ukraine.
30. Simon Vasil'evich Petliura (1879–1926) was a Ukrainian political figure and the chairman of the Directory of the Ukrainian People's Republic in 1919–20. A nationalist and rabid anti-Semite, he emigrated to Paris, where he was killed by an émigré Jew.
31. Pavel Petrovich Skoropadskii (1873–1945) was a Ukrainian political figure and Ukrainian *hetman* in April-December 1918. He headed the Ukrainian state with the support of Germany, after replacing the Ukrainian People's Republic. The military autocracy was, in its turn, overthrown by the Directory, which reestablished the Ukrainian republic. He fled to Germany.

First Impressions

1. Kovalevskii is speaking about the former boundary between Lithuania and the USSR: the Baltic States were absorbed into the Soviet Union in 1940, following the creation of puppet governments.
2. Large covered barn for drying out bales of hay.
3. This is a partially true assertion. Despite the propagandistic declaration on the 'liberation of the peasants', the Germans maintained the former system for tilling the land, issuing the appropriate order at the end of August 1941 and only changed the name 'collective farm' to 'common agricultural farm'. At the same time, it is highly doubtful that the living and working conditions somehow got better: the volume of production which the peasants had to turn over to the occupiers could not have been less than in the previous year; accordingly, the exploitation of the peasants did not lessen, and their life became even worse in light of the marauding practised by the German army. At the same time, the civil administration of the occupied territories did not follow a single policy, and each local leader had the authority to assign his own norms, which often varied from one inhabited area to another. O.Iu. Plenkov, *Tretii Reikh. Sotsializm Gitlera (Ocherki istorii i ideologii).* Saint Petersburg, 2004, p. 212; X.M. Núñez Seixas, *El frente del Este,* pp. 191–8.
4. On 27 February 1942 the Ministry for the Occupied Eastern Territories, under the leadership of Alfred Rosenberg, published a decree on the new order for working the land. The collective farm system was declared eliminated and the transition to individual ownership of the land was to proceed in three stages. The collective farm was to be transformed into a communal farm, with additional taxes on livestock and buildings. It was then planned to transform these farms into agricultural cooperatives. And it was only at the third stage that for which deadlines were not indicated, that the

division of the cooperatives into individual private farms was planned. It's not difficult to see that the majority of these announcements had a declaratory character, and thus the exploitation of the peasants' labour continued throughout the occupation.

5. Kovalevskii's impressions of poverty coincide with the absolute majority of the émigrés who were in the occupied territories and whose opinions have come down to us, as well as a large number of German memoirs. K. Aleksandrov, *Russkie soldaty Vermakhta. Geroi ili predateli: sborniik statei i materialov.* Moscow, 2005, pp. 512–29.

6. Statistics most likely state the opposite. As a Soviet project, the collectivization and sovietization of the peasants was inseparable from the destruction of the church as an institution and faith as a private practice. During the second half of the 1930s the Bolsheviks clearly aimed at destroying the church as such. More than 8,000 churches were closed in 1937 alone. Priests were exiled to camps and even executed. V.S. Batchenko, 'Krest'ianskoe soprotivlenie gosudarstvennoi antireligioznoi politike v 1929–1931 gg. (na materialakh Zapadnoi oblasti)'. Candidate dissertation, Smolensk State University, 2015, pp. 114–17; M.V. Shkarovskii, *Russkaia pravoslavnaia tserkov' pri Staline i Khrushcheve: gosudarstvenno-tserkovnye otnosheniis v SSSR v 1939–1964 godakh.* Moscow, 1999, p. 92; H. Kuromiya, 'Why the Destruction of Orthodox Priests in the Soviet Union in 1937–38?', *Jahrbücher für Geschichte Osteuropas*, 55:1 (2007), pp. 86–93.

7. In the original manuscript there was an addition here on a separate piece of paper. The information is not exact.

    'It is necessary to halt in somewhat greater detail on the land question in the USSR. There exists there two forms of land ownership and, accordingly, different conditions for the peasants. The collective farms, according to wartime information, then occupied two-thirds of all the land, or 85,000,000 *desyatinas*. Within them the peasants were like cooperative members, distributing the collective farm's income after an enormous payment (more than 50%) to the government for everything received, both from the land and from the livestock fund. Depending on the number of collective farms and the amount of land under cultivation and its fertility, the collective farmers' material situation (the phrase was left unfinished).

    The state farms occupied 57,000,000 *desyatinas* (in 1938), predominantly in the former large landlord estates, which in the old days produced the main mass of bread for export, thanks to improved methods of tilling the land. Some, like Koenig's *latifundia* in the Khar'kov governate, with all of its plants and factories, provided work for 200,000 peasants and workers. The state farm, with its *corvée* and wretched payment for work days is an ulcer for both the population and the state.'

8. This is a false contrasting of German orders and Spanish practice. Supplying the army 'from the land' was the norm for the Wehrmacht. This practice was approved and widely employed from the summer of 1941, placing the Soviet population under the threat of death by starvation in the conditions of the approaching winter. As part of the Wehrmacht, the Spaniards were no different in this regard. This campaign, in which military necessity was mixed in with racist ideology, showed the true attitude toward the occupied population. J. Rutherford, *Combat and Genocide on the Eastern Front: The German Infantry's War, 1941–1944.* Cambridge, 2014, pp. 71, 105, 110, 145–7; X.M. Núñez Seixas, *El frente del Este*, pp. 191–206.

9. In this regard, Kovalevskii's opinion once again coincides with the evaluation rendered by other émigrés. On the other hand, the Spaniards' perception of the situation was much more contradictory: at the same time they noted a deference and respect for traditions among the older population, the absence of religious feeling and dissipation was observed among the youth, which had been brought about by the Soviet system;

others regretted the absence of morality among the peasants, which they explained by the evil influence of communism, the specifically Russian self-consciousness and the backwardness of the population. X.M. Núñez Seixas, 'Russia and the Russians in the Eyes of the Spanish Blue Division Soldiers, 1941–4', *Journal of Contemporary History*, 52:2 (2017), pp. 352–74.

10. This is a typical turn of phrase. A *kursistka* was a student in the higher courses for women in Tsarist Russia. Questions of education touched upon rural youth much less than in the city, although in the final years of the Russian Empire active attempts were undertaken to change this situation. By 1941 courses for women no longer existed, because women had been admitted for study in the universities.

11. Lev Nikolaevich Tolstoi (1828–1910) was a writer and classic of Russian literature. Kovelevskii is hinting that Tolstoi was a count, but at the same time sought to draw close to the peasantry and present himself as one who expressed their interests.

12. The emigration was not just a diaspora, but an alternative Russian nation. Without having formal state boundaries, the community of Russians abroad had its own holidays, press, charitable, religious, professional, educational institutions (including universities), culture, military caste and public life. The émigrés constantly asked themselves what was going on with those Russians who had remained in the USSR and often came to a conclusion about their own exclusiveness. From their point of view, *Soviet* people lived in the USSR, and had altered in the religious, political, moral and other senses, which only served to deepen the gap the sense of identity in the two communities. L. Manchester, 'How Statelessness can Force Refugees to Redefine Their Ethnicity: What can be Learned from Russian Emigres Dispersed to Six Continents in the Inter-War Period', *Immigrants and Minorities*, 34:1 (2016), pp. 70–91.

13. It was observed that some of the Spanish soldiers were interested in and were entranced by the traditions of the Russian people. For them the Russians' religiosity was proof of being 'unsullied' and that communism could not penetrate into the intimate recesses of the human consciousness. Such views were held in particular by those who were permeated with the ideas of Christian humanism. Some hoped to find confirmation of the stereotypes formed by Russian classical literature from Tolstoi to Dostoevskii. Striking examples of this are the fervently Catholic medical corps Captain Manuel de Cárdenas, and some Falangists, such as Guillermo Alonso del Real. In 1943 the exarch of the Russian Orthodox Church in the USA, Metropolitan Veniamin, associated with a Russian youth who had arrived in America from Spain. Before this he had lived for half a year in a family of Falangists. The son was a soldier in the division and returned home disappointed following his wounding, about which he told his unusual lodger in November 1942: 'We were repeatedly told everywhere that ours was a holy war against the Reds and that it was a crusade for the faith! But when I arrived in Russia I saw churches. Our detachment was near Novgorod the Great: everywhere there were cathedrals, everywhere icons, and the people prayed without anyone hindering them. We were tricked. And our allies, the Germans; these were the real atheists and materialists, and I saw no signs of faith among them'. X.M. Núñez Seixas, *The Spanish Blue Division*, p. 176; Metropolitan Veniamin (Fedchenkov), *Na rubezhe dvukh epoch*. Moscow, 2016, p. 586.

14. Kovalevskii is obviously confusing two names: the Moscow–Minsk highway, which was begun in February 1936, had no relation to Stalin's name. The 'Stalin Line' was what they called the defensive positions, consisting of fortified areas, along the 1940 border of the USSR. The highway really was a match for the best highways of that time. Due to the mobilization nature of the Soviet economy, the work was rapidly

completed. The greater part of the workers engaged in building the highway was made up of prisoners from the Soviet GULAG NKVD labour camps. O. Kornilova, '"Slavnuiu dorogu stroiat chekisty": stroitel'stvo avtomagistrali Moskva–Minsk v 1936 godu', *Istoricheskii zhurnal: nauchnye issledovaniia*, 6, 2014, pp. 660–76.

15. The Spanish explained their long march to the front as being due to some kind of 'discrimination' on the Germans' part, although this march did not differ from the usual German practice. To imagine the Wehrmacht as a highly motorized army would be a mistake. The Germans employed horses in large numbers: for example, horse-drawn transport was the main means of movement and supply in the Fourth and Ninth Armies. One can say the same thing about the infantrymen: many later recalled the exhausting and endless marches during the summer and autumn of 1941, when the infantry was actually forced to catch up on foot with the tank units which were rushing forward. Even such generals as Gotthard Heinrici complained to their wives that they had to march 30–35 kilometres each day. D. Stahel, *Operation Barbarossa and Germany's Defeat in the East*. Cambridge, 2009, pp. 183–5; J. Hürter (ed.), *Notizen aus dem Vernichtungskrieg: Die Ostfront 1941/42 in den Aufzeichnungen des Generals Heinrici*. Darmstadt, 2016, p. 48.

16. Rostislav Zavadskii, a Russian émigré who served as an interpreter in the Walloon Legion (*Légion Wallonie*, or the German 373rd Infantry Battalion) with Belgian volunteers, saw such scenes. In the beginning of December 1941 he left the following entry in his diary: 'One has to witness disagreeable scenes all the time. The Germans take from the inhabitants their last valuables, that is, hay, a cow, a pig, and similar things. There are cries and tears. What can I do? I was able to save something, but for the most part I was forced to be a witness, while gritting my teeth. And another scene: the Germans were unable to get their transport over a bridge because it was too slippery. They got out of this fix by taking the roof (a straw one) from a nearby house and covered the bridge with it. The transport passed and the inhabitants were left without a roof over their heads. And this was in winter! There's nothing more to add.' R.V. Zavadskii, *Svoia chuzhaia voina. Dnevnik russkogo ofitsera vermakhta 1941–1942 gg.*, p. 135.

17. In September–October 1941 the German occupation authorities and the liaison staff with the Blue Division constantly complained about the low level of discipline in the Spanish march columns, pointing out the peasants' unhappiness with the requisitions. What was paradoxical is that a similar requisition of livestock from the population was an absolutely acceptable practice for the German units as well. X.M. Núñez Seixas, *The Spanish Blue Division*, pp. 93–5 and 173–5.

18. Kovalevskii uses the term *golodukha* (severe shortage of food close to famine). Nonetheless, it is true that post-war Spain suffered from a shortage of food and that a rationing system was employed.

19. Of course, not on the scale sketched by Kovalevskii's perception, but the division really did suffer is first losses even before the start of the fighting: several soldiers blew themselves up on mines and died.

20. The author refers to Claudio Rivera Macías (1893–1971), an experienced commander who had already fought in the Riff wars, where he was awarded the Cross of the Order of St. Ferdinand. In May 1931 he submitted to the military reform of the then-minister Manuel Azaña ('Azaña's law') and retired from the position of commander. Two years later he established contact with José Antonio Primo de Rivera and the group which founded the Spanish Falange, and received membership card no. 29. During the Civil War he became the victim of persecution in the Republican zone and once again took

up an activist role. Upon returning from Russia, Rivera occupied a number of positions, retiring with the rank of division general at the end of his career.
21. Count Petr Semenovich Saltykov (1700–72), Russian field marshal and commander-in-chief of the Russian army during the Seven Years War.
22. This is an incorrect assertion. The soldiers' religious care had existed earlier; some priests served as chaplains as early as the First World War. During the Second World War each German division had an authorized chaplain. Catholics served in this capacity in the Wehrmacht: the latter numbered 550 men, while another 17,000 priests and seminary students served in the army in positions not associated with the care of their flock (as medics and the like). The chaplains' diaries and letters from the front are also distinguished by their particular view of current events. L.N. Faulkner, *Negotiating the Cross and the Swastika: Catholic Priests and Seminarians as German Soldiers, 1935–1945*. PhD dissertation, Brown University, 2009, p. 189; D. Popping, *Kriegspfarrer an der Ostfront: Evangelische und katholische Wehrmachtseelsorge im Vernichtungskrieg 1941–945*. Göttingen, 2017. As regards the Spanish division, see the exhaustive description by P. Sagarra, *Capellanes en la División Azul. Los últimos cruzados*. Madrid, 2012.
23. This probably refers to the breakthrough by the 2nd Shock Army to the western bank of the Volkhov River on 13 January 1942. The Spanish positions were south of Miasnoi Bor, at the neck of the breakthrough. The 250th Division subsequently took part in the creation and elimination of the sadly famous 'Volkhov cauldron'.

Novgorod and Its Environs

1. Joseph Rudyard Kipling (1865–1936), a British writer and poet.
2. He is possibly speaking here of the village of Beregovye Moriny.
3. Kovalevskii's considered opinion on the Spanish officers' lack of skill and the excess privileges of their assistants coincides with the impressions of the German liaison officers. X.M. Núñez Seixas, *The Spanish Blue Division*, pp. 83–5.
4. This was really the case: units of the Novgorod Army Group, stationed on the other side of Lake Il'men, constantly dispatched reconnaissance groups across the lake ice. On 23 November a group from the 225th Rifle Division crossed, 'escorted by the captured Spaniard Marko'. On 25 December, in the same area, a detachment of 185 men crossed under the command of Captain Tatur. Central Archives of the Ministry of Defense of the Russian Federation (TsAMO RF). Fond 1499, opis' 1, delo 11, list 2; TsAMO RF. Fond 1499, opis' 1, delo 8, list 213; TsAMO RF. Fond 1499, opis' 1, delo 11, list 58.
5. In the German camps in the autumn of 1941 8,348 Soviet prisoners of war died each day. By February 1942 about two million prisoners, out of the 3.3 million taken prisoner in 1941, had died from starvation and disease. The conscious murder by starvation of hundreds of thousands of prisoners is the greatest of the Wehrmacht's crimes as an institution. The situation only changed by the middle of 1942, when they began to view Soviet prisoners as a source of free work and to put them to forced labour. For an updated overview, see R. Keller, *Sowjetische Kriegsgefangene im Deutschen Reich 1941/42*. Göttingen, 2011, pp. 320–3. See also C. Streit, 'Soviet Prisoners of War in the Hands of the Wehrmacht', in H. Heer and K. Naumann (eds), *War of Extermination: The German Military in World War II, 1941–1944*. New York, Oxford, 2000, pp. 80–1.
6. Incidents of corruption and favoritism in the Blue Division's quartermaster service were uncovered regularly: they were discovered by both the Germans and the volunteers themselves, including Falangist leaders such as Dionisio Ridruejo. However,

Kovalevskii's assertion that most of the corrupt people among the officers were Falangists raises doubts. X.M. Núñez Seixas, *Camarada invierno*, pp. 122–3.

7. Upon the Wehrmacht's arrival in Pushkin at the end of 1941, the Soviet collaborator Daniil Fedorovich Petrov (1918–2011), more famous under the pseudonym of 'Vladimir Rudinskii', entered German service in the capacity of an interpreter. In Popovka in May 1942 he transferred to the Spanish division and until November served in the 13th Company of one of the battalions. After the war, he left his short memoirs, in which he described a similar situation in which the Spaniards courted the girls, while trying to be of use. 'I remember, by the way, a picture which I had occasion to observe on one of my first days with the Spaniards. Some young peasant girl was working on her plot. A Spaniard came up to her and started to speak with her; within a minute her shovel was in his hands and he began to work at full strength. Before long he had been joined by several other Spaniards; one takes up a bucket and begins to water the beds of plants, while another finds some other kind of work of this type, while all the girl has to do is to issue general instructions. The Germans never resorted to this kind of courtship!' V.S. Rudinskii, 'S ispantsami na Leningradskom fronte', *Pod belym krestom*, 2, April 1952, p. 13.
8. Kovalevskii is speaking about Major Angel Enríquez Larrondo, the commander of the 262nd Infantry Regiment's 1st Battalion.
9. Following the transfer of the Spanish division to the Pushkin area, the German SD organs (*Sicherheitsdienst*, or the SS *Reichsführer*'s security service) made the following note in its reports regarding the population's attitude: 'Concerning the discipline of the Spanish, compared to that of the Germans, they call them gypsies and robbers ... There are rumours that "The Germans are angels compared to the Spanish".' Central State Archive of St. Petersburg (TsGA SPB). Fond 9788, opis' 1, delo 16, list 12. SD-Aussenstelle Pawlovsk, Lage-und Stimmungsbericht 26.8–10.9.1942.
10. The Spanish soldiers' inability to use the stoves in the peasant huts increased the number of accidental fires, which amazed both the local residents and the Germans. X.M. Núñez Seixas, *Camarada invierno*, p. 267.

In the Trenches

1. This is most likely an aberration of memory. The city park is now the Kremlin Park in the city centre. To judge by the description, this is most likely the park near the Antoniev Monastery, in the commercial quarter.
2. It's assumed that the author is speaking about Hipólito Echeverría Ibarrola, a former sergeant from the *Navarra tercio* in the Civil War, during which he was awarded the rank of provisional sergeant. He was assigned to the 262nd Infantry Regiment's 3rd Battalion and during his service was awarded the Military Cross (*Cruz de Guerra*). He returned to Spain in May 1942 from his second tour. AGMAV 4593/7.
3. The Blue Division was a good example of the cohesion created by the 'primary groups' of like-minded confederates, comrades-in-arms from the Civil War, people from the same region and relatives. Even such a man as Kovalevskii could have encountered familiar red berets with whom he had fought in 1938–9.
4. This is a mistake in the company's number. He is speaking of the 3rd Company, under the command of Captain Antonio Leiva Leaniz-Barrutia, who in August 1942 was awarded the Iron Cross Second Class.
5. On 12 October 1941 the Spanish 262nd Infantry Regiment's 3rd Battalion relieved the units of the 18th Motorized Division's 30th Regiment in its positions in the area of the bridge near Bolotovo. National Archives and Records Administration (NARA). T-315.

R. 1726. F. 244. The Germans (the surgeon, Hans Killian) ascribed to the Spanish soldiers the desire to employ hand grenades in fighting.
6. The author is speaking about Captain Sergio Gómez Alba, a graduate of the military academy in Zaragoza.
7. This is a mistake in the regiment's number. Kovalevskii is speaking here of the Blue Division's 263rd Infantry Regiment.
8. This appears to be a mistake in dates and circumstances. Major Rivera Macías commanded the 262nd Infantry Regiment's 1st Battalion from 11–12 October 1942, having relieved Enríquez Larrondo at this assignment. Captain Fernández held the post of temporary battalion commander for only three days – 27 September–1 October 1941.
9. The author is speaking of Manuel M. Gómez y Fernández de Bobadilla, a resident of Irún (Guipuzcoa) and son of a local notary. At the beginning of the Civil War he made his way to the zone occupied by the insurrectionists. He signed up with the Spanish Legion, where he advanced from corporal to temporary junior lieutenant and was repeatedly wounded and decorated. In the Blue Division he served in the 4th Company of the 262nd Infantry Regiment's 1st Battalion. He perished in December 1941. AGMAV 4686/19.
10. Kovalevskii is speaking of Colonel José Martínez Esparza (?–1949), the commander of the Blue Division's 269th Infantry Regiment and a veteran of the Rif war. Although he was praised as a competent military man, many of the division's soldiers were not fond of Esparza. In particular, many Falangists reproached him for his indifference to political ideals, his cruel methods of command, his spiteful treatment of subordinates, and his orders to undertake clearly suicidal attacks. Esparza's reputation outstripped him to such an extent that captured Spaniards complained about him to the Red Army soldiers, which the latter immediately used for propaganda, and the legionnaires returning from the Russian front sometimes sang such ditties: 'Hey, you, Esparza the asshole, where did you come galloping from? I've arrived from Russia, I shit the division away' (¿De dónde vienes, Esparza, de dónde vienes, cabrón? Vengo de Rusia, de joder a la División). In this case, Kovalevskii is expressing a widely-held opinion, which coincides with what the Falangist Dionisio Ridruejo wrote in one of his letters in which he curses 'the monster, Colonel Esparza'. X.M. Núñez Seixas, *The Spanish Blue Division*, p. 109; 'Vechrenee soobshchenie 3 ianvaria 1942 g', *Soobshcheniia Sovetskogo Informbiuro*. Vol. 2. *Ianvar'–iiun' 1942 goda*. Moscow, 1944, p. 10.
11. The Spaniards complained about the meagre German rations, their content and the absence of hot food for dinner, beginning as early as their stay in the Grafenwöhr training camp and did not cease throughout the following months.
12. This is a distortion of memory and the anticipation of events. The Blue Division's soldiers were allowed to receive parcels from their relatives in Spain, and at the end of November 1941 General José Moscardó, who had commanded the troops besieged at the Alcázar of Toledo in 1936 and was quite popular in European anti-communist circles thanks to the Italian film *The Siege of the Alcazar* (1940), personally left for the Russian front in order to award a 'special gift' (*donativo especial*) to the soldiers from Franco – tobacco and wine. The rest of the soldiers had to wait: the German food gift assortment was distributed for Christmas 1941, while the same assortment from the Blue Division – food, drink and clothes, which had been collected by the FET's female section – was received only at the end of January 1942. X.M. Núñez Seixas, *Camarada invierno*, p. 359.
13. Kovalevskii's depressing description is clear hyperbole. Nonetheless, it is known that the division's quartermasters were corrupt and ineffective, which also drove many

soldiers to robbery in the nearby rear. The German liaison officers in the headquarters reported these incidents beginning in October 1941. Ibid., pp. 266–7.
14. Once again, the number of deserters is exaggerated. Five such incidents were noted by the beginning of December, to which may be added unsuccessful attempts to cross the front line: there were twenty-four trials of deserters in the division between November 1941 and August 1942. One of the deserters, whom we were unable to identify, knew Russian and was captured by the Spaniards in attempting to swim across the river. They sometimes employed deserters in radio propaganda and they would appeal to their former comrades to lay down their arms and come over to the Red Army. X. M. Núñez Seixas, *The Spanish Blue Division*, pp. 70–1; Archivo Municipal de Cádiz (FGV-AMC). Report by Dirección General de Seguridad to General Varela, n. d. (early December 1941), p. 115; M.I. Suknev, *Zapiski komandira shtrafbata. Vospominaniia kombata. 1941–1945*. Moscow, 2007, p. 62. On Spanish prisoners of war in the USSR, see: A.V. Elpat'evskii, *Golubaia diviziia: voennoplennye i internirovannye ispantsy v SSSR*. Moscow, 2015, pp. 120–55.
15. Aleksandr Aleksandrovich Tringam (1896–1981) was from Sumy and the son of an officer. He fought in the First World War as a volunteer in the 10th Novgorod Dragoon Regiment. He was wounded in the fighting in February 1915. He was a St. George's Cross holder. In 1917 he graduated from the Elisavetgrad Cavalry School. During the civil war in Russia he served as a staff cavalry captain in the Drozdovskii cavalry battalion. He retreated with the Russian army from the Crimea in November 1920 and was in the camp at Gallipoli. He lived as an émigré in Belgrade. He was a member of the Russian National Union of War Participants (RNSUV) and the 'Russian Falcon' Society. From July 1938 he took part as a volunteer in the Spanish Civil War as a traditionalist volunteer, first in the *Navarra tercio*, and then in the *Doña María de Molína tercio*. He was seriously wounded in January 1939 with a bullet in his hand and grenade fragments in his head, and was evacuated to a hospital in San Sebastián. Despite his wounds, he was recognized as a 'useful invalid'. He left the hospital at the end of May. In September 1939 he received Spanish citizenship. Upon settling in Madrid, he worked as bookkeeper's assistant at an electrical factory. He volunteered to go to Finland in December 1939, but was not accepted. In July 1941, while working in the headquarters of the National Militia in Madrid, he signed up as a volunteer in the Blue Division after lying about his age (he took off ten years). He served in a veterinary company until October 1942, when he was transferred to the position of translator in the Second Section of the division headquarters. In May 1942 he had the rank of *Sonderführer* (a civilian specialist with knowledge useful to the army; such specialists were part of a parallel system of ranks corresponding to army ranks), which corresponded to the rank of sergeant. In November 1943 he was transferred to the first section of the headquarters and that same month married Tat'iana Shitnikova (Filonova). In February 1944 he returned to Spain with his wife and her mother, after which he was decorated several times, received the rank of honorary junior lieutenant of cavalry and the rank of permanent sergeant-invalid of cavalry. He worked with the journals *The Military Past* and *The Sentry*. He lived on the outskirts of Madrid, in Pinto, where he passed away in February 1981. A.V. Okorokov, *Molodezhnye organizatsii russkoi emigratsii: 1920–1945 gg*. Moscow, 2000, p. 18; AGMAV 4390/112, 5347/4; Sht.-rotm. A.A. Tringam, 'Peshii boi 10 drag. Novgorodskogo polka', *Voennaia byl'*, 79 (May 1966), pp. 22–5; 'Spisok sotrudnikov zhurnala "Voennaia byl'" (s 1952 po 1967 g.)', *Voennaia byl'*, 85 (May 1967), p. 45; 'Nezabytye mogily', *Chasovoi*, 630 (2) (March–April 1981), p. 18.

16. Lev Georgievich Totskii (Lukin) (1898–1983) was a cadet from Sumy. He fought in the First World War and the civil war in Russia. As an émigré in France he worked as a taxi driver. From March 1937 he fought in Spain and served in the *Doña María de Molina tercio*. He was granted Spanish citizenship in August 1939. In July 1941 he joined the Blue Division and worked as an ambulance driver; in December he was transferred to the position of translator to the Spanish hospital in Grigorovo and later served with the artillery and in two regiments at the same position. He was distinguished by his cynical careerism and unpardonable behaviour, and he robbed the Russian population. The intentional distortions of his 'transfer' were recalled even by the Spaniards. He returned to Spain with a Russian wife, Irina Stepanovna Parysheva. He resided in Madrid until the summer of 1945 and soon migrated to Argentina, where he lived with his wife until his death. See E. Errando Vilar, *Campaña de Invierno*. Madrid, 1943, p. 144.
17. The author is speaking about the 'iron ration' (*Eiserne Ration*), a hermetically sealed food assortment for the Wehrmacht's soldiers, which could only be opened on strict orders by the commander in cases of extreme necessity and the cessation of regular supply. The ration included 300 grams of biscuits and hard barley bread (*Knäckebrot*), 200 grams of preserved meat, 150 grams of oatmeal, and 20 grams of ground coffee. Many Spaniards, eaten up by curiosity, set about consuming their 'emergency rations' as early as the camp in Grafenwöhr.
18. Spanish thievery was so unbridled that Soviet prisoners looked to the Germans for protection (!). In the documents of the XXXVIII Army Corps there are various notes of this sort. In the beginning of December 1941 the deserter Ivan Ryzhkov, from the 305th Rifle Division's 1002nd Rifle Regiment, complained that the Spaniards had immediately taken his warm clothing and had not fed him at all (they ate his ration) and that they also constantly and without reason beat him. Grigorii Khramov from the 1004th Rifle Regiment of the same division complained on the insufficient food with the Spanish. NARA. T-314. R. 900. F. 1104, 1111–1113.
19. This should be sub-lieutenant or ensign (*alférez*).
20. Konstantin Andreevich Goncharenko (Chudov) (1902–42) was a graduate of the Konstantinv Military School in Kiev. He was a St. George's cavalier. He took part in the civil war in Russia and was a second lieutenant in the Markov Regiment. He later emigrated. From August 1937 he fought in the Spanish Civil War, with the rank of sergeant. In 1941 he was an honorary junior lieutenant in the Spanish Foreign Legion's 3rd *tercio*. In July 1941 he joined the Blue Division as a volunteer with this rank and was appointed to the headquarters of the 263rd Infantry Regiment. He married Anna Zhemchuzhina. He was killed at the end of March 1942; on 22 March funeral services were held according to the Orthodox rite and he was buried in Grigorovo. He was posthumously awarded the Iron Cross Second Class at the end of April. The Gallipoli veterans remembered him in Paris six months after his death. He was reinterred in the Spanish sector of the German military cemetery in Pankovka, near Novgorod the Great. AGMAV 4688/11; 'Nekrolog', *Parizhskii Vetsnik*, 13, 6 September 1942, p. 6.
21. Goncharenko was the interpreter for the 263rd Infantry Regiment's 2nd Battalion, according to C. Ibáñez Cagna, 'Los voluntarios rusos en la División', *Blau División*, 385 (1991), p. 4.
22. The episode being described may be dated to the middle of November 1941. Stalin read a report in honour of the twenty-fourth anniversary of the October Revolution on 6 November, at a solemn meeting of the Moscow Soviet of Worker's Deputies and party and social organizations of Moscow. On 7 November he gave a speech before

the participants of a military parade on Red Square. Both speeches were distributed as leaflets.
23. This took place on 21 March 1942.
24. This is a slight aberration in Kovalevskii's memory, and it is also likely he heard the story from someone else. The following picture emerges when comparing the sources. On 21 March a Spanish reconnaissance group left Khutyn' before daybreak; their task was to cross the frozen Malyi Volkhovets and to launch a raid on the village of Novonikolaevskoe, which was occupied by the soldiers of the 225th Rifle Division's 299th Rifle Regiment. The Spaniards covered about three kilometres to the east. The Soviet division's combat journal states that the enemy reconnaissance group, numbering up to forty men, left Khutyn' and as early as 0300 attempted to infiltrate into the depth of the defensive line. Upon reaching their goal, the Spaniards opened close-range fire. The Red Army troops immediately threw in a group of twenty-five men from the neighbouring sector and began to fire back in an organized fashion. Following a brief fight, the Spaniards fell back to their own lines, leaving several rifles, grenades and helmets, and also a greatcoat and camouflage clothing in the snow. According to Spanish sources, both sides sustained losses: in the 299th Regiment's combat journal it was noted that on 21 March, as the result of enemy fire, a junior commander in the 3rd Battalion was killed. Goncharenko was shot in the left hip, after which he was taken to the hospital, where he soon died from loss of blood. The exact circumstances of Goncharenko's death are obscure and for some reason the émigrés, having gone through so many wars, saw in this a strange symbol. Shinkarenko: 'As the young Bibikov later told me, Goncharenko was wounded in some kind of search on the ice of a lake, in the fleshy part of the leg. It was a slight wound [Editor's note. According to Spanish sources it was a serious wound]. He was bandaged up and placed on a cot at the dressing station, or in the first hospital detachment. And there he died. There is something unbelievably mysterious in Goncharenko's death and even wounding.' At the end of April a Madrid newspaper placed a short obituary. TsAMO RF, fond 6835, opis' 68938, delo 1, list 40; TsAMO RF, fond 1499, opis' 1, delo 17, list 16; Stanford University Hoover Institution Archives. Nikolai Vsevolodovich Shinkarenko Memoirs (HIA/Shinkarenko). Box 6. Chapter XII. 'V Ispanii. O godakh voiny, v kotoroi ia ne uchastvoval. I besplodnye popytki, kotorye ia delal, chtoby priniat' v nei uchastie', p. 171.
25. Sergei Konstantinovich Gurskii (Ali-Riza Magometov-Gurskii) (1895–1966) came from the hereditary nobility, born in Sebastopol and was of the Orthodox faith. He was a graduate of the Naval Corps. In 1915 he completed the Nikolai Cavalry School in St. Petersburg. During the First World War he was a cavalry staff captain in the Empress Catherine the Great Glukhov 6th Dragoon Regiment. He took part in the civil war in Russia. In the Northern Caucasus he converted from Orthodoxy to Islam and commanded a company. He left the Crimea and resided in Berlin. He had made an attempt to join the Freemasons, but was eventually turned down. By mid-1920s he moved to Prague, where he became a member of a branch of the ROVS and the 'Second Generation' (*Vtoroe pokolenie*) organization; in the latter he was one of the editors of the weekly under the same title. He worked as a secretary in a theatre, where he met the famous dancer and choreographer Nina Jirsíková. They got married in February 1927 but divorced in 1930. From February 1937 he served in the ranks of the 4th *Bandera* of the Spanish Foreign Legion, where he spent 16 months; he later served in the *Doña María de Molina* and *Montejurra tercios*. He was wounded four times, twice in the head. He was decorated several times. He was recommended for an officer's rank in the Legion, but was nevertheless not promoted because he was a Russian, and thus only received the rank of corporal. He knew cartography well and following Franco's

victory he was head of the map section in the Higher Army School. In July 1941 he was a volunteer in the Blue Division. In June 1942 he returned to Spain. Iaremchuk wrote: 'Gurskii returned within a year and I asked him: what right did he have to return, but he replied that he could not withstand air attacks. He became extremely insulted . . . ' In October 1944, he finally received the honorary rank of lieutenant in the Legion. He was the editor of one of the Russian sections of Spanish radio. He died in Madrid. AGMAV 1978/3; 'Nezabytye mogily', *Chasovoi*, 485 (11) (November 1966), p. 23; A. Gabrieli [A. P. Iaremchuk II], 'S ital'ianskoi armiei v Rossii', p. 84.

26. Once again, he's laying it on thick.
27. The author is speaking about Anna Zhemchuzhina, the 35-year-old chief of the section for weak patients in the Kolmovo psychiatric hospital and a participant in mass murders. In the autumn of 1941 about 250 patients were 'removed' from their rooms. Upon being 'quieted down' by injections, the patients were transported in trucks 20 kilometres outside of Novgorod, where they were placed in a large barn and killed. Zhemchuzhina's name figures in post-war interrogations among those who approved of a similar practice of destroying patients. Zhemchuzhina took part in injecting narcotic drugs into patients as they were being loaded onto trucks. In the beginning of 1942, within a month after her wedding to Goncharenko, she died of the galloping flu. B.N. Kovalev, 'Palachi i zhertvy Kolmovskoi bol'nitsy', *Peterburgskii istoricheskii zhurnal*, 3 (2016), pp. 254–6.
28. This 'secret' is nothing but the fruit of the author's imagination. However, the fact remains that neither Goncharenko nor Zhemchuzhina survived the winter of 1941–2.

Main Headquarters

1. The following episode characterizes the war during this period and in this place. On the night of 26 October a patrol of thirteeen men, from the 3rd Tank Division, reached the Spaniards' strongpoint in the Kirillov Monastery. 'The enemy, who was in the monastery, fell back behind the Levoshnia River, and while retreating kept up a disorganized rifle fire.' The group attempted to burn down the stone building with bottles filled with flammable liquid and fell back. Later on the Soviet forces tried repeatedly to take the strongpoint, which was located on an island in the middle of a swampy flood land, and suffered heavy losses. TsAMO RF, fond 3003, opis' 1, delo 1, list 519.
2. The Spanish, who were experiencing a great shortage of personnel, selected Soviet citizens who knew the language. Aleksei Inosemskii (Inozemtsev) (1924–after 1990) worked as a glazier in Pushkin. At the end of the 1930s he met the children of Spanish Republicans who had left for the USSR, and from 1937 to 1941 was a student at the Pioneer Palace in Leningrad, where he learned Spanish. While under occupation at the end of the summer of 1942 he became acquainted with the Spaniards and accepted their invitation to enter their service. As a private in the 262nd Infantry Regiment's 15th Company, he took part in the fighting against the Red Army around Volkhov and Tikhvin and was decorated with the Red Cross of the Order of Military Merit (*Orden del Mérito Militar con distintivo rojo*). Under the name of 'Aleksei Konstantino', he left the USSR at the end of 1943 with a Spanish contingent for Königsberg, and from there to San Sebastián. He joined the Spanish Foreign Legion in Morocco and served for two years. He left to work in Barcelona and began work in the American consulate, and was then transferred to Paris. He got in touch with the Soviet-émigré organization 'Soviet Patriot', and under unclear circumstances left for the USSR in 1948. He got a sentence of 25 years in the camps on the charge of betraying the motherland.

He was amnestied in 1955. He lived in St. Petersburg in the beginning of the 1990s and demanded that he be recognized as a victim of political repression. His appeal was declined.

The philologist Iuliia Abramovna Dobrovol'skaia spoke about her classmate, the Novgorod resident Aleksei Ardalionovich Almazov (1917–2004): 'His father, a lawyer, rotted in the camps, and Lesha also rotted in his own way. His mother, following the university, never saw her only son again. At the beginning of the war he joined the Militia [Editor's note. The 3rd Guards People's Militia Division]. The Spanish "Blue Division" was stationed near Leningrad, and he was captured [Editor's note. This was at the end of the summer of 1941, in the Krasnoe Selo area, and he at first served in German units] and was assigned as an interpreter. That's it! The way back is barred: a collaborator! He ended up in Germany with the retreating units and then travelled to Argentina. In Buenos Aires he married a cultured Russian girl, Vera, and they moved to the States, to Washington, where he taught Spanish. They had three children, two sons and a daughter, and one son was a diplomat. A good and decent family.' B.N. Kovalev, *Dobrovol'tsy na chuzhoi voine. Ocherki istorii Goluboi divizii*. Velikii Novgorod, 2014, pp. 316–18; B.V. Bjorkelund, *Puteshestvie v stranu vsevozmozhnykh nevozmozhnostei*. Edited by S.A. Man'kov. St. Petersburg, 2014, p. 212; Iu.A. Dobrovol'skaia, *Post Scriptum: vmesto memuarov*. St. Petersubrg, 2006, p. 43. On Spanish children in the USSR, see: K.D. Qualls, *Stalin's Niños: Education of Spanish Civil War Refugee Children in the Soviet Union, 1937–1951*. Toronto; Buffalo; London, 2020.

3. In order to create a military police (field *Gendarmerie*), the army ministry announced the enrollment of volunteers from the Civil Guard, a Spanish police corps deployed in the countryside under military command. Their task consisted of controlling movement in the division's rear and in escorting arriving and departing Spanish soldiers to the deep rear (*Zona de Retaguardia*). Police posts were established in Berlin, Bruchberg, Vilnius, Königsberg, Riga and Hof, as well as on French territory. Two mobile 'mini-brigades' were created and located in Berlin, Königsberg, Riga and Pskov, whose tasks included intelligence and counterintelligence regarding the enemy, civilians and their own troops. The division headquarters' Second Section headed the anti-partisan struggle in the rear. The initial complement of fifty-four Civil Guards gradually increased due to the arrival of those from Spain. Five captains, 16 Lieutenants and 320 NCOs from the Civil Guard saw service in the Blue Division. J. García Hispán, *La Guardia Civil en la División Azul*. Alicante, 1991; J.N. Núñez Calvo, 'La Guardia Civil en la División Española de Voluntarios', *Aportes*, 61 (2006), pp. 86–118; V.J. Hall, '"For a better Spain and a Fairer Europe": A Re-Examination of the Spanish Blue Division in its Social, Cultural and Political Context, 1941–2005'. Master Thesis, National University of Ireland. Maynooth, 2005, pp. 100–06.

4. In this case, Kovalevskii is quite evenhanded and not far from the truth. Despite the praise for the Blue Division in the OKW daily reports, 'on the ground' many German commanders had a negative opinion of the formation, in the professional sense, particularly of the officer and NCO corps. At the same time, the Wehrmacht's rank-and-file infantry soldiers (*Landser*) valued some of their Spanish comrades' qualities, from which there very quickly began to grow the romantic myth of the Spaniards' 'heroism' and 'warmth'. Pre-existing stereotypes on Spain played an important role in creating the myth. X.M. Núñez Seixas, *The Spanish Blue Division*, pp. 83–4.

5. José Miguel Guitarte Yrigaray (1914–43) was a former communist and involved in the founding of the Spanish Falange and the Spanish University Union (*Sindicato Español Universitario*, or SEU), whose leader he was in 1941. In April 1942 he took part in the

European University Congress in Dresden. Several months after his return to Spain he was appointed to the post of member of the *Cortes*, but died of a disease he picked up in Russia.

6. José Enrique Varela (1891–1951), a general and an outstanding Spanish military personage, took part in the African campaign and was one of the plotters against the Spanish Republic and played a notable role in the Franco camp during the civil war. During August 1939–August 1942 he occupied the post of army minister while distinguishing himself by his hostility toward the Falange. He later accepted the post of supreme commissar for Morocco. Varela often expressed his delight with the Wehrmacht, but this did not prevent him from taking enormous bribes from the British, who were attempting to secure Spain's neutrality in the war.

7. Kovalevskii is speaking of the Cross of the Order of Saint Ferdinand – the highest medal, which Varela was awarded twice for his actions during the war in Africa.

8. It's assumed that he is speaking of Colonel José M. Troncoso Sagredo, the chief of the division staff.

9. It's implied that this was the strategy of creating fortified points, so-called *blocaos* (from the German word *blockhaus*), in which a detachment of soldiers was housed, controlling the sector assigned to them. A German officer from the First World War, Werner Beumelburg (1899–1963), who later became a convinced Nazi and journalist writing on military affairs, published a book on the experiences of the Condor Legion, which fought in Spain. W. Beumelburg, *Kampf um Spanien. Die Geschichte der Legion Condor.* Berlin, 1939.

10. This should be the 269th Infantry Regiment.

11. Of course, the sortie to the Volkhov, which was carried out by the 269th Infantry Regiment and German sub-units, was not Martínez Esparza's plan alone, but was part of a large-scale operation by the entire Army Group. Its goals were to seize the Tikhvin transport hub and all Soviet forces south of Lake Ladoga, and to link up with the Finns beyond the Svir' River. Moreover, it was planned to break through to Vyshnii Volochek south of Lake Il'men. On 19 October the Spaniards forced the Volkhov River and, during the course of bitter fighting in conditions of extreme cold, seized several inhabited locales. In the beginning of November the Spaniards relieved the Germans in their positions in Posad, Otenskoe and Poselok. In Posad the division's soldiers maintained a defence for several days against desperate Soviet counter-attacks, while being bombarded with light artillery. In December the German command ordered the Spaniards to fall back to the river's western bank. The division's losses were significant: no less than 700 killed, 1,800 wounded and 1,300 sick. The division's military press and the Falangist media zealously glorified those who died, among whom were such noted Falangist leaders as Enrique Sotomayor. An entire propaganda campaign, which actually sought to cover up a local retreat and no small amount of losses, inflated the fighting in Posad and Otenskoe to the height of the heroic literature of antiquity. Besides this, the Blue Division received a proportionately larger number of Iron Crosses than did the German units. X.M. Núñez Seixas, *The Spanish Blue Division*, pp. 109–10.

12. This episode took place not on the Orthodox Christmas (7 January) but on 9 October 1938. On the day, Protopresbyter Aleksandr Shabashev arrived at Cerro del Contadero to the Russian detachment of the *Doña María de Molina tercio*. In his memoirs, penned only a few weeks after the events, Shabashev wrote: 'On that day we had guests arriving from [*tercio*] Navarra – Colonel Vladimir Avramovich Dvoichenko and Lieutenant Kovalevskii. The cavalry officers from a nearby regiment were invited to come over as well. We have had one blast of a celebration. To use Colonel Boltin's

colloquial expression, "one cannot walk out sober from a Russian regimental holiday". [. . .] Suffice it to say many of us, especially the Spaniards, grew weak in flesh, and few of us could stand up straight on their own two feet. [. . .] We waved our guests goodbye with a rifle salute, which had later brought troubles for the Russian detachment: seen from afar, the cavalry movement and the shooting on the mountain ridge had alarmed the neighbouring units – the latter immediately arrived to lend a hand to "the Russian unit attacked by the red cavalry". In the end, we even had to report back to the HQ, confirming that we were indeed safe, and that the key to the Aragonese front still remains in reliable Russian hands.' Russian State Library (RGB). 'Na ispanskom fronte. Rasskaz protopresvitera o. A. Sh', *Nasha gazeta (Sofia)*, no. 12, 4 January 1939, p. 7.

13. These are inaccurate evaluations, although it's possible that they reflect the opinion of part of the division. From 11 November 1941 through 31 March 1942 the Spaniards received 159 Iron Crosses Second Class, while the other German units of the XXXVIII Army Corps received 161. The Spaniards received 325 Military Merit Crosses and the Germans 210.

14. Kovalevskii refers here to Captain Teodoro Palacios Cueto (1912–80), who was taken prisoner at the battle of Krasnyi Bor (10 February 1943), and returned from Soviet captivity in April 1954 alongside 247 Spaniards released by the Soviet regime, most of them war prisoners of the Blue Division, but also some civil inmates. Palacios was treated as a hero by the Franco regime, as well as his comrade Captain Gerardo Oroquieta, and even exalted as a model of Spanish military character, as he acted as the leader of all Spanish POWs and refused to cooperate with the Soviet authorities. His autobiography, penned with the help of journalist Torcuato Luca de Tena, *Embajador en el infierno. Memorias del capitán Palacios: once años de cautiverio en Rusia* (Madrid, 1955) became a best-seller and also inspired the film *Embajadores en el infierno* (1955, José M. Forqué). Palacios was given control over seven later expeditions to repatriate 'war children' from the Soviet Union, until 1959. He was promoted to general, yet he always remained as 'Captain Palacios' in Spanish popular culture.

15. An inaccurate generalization. The Bolshevik regime indeed mistreated and mistrusted its own returnees and those who had managed to survive in the German camps. However, the policy did not entail arbitrarily sending all of the former prisoners to Siberia: instead, the prisoners underwent a 'filtration' process and were interrogated, which most of the time resulted in a release. The problem was that in the USSR the fact of being captured or having lived in the occupied territory was a social stigma like no other.

16. From *odalık* (Turk.), meaning servant or housemaid. The word is used here in the sense of 'concubine' or 'available girl'.

17. A number of reliable cases have been confirmed when an officer took on a Russian mistress. There are repeated mentions of Russian girls ready to enter into relations with various ranks in exchange for food and protection. It's hard to confirm Kovalevskii's stories about the mores reigning in the division; in any event, they appear to be quite subjective. X.M. Núñez Seixas, *The Spanish Blue Division*, pp. 179–80.

18. Spanish sources state that Gurskii did not just take part in drinking bouts. According to a note by the General Director of Security, for 9 December 1941, addressed to General Varela, Gurskii had written several letters to officers studying at the Higher Army School in Madrid. Army censorship intercepted these letters: they testified that 'the Spanish officers' conduct in Russia was absolutely scandalous. Gurskii's main task was to deliver Russian prostitutes to the Spaniards, who organized orgies and drinking

bouts every day. Morals have really gone downhill in this regard.' FGV-AMC. Box 115. Report by Dirección General de Seguridad to Varela, 9 December 1941.

19. The correct name is Konstantin Aleksandrovich Gogidzhanoshvili (earlier, Gogidzhanov, as well as the corrupted versions: Gognidzhanoshvili, Gogidzhonashvili) (1895–1965), from Batumi, the son of a Georgian and a German woman, Matilda Strauf. He was a graduate of the Odessa Cadet Corps. During the First World War he completed the Elisavetgrad Cavalry School and served as a cavalry captain in the Caucasus Native Division. He took part in the civil war in Russia and served in the cavalry under General Barbovich. He was an émigré in France. He joined the *Navarra tercio* with a group of Georgians in San Sebastián in November 1936 and distinguished himself in the fighting on several fronts, for which in April 1937 he was promoted to a red beret lieutenant. He was wounded several times and lost an eye. After the war, with the rank of honorary lieutenant in the Spanish Foreign Legion, he was dispatched for military-historical service. His nickname was 'teniente Konstantino', because his surname was so hard for the Spaniards to pronounce. In December 1939 he attempted to volunteer for Finland, but he was not accepted. He enrolled as a volunteer in the Blue Division in July 1941 and was assigned to the information service (intelligence) in the headquarters' Second Section, and later served in the 269th Infantry Regiment's headquarters. In January 1942 he fought in a ski company on Lake Il'men and suffered frostbite and was back at headquarters at the end of the month. He distinguished himself in the fighting for Krasnyi Bor: on the morning of 11 February 1943 a group of Spaniards under his command knocked out a medium tank, after which he later knocked out a heavy tank, which had driven up to the headquarters, and dragged a wounded German soldier from the battlefield. From the middle of February 1943 he held the post of the Second Section's (intelligence and counterintelligence) head officer in the division's headquarters. His service record mentions that he exposed some kind of 'Russian espionage plan' in the area of Lake Il'men, 'arresting a large number of communist spies who had escaped from the concentration camps', and also carried out 'propaganda against the Red forces'. Following the division's withdrawal from the front in November 1943, he remained with the Blue Legion. He returned with the Legion to Spain in April 1944. He was decorated several times. He was distinguished by his cruel treatment of the Russian population and prisoners of war. Colonel Esparza recalled him as a good rider, while another of the division's officers described him as a reserved and solitary man of few words and no friends. In 1946 he did construction work in Barcelona. From 1947, having confirmed his knowledge of Russian before a special selection committee, he was accepted as an interpreter and honorary Legion captain into the army general staff, where he served up to the time of his death. Following the signing of the Madrid Pact in 1953, he also cooperated with the Americans; he was involved in the Society of USSR Repatriates (*Delegación de Repatriados de la URSS*). This is how Shinkarenko recalled him: 'This Konstantino was a very relative Georgian [. . .] In 1937, at least, he probably only knew such Georgian words as '*mravaldzhamie*' [Editor's note. A Caucasian drinking song] [. . .] He was a brave officer, but suffered from a certain elementary level of education, which is why he would insert clumsy translations of Spanish terms into ordinary Russian conversational speech and began to speak Russian worse than he spoke it before [before 1959]. He Georganized his surname: It's now written as Gogidzhanoshvili. Our relations came to an end. However, that does not prevent me from saying right now that as a combat officer he was, and probably still is, brave and diligent.' He died under the wheels of an automobile on the streets of Madrid. AGMAV 3784/6, 4678/37 and 4702/37, as well as his service record in AGMS 2262; J. Martínez Esparza, *Con la*

División Azul en Rusia. Madrid, 1943, p. 83; E. Errando Vilar, *Campaña de invierno*, p. 222; HIA/Shinkarenko. Box 4. Chapter II. 'Pulia v golovu', pp. 20–1; 'Nezabytye mogily', *Chasovoi*, 476: 2 (February 1966), p. 24.

20. Igor' Perchin [Pershin] (Pozniak) (1917–79) was from Mogilev and the son of Russian émigrés. He grew up in Madrid. He worked as a translator in the *Havas* Agency and cooperated with the censorship authorities. He enrolled as a volunteer in the Blue Division in 1941. He was the only one of the division's Russian volunteers who was a civilian and not a military man; at the time he joined he explained that he was a Catholic and an editor. In October 1941 he was assigned to the division's Second Section and in February 1942 was awarded the rank of *Sonderführer*, which corresponded to the rank of sergeant. Perchin returned to Spain at the end of May 1942, where he resided until the end of his life. He worked for Air France. In 1954 he was awarded Spanish citizenship. He died in Madrid. AGMAV 4336/30.
21. No reference has been found for this story, which seems to be an invention by Kovalevskii, perhaps based on rumours.
22. Many accounts by the division's soldiers present the stereotype of the Russian peasants as people devoid of morality and victims of Soviet atheism. D. Ridruejo, *Cuadernos de Rusia*, p. 262 (entry of 28 October 1941).
23. As explained above, Martínez Esparza had quite a bad reputation among many Blue Division soldiers, particularly the Falangists, for his brutal behaviour towards his subordinates. However, he was also valued as a good military commander. Nothing indicates that his death was plotted by any conspiracy, as Kovalevskii suggests.
24. Kovalevskii relates the story of the famous General Erwin Rommel, the 'Desert Fox'. Implicated in the 20 July 1944 plot to assassinate Hitler, Rommel was given a tough choice between committing suicide, with assurances that his family would be taken care of, or facing a military trial, which would have ended in a hanging sentence. Rommel chose the latter and committed suicide with cyanide. As a result, he was given a lavish state funeral.
25. This is a mistake. There were three regiments in the Blue Division: 262nd, 263rd and 269th.

The Russian Interpreters

1. In 1930 only 171 Russians lived in Spain, of which the majority resided in Barcelona and Madrid. This geographical fragmentation hindered the creation of a firm community, and it was only in Barcelona that several Russian aristocrats established joint services in an Orthodox chapel. Forty-eight White Guards, who had gone through the civil war in Spain, joined this small diaspora, as well as twenty or thirty Russian soldiers from the Spanish Foreign Legion.
2. Once again an exaggeration, this time on the basis of retelling stories from third persons. Very little is known about Sergei Ponomarev's life before 1941: he was from St. Petersburg and served as a cavalry captain during the civil war in Russia. At some point he made his way to Spain and was a member of the Spanish Falange from 1934. During the Civil War he fought on the Teruel front with the rank of infantry sergeant. He was living in Barcelona in 1941 and was engaged in trade. At the end of June 1941 he volunteered for the Blue Division. On 17 April 1942 a session of a military tribunal was held, under the chairmanship of Lieutenant Colonel Ramon Rodriguez Vita, which was investigating the case of Ponomarev, who was accused of activities contrary to international law (*un supuesto delito contra el derecho de gentes*) committed at the end of January 1942. According to the indictment, in the village of Chechulino, the interpreter

was negotiating for the 'delivery of food and materials for his regiment'. Pomomarev carried out a search in the home of Vera Koricheva, the wife of a local communist, who 'undoubtedly ran off with the enemy army', and whom they also suspected of hiding weapons. According to several Russian witnesses, Ponomarev raped Koricheva during the search, and then robbed her, taking her money and possessions. However, the accused was exonerated: the Spanish 'tribunal' preferred the testimony of two Spaniards who accompanied him, and the settlement elder, while the latter had been appointed by Ponomarev, having removed the previous village chief. Ponomarev's 'defence' in the person of the two Spaniards and the Russian elder, confirmed that there had been no rape, nor robbery, nor any other abuses: besides this, Ponomarev had supposedly been following the orders of his chief, Lieutenant Fernández Carnicer. The testimony of the Russian peasants, who maintained just the opposite, was considered just 'testimony by Russian civilians, whose relatives are fighting in the ranks of the enemy army and who are undoubtedly trying to defame the occupation forces'. Ponomarev was exonerated, although they sent him to a punishment platoon for three months for exceeding his authority and for 'unnecessarily frightening the population, which he threatened'. On 5 May 1943 he returned to his old sub-unit. He was demobilized two months later and returned to Barcelona. His further fate is unknown. The tribunal's verdict of 7 April 1942 and the record of the Blue Division's auditor of 7 March 1942 are available: AGMAV 3791/30. His service record is in AGMAV 5126/58.
3. *La medalla de la Vieja Guardia* was introduced in March 1942 to reward those members of all parties that merged with the FET in March 1937, who had enlisted in them before mid-February 1936. In practice, just the former members of the Fascist Falange were really interested in applying for such a distinction.
4. Gogidzhanoshvili treated the Russian population disgracefully, for which there is confirmation in other sources. Iaremchuk, an officer and interpreter in the Italian army, following his demobilization, ended up in the camp at Hof, where he tried to enroll in the Blue Division together with other fellow émigrés. 'At this time the entire "Blue Division" was returning to Spain through Hof, and they arrived from the front in German uniforms, after which they sent them to the showers and dressed them in Spanish uniforms and lined them up, a German general made an appropriate speech, and then they sent them to the railway station. All of the soldiers and officers spent the night in our barracks and we met familiar officers and asked them about our émigré interpreters. Everyone had a very high opinion of them. To be sure, when they began to speak about one Georgian, a Legion officer (his pseudonym was "*teniente* Constantino", because his Georgian surname was difficult to pronounce), the Spanish officers would observe an embarrassed silence. We found out later that he had treated the Russian population bestially and one officer acquaintance openly said: we despised him because he supplied the senior officers with Russian women. We avoided him for a few years upon returning to Spain, but we later got used to him.' A. Gabrieli [A. P. Iaremchuk II], *S ital'ianskoi armiei v Rossii*, p. 118.
5. The text is somewhat different in the typed version of Kovalevskii's memoirs: '[He] was in the grip of a sort of mania for being a toady: he was ready for any base act in order to earn the praise of his lords, who sincerely despised him for this . . . He, in order to make his way to General Muñoz Grandes, like a dog, ran after every general or colonel, while praising his non-existent feats. He, in order to get the Iron Cross, denounced without even thinking, innocent people and led them to their execution.'
6. In the Wehrmacht cultural 'enlightenment' and the maintenance of morale among the troops were considered priority tasks. A wide-ranging propaganda apparatus constantly worked on the soldiers, and even trench newspapers were published in many

units. The first few wall newspapers were prepared for the Blue Division as early as the training period in Grafenwöhr and during the march to the front. Upon arriving at the front line, these homemade leaflets gave way to the regularly issued *Campaign Leaflet* (*Hoja de Campaña*), which was first issued in Grigorovo, and then in Riga, and later in Tallinn. Up until the beginning of March 1944 the paper was run by Lieutenant Colonel Manuel Ruiz de la Serna. Several of the division's 'cultured' soldiers worked in the paper, such as Professor Fernando Castiella, who later became the Spanish minister of foreign affairs, and the satirical writer Alvaro de Laiglesia, who later embraced a critical stance towards the Franco regime.

7. There is a great amount of material on Soviet prisoner interrogations in AGMAV 2005/6, 2005/7/3, and 2005/9.
8. Here and later on Kovalevskii mistakenly cites the number of the division. The 88th Rifle Division fought on the Karelian front, and not in the Novgorod area. In the first edition we mistakenly assumed that he was perhaps speaking of the 188th Rifle Division, although it made no sense for the division's surrounded personnel to fall back from around the Kholm area to the north-west, because it was simpler to get lost or to cross the front line there, in the swampy and wooded terrain. The general direction of the breakout was the opposite: in the autumn of 1941 the surrounded soldiers and partisans left the hungry and dangerous areas for the zone south of Lake Il'men. The main mass of the surrounded troops in the 'Spanish' area belonged to units of General Andrei Nikitovich Astanin's Luga Operational Group (LOG). In September 1941 the 111th, 177th and 235th Rifle Divisions and the 24th Tank Division, plus militia from Leningrad, ended up in the Luga cauldron – for a total of about 43,000 men. 13,000 men came out of the cauldron in September and October; 20,000 out of this group ended up as prisoners. Not all of the remaining 10,000 died, but part of them roamed around the forests. In the German documents it is mentioned that many men from the group tried to break out to the south-east, to the areas south of Lake Il'men, that is, where it was easier to cross the front line. It was precisely the surrounded men from the LOG that the Germans caught in the Sixteenth Army's rear. Taking into account that two Red Army soldiers on the list belong to one and the same 111th Rifle Division, then we are speaking of it in all cases. NARA. T-501. R 79. F. 1143–1184, 1231; I. Khomiakov, *Luzhskii rubezh. Khronika geroicheskikh dnei*. St. Petersburg, 2014, p. 234.

The Second Section and the 'Guardia Civil'

1. This was infantry Captain Manuel Ruiz de la Serna (?–1952), who, following his return to Spain, became a General Staff colonel as well as the civil governor of Huesca and Badajoz.
2. Pedro Martínez de Tudela García (1905–?) was a captain in the Civil Guard and in October 1934 distinguished himself as a commander during the miners' uprising in Asturias, where he captured a number of villages. Following the start of the civil war, he was arrested in Bilbao. He was able to escape and joined the rebels. Martinez de Tudela was responsible for the organization of the Spanish Division's internal information service, which was directly dependent on the Second Section (intelligence and counterintelligence). Several motorized vehicles were at the disposal of his organization.
3. He is probably speaking here about Enrique Sáez Jiménez (1903–?), a sergeant in the Civil Guard, whose surname sounded strange to Kovalevskii, so he transcribed in the German manner as *Zeiss*. Sáez served in the Civil Guard's 1st 'Madrid' Mobile

Company. In December 1941 he put in a request for promotion to *brigada*; in May 1942 his request was granted (backdated to 1 June 1940). This explains why Kovalevskii always calls him by that rank. AGMAV 4982/27.
4. Another typical instance of Kovalevskii manifesting his psychological traumas.
5. The author is speaking of Francisco Galeote Cortés (1895–?), a corporal in the Civil Guard. He served in Madrid in the Civil Guard's general directorate. He fell ill in May 1942 and was repatriated. AGMAV 4643/18.
6. Other sources paint a different picture of events. This concerns the murder of the mayor of Novgorod, Fedor Ivanovich Morozov, who took up the position in November 1941. There follow data generally accepted today. The distribution of milk was organized in the city hall to its employees, children and pregnant women. Spanish soldiers also began to arrive for the milk, which caused dissatisfaction among the citizens. On 17 November 1941 they once again came to the town hall, demanding that they be given milk. Morozov was in a state of drunkenness: dissatisfied with the Spaniards, the burgomaster began to make a stink with them. During the skirmish Morozov threw one of the Spaniards down the stairs. The insulted Spaniard grabbed his pistol and killed Morozov with two shots. Other testimony states that the victim was the village elder of Grigorovo. It was only after the German command's very harsh demands to turn the accused over to a court that the Spaniard was sentenced to three years in prison and in January 1942 he returned to Spain. This was a very young soldier, only 17 years old, whom his fellow soldiers gave the nickname of 'mayor killer' (*Mataalcaldes*). X.M. Núñez Seixas, *The Spanish Blue Division*, p. 175; M. Iglesias-Sarria y Puga, *Mi suerte dijo sí. Evocación autobiográfica de guerra y paz (1918–1936–1945)*. Madrid, 1987, p. 282; B.N. Kovalev, *Povsednevnaia zhizn' naseleniia Rossii v period natsistskoi okkupatsii*. Moscow, 2011, p. 21.
7. While carrying out reconnaissance in Novgorod, the partisan Surgucheva encountered the Spaniards: 'I was passing through the area near a military installation and asked the Spanish sentry to let me go straight ahead. He grimaced and pointed to the window, where an officer was sitting. I asked him: "Are you Spanish?" to which he replied: "Yes", and in turn asked: "Are the Spanish not good?" I replied: "The Spanish are good and the Russians are good, but the Germans are not good." The sentry laughed and added: "The Spanish officer is not good either." I advised him to go over to the Russians. He indicated with his hand that the Russians were far off. He then led me along a path and I saw everything that I needed.' Another Spaniard complained about the Germans and got upset that the Finns, who were supposedly going to relieve the Blue Division, never seemed to arrive. Central State Archive of Historical and Political Documentation of St. Petersburg (TsGAIPD SPB), fond O-116, opis' 1, delo 348, list 47.
8. This is presumably the Civil Guard José López Martínez.
9. As is admitted in a number of memoirs and eyewitness accounts, the Orthodox icons were valued by both the Germans and the Spanish. X.M. Núñez Seixas, *The Spanish Blue Division*, p. 173.
10. The author is speaking of the wreck of the Russian emperor's train, which took place on 29 October 1888. Borki station is located 50 kilometres from Khar'kov.

Hunting for Partisans

1. Many of the division's soldiers shared to a certain degree Kovalevskii's perception of Russian peasant children. This group of Spaniards most likely had warm feelings for the children, considering them to be victims of communism, while for more devout

Spaniards the children's innocent nature meant that Russia still had the chance of 'once again being converted' to Christianity. Aside from this, the Spanish saw that the children had grown up in poverty; groups of orphans were often encountered, who gathered into bands and carried out petty thievery for the purpose of simply surviving.
2. In this sense, the dual character of the relations between the occupiers and the local residents is noted in other testimonies. The soldiers who were quartered in the huts ate up or requisitioned the peasants' meagre reserves, while manifestations of friendship or warmth, like occasional presents (they would share sweets or part of their own rations) could in no way compensate for their losses. The Spanish saw that the peasants lived in poverty and sought to hide from their uninvited guests everything they possibly could. X.M. Núñez Seixas, 'Good invaders? The occupation policy of the Spanish Blue Division in Northwestern Russia, 1941–1944', *War in History*, 25:3 (2018), pp. 361–86.
3. The author is probably speaking of here and further on about the village of Nekokhovo, in the Novgorod *oblast'*.
4. According to a list of village elders in the Novgorod area and partisan reports, this was Kirill Afanas'ev. TsGAIPD SPB. Fond O-116, opis' 1, delo 32, list 51.
5. 'The former chairman and the secretary of the B[ol'she]zamoshsk v[illage] s[oviet] live in their village of Osiia. The former chair[man] of the collective farm "Paris Commune" E. has been elected village elder': 'Raport byvshego direktora Novgorodskogo gortopa, byvshego partizana Z. I. Sverdlova sekretariu Novgorodskogo raikoma VKP(b) P. I. Sokolovu o deistviiakh otriada i polozhenii na vremenno okkupiirovannoi territorii. 17 oktiabria 1941 g.', in V.G. Kolotushkin (ed.), *Iz istorii organizatsii partizanskogo dvizheniia na novgorodskoi zemle v 1941–1942 godakh: Sbornik dokumentov*. Velikii Novgorod, 2017, pp. 159–60.
6. Given the use of the singular and the preceding words regarding 'hysterical bravery', Kovalevskii is most likely speaking again of Gogidzhanoshvili.
7. This is the latest mistake in the regiment's designation: presumably he is speaking of the 269th Infantry Regiment's music teacher.
8. The correct name is Selo-Gora.
9. And even though we might be dealing with *a posteriori* reflections, Kovalevskii noted with discernment that effect which the Bolsheviks' patriotic propaganda had, appealing to defend the motherland, and not the party, and for this resorting to Great Russian patriotism. As early as the late summer of 1941, appeals to defend the revolution or to the working masses' abstract anti-fascism began to disappear.
10. This village no longer exists, having become part of the settlement of Tesovo-Netyl'skii.
11. This incident took place on 3 December 1941 and coincided in time with a significant increase in partisan activity bordering on the Spanish zone of responsibility. According to the daily report of the 250th Division to the XXXVIII Corps, which was compiled on the following day, they managed to detain several participants in the underground and their accomplices. One of the peasant women was a witness as to how a partisan, with the surname of Tumanov, who was just a teenager, was hanged. X.M. Núñez Seixas, *Camarada invierno*, p. 290.
12. The distance from Podberez'ia to Rogavka is 44.6 kilometres to the north-west.
13. As early as August 1941 *Einsatzgruppe* A was reporting: 'The tactic of replying to terror with terror has brilliantly justified itself. The peasants, out of fear of punitive measures [*Vergeltungsmassnahmen*] have travelled 20 kilometres on foot or by horse to the headquarters of the *Einsatzgruppe*'s sub-command with reports on the appearance of partisans. The majority of these reports proved to be true. In all, 48 partisan supporters were shot, including six women.' NARA. T-175. R. 233. F. 656.

14. This may be Ivan Petrovich Novikov, from the detachment of the Novgorod district committee's secretaries. In the autumn of 1941 the partisan detachment of Anton Mikhailovich Novikov was also operating in the area, among whose soldiers including Aleksandr Nikolaevich Treshov. TsGAIPD SPB. Fond O-116, opis' 1, delo 1045, list 2.
15. 'The form[er] chief of our detachment, com[rade] Laskovskii went with me to the Ermolino v[illage] c[ouncil], in the "Truzhenik" Collective Farm, where he remained with our soldier, Nikolai Gavrilov'. Raport byvshego direktora Novgorodskogo gortora, byvshego partizana Z. I. Sverdlova . . ., pp. 160–1.
16. The author is speaking here of Fernando-María Castiella (1907–76), a doctor of law and a professor at the University of Madrid, and a Falangist since 1935. That same year he published the book *Reivindicaciones de España* (*Spain's Demands*), with José M. de Areilza, which outlined the maximum programme of the Falange's imperial ambitions. He was assigned to general headquarters in occupied Soviet territory as a liaison and, as opposed to Kovalevskii's assertion, wore a German uniform like any other of the Blue Division's soldiers. Upon his return to Spain, he held the posts of president of the Falangist-oriented Institute of Political Studies (1943–8) and ambassador to Peru and the Vatican (1951–6), after which he became minister of foreign affairs (1959–69).
17. In December 1941 the partisan war in the occupiers' rear was poorly coordinated by the Soviet centre. The situation was desperate around Leningrad: on 25 October there were no data on 86 of the 194 detachments that had been formed, and they had perished for the most part. Those who survived had no resources for surviving the winter and sought to return to the Soviet rear. Those who remained had no opportunity for waging full-fledged and coordinated military operations and hid in inaccessible and swampy 'bear corners'. Relations with the local population during this time were very complex. On 23 November 1941 the commander of the 285th Security Division reported that, according to testimony from captured partisans, they were sending out liaison personnel from Leningrad with orders to gather Red Army soldiers in the rear and to break through the front line. The Oredezh partisans, who were also operating in the Rogavka area, were ordered to break out toward Novgorod. P. Gavrilov, '"Naselenie stanovitsia ne za nas, a protiv nas": partizany Leningradskoi oblasti, sovetskaia identichnost' i natsistskaia okkupatsiia', *Neprikosnovennyi zapas. Debaty o politike i kul'ture*, 3 (131) (2020), pp. 70–95; A. Hill, *The War behind the Eastern Front. The Soviet Partisan Movement in North-West Russia 1941–1944*. London, New York, 2005, pp. 69–80; NARA. T-315. R. 1878. F. 721.
18. Nikolai Petrovich Zotov was born in Russia and was the youngest of the division's interpreters. During the Russian Civil War he was a Lieutenant in the Alekseev Infantry Regiment. He took part in the Spanish Civil War: he first fought in the ranks of the Spanish Foreign Legion and later with the Falange on the Teruel front. He was a corporal (according to other sources, a sergeant) and was wounded twice. In July 1941 he signed up with the Blue Division as a volunteer; despite his serious wounds and being partially unfit for duty, he was accepted and appointed interpreter with the headquarters of the 263rd Infantry Regiment. He returned to Spain in June 1942 and remained in the Spanish Foreign Legion and serving to the rank of lieutenant. He died in Madrid.

Denouement
1. This refers to the directive on the treatment of political commissars (*Kommissarbefehl*, or Commissar Order) of 6 June 1941, ordering the execution of the Red Army's

commissars as bearers of a hostile ideology. The Blue Division most likely also received the directive. The order was rescinded on 6 May 1942 because it stimulated resistance: the political leaders understood that they had nothing to lose and that captivity would end in death, and thus fought to the last man. By this time, in accordance with the order, several thousand captured political workers had been executed. Circumstantial evidence indicates that the order was also carried out in the Blue Division. See F. Römer, *Der Kommissarbefehl. Wehrmacht und NS-Verbrechen an der Ostfront 1941/42*. Paderborn, 2008.

2. The author is speaking here of plexiglass – organic glass used in aviation. It burns easily and for an extended time. The surrounded soldiers, most likely, used the pieces of glass for lighting fires and as a source of light (a primitive oil lamp), or they melted snow to get water.
3. This evidently refers to those soldiers from the Luga Operational Group who were surrounded. A report by the XXXVIII Corps of 21 December 1941 speaks of capturing six prisoners who emerged from the Luga cauldron. NARA. T-314. R. 901. F. 581.
4. Not identified.
5. Not identified.
6. Not identified.
7. The author is presumably speaking of Ivan Vasil'evich Vagin (1907–41), the political leader for the 111th Rifle Division's 399th Rifle Regiment. The division was part of the Luga Operational Group and got into an encirclement. He is officially listed as missing in action in August 1941.
8. The author is presumably speaking of Veniamin Matveevich Belolipetskii (1909–41), a senior lieutenant who served as senior adjutant in a battalion of the 111th Rifle Division's 399th Rifle Regiment. He was officially declared missing in action in December 1941.
9. Not identified.
10. A Soviet citizen, Olimpiada Georgievna Poliakova ('Lidiia Osipova'), who worked for the Spaniards, wrote in her diary on 17 September 1942: 'Upon seeing my laundresses, the Captain began to roar in a frenzy for them to go and help out. By the way, when they're upset the Spanish howl as if they were being cut. And they are always very pointedly and loudly upset, so that an unending howl hangs over the city as if it were doomsday. The population was afraid earlier, but now they've gotten used to it.' 'Svershilos'. Prishli nemtsy!', reproduced in O.V. Budnitskii (ed.), *Ideinyi kollaboratsionizm v SSSR v period Velikoi Otechestvennoi voiny*. Moscow, 2012, p. 141.
11. An indication of when the text was written, that is, in November-December 1951.
12. Here the author clearly meant a 'raid'.
13. The village's correct name is Selo-Gora.
14. 'In January 1942 in the village of Dolgovo, Arkadii Vasil'evich Davydov was executed and his body lay uncollected in the yard until May 1942, because the Germans forbade him to be buried.' 'Iz akta novgorodskoi raionnoi komissii ob itogakh rassledovaniia zlodeianiii nemetsko-fashistkikh zakhvatchikov na territorii raiona. 20 aprelia 1945 goda', S.F. Vitushkina, T.A. Dan'ko, et al. (eds), '. . . *I nichto ne zabyro'. Dokumenty i materialy o zlodeianiiakh nemetsko-fashistskikh okkupantov na Novgorodskoi zemle (1941–1945)*. Novgorod, 1996, p. 59.
15. Yet another typical turn of phrase; this is an anachronistic term, referring to the students of a military school in Tsarist Russia.
16. 'In November 1941 in the Bol'shoe Zamosh'e village soviet at Tatino station, during their occupation the German cannibals shot, following prolonged tortures and

torments, the school director – a labour invalid, Kuz'min Ivan Mikhailovich'. 'Iz akta Novgorodskoi raionnoi kommissii . . . ', p. 59.
17. Kovalevskii obviously wrote his memoirs during 1948–51, when Castiella held the post of Spanish ambassador to Peru. The fact that he earlier mentions Castiella's subsequent service as minister of foreign affairs gives enables us to assume that small corrections were later inserted into the original text.
18. An alternative and less partisan description is contained in the following work: J. García Hispán, *La Guardia Civil*, pp. 46–7. Pedro Martínez de Tudela, his orderly, Florentino Cortijo Marín and Enrique Sáez Jiménez were also decorated; no information that José López Martínez was also awarded a medal has been uncovered. A.G. Pinilla, *Héroes entre valientes. Los condecorados en la División Azul.* Madrid [n. d.].
19. He refers to Francisco Pizarro and Hernán Cortés, the Spanish conquerors of Peru and Mexico in the sixteenth century.

Index

Abraham Lincoln International Brigade, 18
anti-Bolshevism, 11
anti-communism, 6, 26, 32
anti-democracy, 26
Azar, Vladimir, 57–9

Badajoz front, 52
Baltic Germans, 25
Barcelona, 6–7, 10, 33, 47, 72
Belgrade, 11, 51, 153
Beliaev, Ivan, 8, 50, 183–5
Belorussian villages, 111
Berlin, 5, 16, 28, 30–1, 45, 85, 118, 145
Bibikov, Aleksandr, 148
Blue Division, the, 29–33, 35–8, 40–1, 43–5, 47–8, 50, 54, 63–5, 69–71, 73, 102–03, 136–8, 142–4, 151–2, 154–5
Blue Legion, the, 35, 45
Bobadilla, 131–2
Bogacheva-Baskakova, 39
Bolshevik Intelligence, 15
Bolsheviks, 3, 6, 11–13, 15, 20, 22, 30, 32, 67, 79, 85–6, 103, 105
Bolshevism, 6, 25, 29–30
Boltin, Nikolai, 20–1, 30–1, 33, 53, 84, 145
Bulgaria, 3–4, 14, 22
Burgos, 15, 86, 88–2, 96, 129

Carlists, 13, 16–17, 20, 32, 64, 155
Catalonia front, 23
Catholics, 28–29, 104–5
    anti-communist, 29
communism, 22–25, 31, 33, 61, 182
Civil Guard, the, 54, 64, 69, 175
comrades-in-arms, 5, 30, 33, 45, 53
Corpo Spedizione Italiano in Russia, 30
Cortez, Sergeant 99

Davydov, Arkashka, 176–7, 195
Dolgovo, 169, 182–6, 195–96, 198
Don front, 37
Dona Maria de Molina tercio, 12–13, 32
Dvoichenko, Vladimir, 14, 33, 54

émigrés, 14–17, 19–20, 22–3, 25–7, 29–31, 33–5, 42–4, 46, 49, 51, 53, 56, 58–61, 67, 153–4

Esparza, Colonel, 132, 144, 147–9, 175

Falange, the, 29, 33, 53, 64, 85–6, 134, 155
Falangists, 29, 32, 45, 63–4, 88, 145, 160
Fernandez, Captain, 119, 128, 131
Filistinskii, Boris, 42–3
Fok, Anatolii, 12, 18–19, 47
France, 4–6, 10–11, 14, 17, 21–2, 24, 47, 53, 71, 92, 153
Franco, General Francisco, 5, 10, 13–15, 18–21, 32, 45, 55, 86
Francoists, 14, 17–18, 21, 29, 86
French Foreign Legion, 8, 51, 54, 100
French Reds, 24

Galeote, Corporal, 160, 165
Gallipoli, 8, 46, 50
Gendarmerie, 69, 142, 156, 158, 160–1
Georgia, 13, 17, 71
German alliance, 83
German-Soviet front, 31, 37
Gogidzhanov, Konstantin 13, 42–3, 45, 139–40
Gory, 177, 195
Grafenwöhr, Camp, 95
Grodno, 44, 106
Guipúzcoa, 32, 53
Gurskii, Ali, 12, 32–3, 140, 142, 150, 156–7, 192

Higher Army School, 32, 47
Hitler, Adolf, 25–27, 30, 32, 45, 83
Hof, 45
Hoover Institution, 56–7, 72

Iaremchuk, Anton, 24, 30–1, 45, 51, 53, 55, 58

Jews, 17, 32, 70, 83, 106

Kampf um Spanien, 144, 185
Klimov, Semyon, 174
Kornilov campaign, 17
Kovalevskii, Vladimir, 42, 44, 46–7, 50–1, 53–5, 58, 60–71, 73, 75, 134, 162–3, 169–70, 186–9, 194, 196–7
    memoirs, 56, 65, 72
    notebook, 58

251

Krasnyi Bor, 36–37
Krivosheia, Nikolai, 45

Lampe, Aleksei, 27, 49
Lamsdorf, Grigorii, 35
Leiva, Captain, 130
Leningrad, 36, 70
Lithuania, 36, 60, 69, 105, 107, 111
Lithuanians, 60, 105
López, Gendarme, 161–63, 165, 171, 173, 176, 183, 185–86, 198

Madrid, 6, 30, 33–34, 45, 49, 53, 58, 134, 136, 146, 155
Maksimovich, Captain, 15
Maloe Lobanovo, 119
Martínez, Captain, 157–9, 165, 174, 177–8, 183, 185, 194–5, 198
Mein Kampf, 25–6, 144
Melilla Battalion, 52
Moscow, 13, 16, 24, 56–7, 83, 85, 103, 106, 114, 135
Muñoz Grandes, General, 30, 31, 48, 97, 143–5, 147, 149–50, 175

Nekhotovo (Nekokhovo), 167–8, 172, 180, 182
Nestor Istoriia publishing house, 72
Nikitin (depot chief), 169, 171–2, 176–7, 195
Nikulin, Nikolai, 70–1
Novgorod, 36, 39, 118–19, 121, 123, 125, 137–8, 140, 160–1, 163, 169, 171–2, 176, 178, 185–6

OKW, 27–8
Oseja (Osiia), 169, 171, 174, 182, 186, 192, 195

Paris, 4–5, 10, 14–15, 23, 92
partisan movement, 176, 178
Perchin, Igor, 148, 152–3, 155, 159, 187, 196–8
Peru, 144, 198
Petrov, Count Ivan, 22
Pobereja, 174, 184, 186, 194
Poland, 83, 94, 104, 111, 137
Polukhin, Captain 12, 18–19, 23, 47, 155
Ponomarev, Sergei, 33, 66, 155
Posad, 144
Pushkin, 39, 77, 188

Red Army (RKKA), 13, 16, 36, 60, 71, 112
Republicans, 16, 18–19, 51
ROA, 34
Rogavka, 180–1, 186, 195
ROVS, 4, 10–11, 14–15, 17, 21, 23, 26, 28, 33–4, 49
  chiefs, 27
  delegates, 14
Rudinskii's memoirs, 44
Russian Civil War, 6, 17
Russian Imperial Union Order (RISO), 23
Russian interpreters, 141, 148, 151–3, 155, 179
Russian Liberation Army, 34
Russian volunteers, 12, 14–16, 20, 22–4, 49, 144

Saltykov, General, 118
San Francisco, 56
San Sebastián, 19, 53–5, 83–5, 87, 90, 92, 153
Scheubner-Richter, Max von, 25
Second World War, the, 50, 53, 57–58, 60–1, 149
Shinkarenko, Nikolai V. 11–13, 16–18, 33, 47, 53
Sholokhovo, 144
Sitno, 144
Solonevich, Ivan Luk'ianovich, 103, 180
Soviet Union, the, 4, 5–6, 9, 24, 28–30, 34, 53, 60, 68, 73, 79, 83, 103–04, 172, 174, 180–1
Spain, 6, 9–19, 21–4, 29–37, 44–9, 51, 53–5, 57–8, 61–3, 79, 83–5, 87–9, 115, 125, 134–6, 144, 146, 154–5, 158–61, 184–5
  post-Franco, 46
Spanish Republic, 13–14, 22, 46
Spanish soldiers, 37–9, 65, 84, 149, 169, 183–4
Spanish Volunteer Legion, 45
St George's Company, the, 50

Tomillo, Sergeant, 99
Totskii, Lev, 43, 45, 136–37
Tringam, Aleksandr, 44–45, 48, 51, 53, 67, 136
Tsarist army, 41, 45

Ukraine, 30, 71, 115

Valencia, 6, 20, 52
Vasil'eva, Kseniia, 181
Vicente, Emilio, 12
Vitebsk, 115–17, 119

Wehrmacht, 27, 30–31, 38, 40, 61
　　Propaganda Company, 45

White George organization, 13
White Guards, 3–4, 8–9, 12, 18–19, 21, 32, 46
White Russians, 3, 5, 9, 18, 21, 31–2, 34, 47, 72, 84

Yugoslavia, 3–4, 8, 14, 51, 83, 136, 153